THE INNER LIGHT & WORLD RELIGIONS

In this new book, Philip Nicholson follows up and expands on his earlier studies of light visions in a number of current and ancient societies. He highlights how self-induced visions, whether through sleep deprivation, strenuous ritual or meditation, lead to the integration of such experiences in emerging religions. In doing so, he discusses a number of prominent prophets and founders of world religions, their traumatic experiences and the outcome in the teachings they promulgated. This book will be a welcome addition to the ongoing studies of the emergence and development of ancient and current religions.

—Dr. Michael Witzel,
    Ph.D., Wales Professor of Sanskrit Studies, Harvard University
    President of The International Association for the Study of
    Comparative Mythology
    Author of *Origins of the World's Mythologies* (Oxford University Press, 2012)

THE INNER LIGHT & WORLD RELIGIONS

How Meditating Mystics Use Sleep as a Ladder
to Trigger Ecstatic Visions

Philip T. Nicholson

Book design by Launch My Book, Inc. (www.launchmybook.com)
with cover design by Erika Alyana Duran (easduran.myportfolio.com)
using a photograph by the author's wife, Beth Nicholson,
and interior design by Booknook.biz.

ISBN 979-8-9897878-0-7 (Paperback)
ISBN 979-8-9897878-1-4 (Ebook)

*This book is dedicated to
my supportive and loving wife*

Contents

PART I.

Visions of
Fiery Light

Introduction

The Visions that Gave Rise to World Religions

The founders of all of the world's major religions—Hinduism, Zoroastrianism, Judaism, Buddhism, Daoism, Christianity, Manichaeism, and Islam—were inspired to do what they did by seeing a vision of fiery light. These visions were said to be so unlike any lights seen in nature that the seers understandably concluded that the visions must have come from God or from some other supernatural agent and that therefore they must encode some divinely inspired message that needed to be deciphered. Many other mystics seers also saw visions of fiery light and used their visions, not to found new religions, but rather to revitalize their existing traditions. Visions of fiery light continue to be prized today by all of the world's major religious traditions as being among the most powerful of all human mystical experiences.

But there's something puzzling about all these accounts. The founders of the world's major religions and the other mystic seers all describe their visions of fiery light in remarkably similar ways. They say they saw flashes of lightning. Leaping flames. Blazing suns. Sun-filled clouds that were blindingly bright. Oceans of light. There are superficial differences, but all of these metaphors indicate that the person's visual field was filled with flashes of bright light. How is it possible that so many different individuals with different personalities, living in different cultures and in different historical eras, would all end up seeing visions of fiery light and describing their experiences in such similar ways? And if these visions were so similar, why did the seers interpret their meaning of their visions in such radically different ways? These are important questions that deserve answers.

All of the world's major religions describe the visionary experiences of their founders in ways that depend on the metaphysical doctrines of that religion. So far no one has been able to provide a detailed, comprehensive, science-based explanation for this phenomenon that surfaces time and time again to change the course of human history. Not until now.

When I set out to track down answers—answers that would not require the reader to accept any particular set of metaphysical doctrines—I knew I had a special qualification that would give me an advantage not available to others who've attempted to address this subject. And what was that special qualification?

I've seen a vision of fiery light myself.

But, in my case, this vision was triggered by accident. I wasn't engaged in any kind of mystical spiritual practice; I was just lying in bed and using my familiar meditation skills to become relaxed enough to fall asleep. And I'm not the kind of person anyone would expect to see visions: I'm not a religious mystic; I'm a professional medical writer. My primary orientation in life is scientific and secular.

It turned out that this "accident" was fortuitous indeed, because knowing what a vision of fiery light actually looks like proved to be quite useful for the project I had in mind. As a medical writer, what fascinated me about this visionary experience was the idea that, given the current state of scientific knowledge about our human visual system, it might now be possible to do something that couldn't have been done before: it might now be possible to carry out a neurologically-grounded, reverse-engineering analysis of the specific characteristics of the light visions I'd just seen myself—an analysis of their shapes, sizes, colors, directions of movement, and timing intervals. Then, with that information in hand, I could dig into the scientific literature to search for descriptions of neural mechanisms in the human brain—in *any* human brain—that would have to be activated in a certain sequence in order to see the visions I'd just seen, including the vision of a bright, flashing light similar to what the founders described. What if the brain mechanisms that generated those visions of bright, flashing lights could be shown to have certain neurological constraints that limited the amount of variation that could occur in the visions they generated? Then it might be possible to demonstrate that the metaphors used by influential mystics to describe their visions were similar because the visions they saw had to be essentially the same.

What follows is a scientific detective story in which I interweave my own experiences and my neurological analysis of meditation-induced light visions with colorful threads drawn from the history of religions, biographies of religious mystics, and psychological insights about the effects of child trauma on adult beliefs. I'll also examine anthropological theories about the cultural conditions in which charismatic prophets are more likely to surface and more likely to succeed.

Then there's the role played by chance. That's where I'll begin the story—with a chance encounter...

CHAPTER 1

The Vision of Fiery Light: A Personal Account

A Chance Encounter

It was summer, and I was driving south through Wyoming, trying hard to keep my attention focused on what seemed like an endless road that stretched straight all the way to the horizon. Out of the corner of my eye I saw a small, hand-lettered sign posted along the side of the highway that read "Sun Dance". An arrow pointed toward a dirt road that veered off to the east, and I could see sunlight reflecting off the chrome surfaces of cars and trucks parked in a ravine not too far away. I decided to take a chance. I stopped, backed up, turned onto the dirt road, and drove to where the cars and trucks were parked. No one was around. I opened the door, stepped out into the hot, dry wind, and started walking cautiously through the tall grass, taking care to dodge the cactuses and sage bushes that dotted the hillside. I couldn't see the crowd, but I could hear the sound of drumming and headed in that direction. I didn't know if I'd be welcome, but I told myself that the only way to find out was to give it a try. This was something I'd always wanted to see since

I was a young boy. Back then I'd read every book I could find about Native American vision quests.

As I topped the crest of the hill, I saw below what I'd come to see. Nested in a valley between the rolling hills was a thick bower of tree branches, woven together in tight bundles and mounted on a frame of wooden posts arrayed in a huge ring. The men, women, and children from an unidentified Sioux tribe were massed together, shoulder to shoulder, beneath that ring-shaped shelter that protected them from the merciless sun. They were all watching what was happening in the inner circle which had been rendered sacred by the enclosure that set this space apart from the surrounding prairie.

I was unsure how the presence of a stranger would be received. One tribesman turned and watched me approaching, but he turned back toward the inner circle, apparently not disturbed by my approach. I took that as a sign that outsiders would be tolerated.

The deep bass boom of the native drums and the high-pitched, falsetto chanting of the singers made the whole scene vibrate with an exciting pulse. As I looked around me, I realized that not only was this was something I'd read about and hoped someday to see—a real Sun Dance ceremony—but I'd arrived on the fourth and final day when the tribesmen who'd chosen to take part in the traditional "piercing" ritual perform their sacrificial act.

As I mingled with the crowd, I saw that the shamans had erected in the center of the sacred circle a tall tree trunk shorn of its branches with a buffalo skull impaled over the top. My timing was perfect: a few minutes after I arrived, the crowd of onlookers across from me made an opening to let the male dancers stride single file into the center of the circle. As the men approached the sacred pole, all of them stared straight ahead, expressionless, although the signs of exhaustion in their gaunt faces were easy to see. Based on what I'd read about this ritual,

I knew that, for the first three days of the ceremony, these men were not allowed to eat or sleep and that their only sustenance would have been an occasional sip of water. As the men stood at attention, the tribal shamans stepped forward, moving from man to man. The shamans grabbed eagle talons out of their ceremonial pouches, pinched a patch of skin on the upper chest of each man, and pierced the skin with the sharp point of the talon. They pierced the skin on both sides of the men's chests. Then, before the shaman moved on to the next dancer, he hooked each of the two talons to a rope hanging down from the pole topped with the buffalo skull.

The drums began pounding louder and with a more insistent beat, matched by the high-pitched, falsetto chants of the singers. The tension rose in the crowd of onlookers as we stared fixedly at the scene in front of us. What happened next would be crucial to the success of this Sun Dance because it would determine who among the dancers would be rewarded by the Spirit World with a vision commensurate with the purity of their hearts and the rigor of their sacrifices—their long fast, the loss of sleep and the unremitting pain of the eagle claws piercing their chests. Now the dancers started to move, shifting their weight from foot to foot and skipping back and forth in a trance-like shuffle. They also pulled away from the central pole, stretching taut the ropes attached to the eagle claws implanted in their chests in order to increase the pain. This was how the dancers demonstrated their courage, their fortitude, and the intensity of their desire to be granted a vision. As the drums and the high-pitched chants became ever more forceful, a surge of emotion swept through the crowd. It was contagious; I felt it surging in me as well, even though I was only an outsider for whom the significance of this tribal ritual had not been inculcated in me from an early age. But I suspect that the vibrations would affect anyone standing there, anyone who heard the crescendo of drums and chanting, anyone who kept eyes fixated on the dancers, waiting for the moment everyone knew was now imminent.

One dancer decided to make his move. He threw his body backward, the ropes pulled taut, the claws ripped out of his skin, and the man fell onto his back. All of us standing nearby could hear the loud pop as his skin parted and tiny pieces of flesh careened through the air. Another dancer followed that man's lead, then another and another, each one throwing himself backward and ripping the skin that bound him to the eagle claws and the central pole. Once on the ground, none of the men tried to get up. They remained immobile, eyes closed, each hoping he would be the one to receive a vision.

This was the moment that brought the members of the tribe together. They assembled not only to honor a ritual sacrifice that had been a tribal tradition since time immemorial, but also because they believed that some dancers would see visions that would endow them with supernatural powers. The dancers yearned to be blessed with that animistic power that the anthropologists call *mana*, a power that would enable the recipients to command the presence of spirits who could help them perform extraordinary deeds. As I glanced around the circle of onlookers, I noticed that some members of the tribe had been pushed forward because it was known that they were suffering from some medical condition or struggling against the infirmities of old age. These men and women were especially keen to see which dancers acquired *mana* and to see if they could attract that blessing to themselves. It was deeply moving for all of us to watch the dancers pick themselves up off the ground and to begin moving around the circle of onlookers with the same slow, trance-like shuffle that they'd performed when they first entered the ring now timed to a very slow, steady drumbeat. As the dancers moved past the onlookers, they reached out with their electrified fingers to touch an old man's weather-beaten face, to comfort a woman who'd begun to weep, to bless a young boy standing alongside his parents, and to channel the healing powers of the spirits to all who were in need of a cure. I could not look away. No one could look away.

Then it was over. The dancers left. The drummers and singers went silent. The members of the tribe began engaging one another in conversation, marveling at what they'd just seen and sharing memories of ceremonies past. I made my way back to the car and then, all too soon, I found myself back on the highway, worried that now I had to concentrate on making up for lost time if I hoped to reach my destination before sunset. It felt strange to be back again inside the secure cocoon of a modern car with its cool, air-conditioned cabin. I tried to keep my attention focused on the highway stretching out in front of me, but my mind kept drifting back to the unforgettable scenes of physical trauma and spiritual rapture.

What I didn't know then, and what I realize only now, is that this fortuitous encounter would pull me back on a path I'd once explored as young child but had long since abandoned, that it would reawaken a desire to open myself to a connection with some spiritual being more trustworthy than fellow humans. Re-entering this path would ultimately propel me into a moment of ecstasy that was as physically and psychologically piercing in its own way as what I'd observed happening to those young men at the Sun Dance. When that did happen, it didn't happen in the way that I would have expected. But now I'm getting ahead of myself...

The "Spiritual Experiments"

As I continued driving south, I found myself fantasizing about what it would be like if I got a chance to become one of those trance dancers. That would never happen, of course, not as part of an authentic tribal ceremony. Even if I were offered the opportunity, I knew I wouldn't accept. It would obviously be much too painful, and, even if I were able to withstand the pain, it would be unlikely that someone like me, an outsider who hadn't grown up in the tribe, would be invited to participate. If I wanted to have a transformative spiritual experience, I'd need to find some way to stir something deep inside myself. I wondered if I could find a setting that was profoundly evocative and immerse myself in that space and in that moment of time, opening my heart to whatever might come to pass. If that was to be my goal, then the most efficient and expeditious way to me to achieve the requisite blend of mental preparation and evocative setting would be to go on a solitary retreat. As I drove south, I kept imagining scenarios in which I might begin testing my new determination to go on a spiritual quest of some kind.

By the time I arrived back at the family cabin, I had an idea for a first retreat that would be relatively easy to implement because it wouldn't require much advance planning. The cabin was located at the base of a steep mountain slope formed by clusters of huge granite boulders piled all the way to the top of a ridge that commanded a view of the entire valley and the front range of the Rockies. What would it be like to hike up to the top of that ridge, spend the night in a sleeping bag, then get up before dawn and… and then do what? That's when it occurred to me that, while I watched the sun rise, I could mimic some of what I'd seen at the Sun Dance—I could do that slow, ritual shuffle back and forth, and I could do a passable impression of the high-pitched chants sung by the singers. It would be worthwhile to see what kind of reaction I'd get if I performed this "experiment". So why not? There were plenty of activities going on at the cabin to keep my wife and the three girls occupied. I put the question to my wife and did not encounter any serious resistance, so I grabbed a pack, stuffed it with a sleeping bag, some beef jerky, and a bottle of water bottle, then headed north up the boulder-strewn slope, carefully sorting a path that wouldn't end with me facing a dead-end. It was a challenging climb, but back then I was in pretty good physical shape, so it didn't take all that long to reach the top. I dropped my pack in a flat space behind a rocky ledge that jutted out over a steep cliff, rolled out my sleeping bag, and munched on the beef jerky. By now it was twilight and much colder than I'd anticipated because there was a stiff wind blowing out of the northwest. I crawled into my sleeping bag just as it was getting dark, and I was tired enough to fall asleep.

I awoke, as planned, just before dawn. I slipped out of the sleeping bag, dressed in the dark, and got ready to perform my experiment. I walked to the edge of the rocky rim and faced the eastern horizon where I knew the sun would soon appear. Then I began to dance: I shuffled forward a few steps, then back, then forward again, all the while singing "ah" and "oh" in a high-pitched, falsetto voice that mimicked what I'd heard at the Sun Dance. What I told myself—and what I willed myself believe, because I knew that if I didn't believe, it wouldn't happen—was that now I might be able evoke an emotional connection with the magnificent natural panorama spread out in all directions and with the rising of the sun. If I sensed any glimmer of an emotional stirring, I intended to nurture it and help it grow while I kept singing and dancing—and that's what I was doing now. But all the while I was also keeping watch on my inner response, assessing what it felt like for me to be doing what I was doing.

Splitting attention between what's happening on the outside and what's happening on the inside is a technique that anthropologists often use. They call it "participant observation." It's what anthropologists do when they want to document the practices of people about whom little is known: they might get invited to a ceremonial function, one that's rarely seen by outsiders, and while they watch, they're careful to maintain a dignified presence and an appreciative expression, behaving in ways that are appropriate for the circumstances. All that time they also keep a small portion of consciousness split off to monitor their personal reactions to whatever is taking place, because that tells something about the differences between the culture being observed and the culture of the anthropologist. This participant observation technique came in handy now as I began my test.

As I shuffled back and forth, chanting nonsense syllables in a high-pitched falsetto voice, I discovered, to my astonishment and delight, that despite my having cultivated a somewhat detached, experimental attitude—despite the split in consciousness—I did feel an emotional response as I welcomed the rising sun with song and dance. The response was authentic and surprisingly powerful; I genuinely felt I was a participant in helping the sun rise, or to be more precise, that the sun and I were collaborating to ensure that the new day would begin with an auspicious start. This experience, undertaken as the result of a casual, spur-of-the-moment decision and begun as a mere experiment, left a deep impression. It taught me that even when a person makes a relatively minor effort to simulate a ritual from some human religious tradition, it's possible to evoke an emotional response that's powerful, positive and personally meaningful.

Since that hike to the ridge worked so well, I wondered if it would be possible to evoke a comparable response by reacting spontaneously to a spur-of-the-moment impulse. One day when the rest of the family were in town shopping for groceries, I took the opportunity to perform another test. I found a grassy space between some boulders, knelt down on my knees, spread my arms wide apart, and told myself to open my heart to let it feel inspired by the beauty of the nature all around me. And it worked again. This time I felt the emotional response without the benefit of having sought out that remote aerie with a magnificent view.

The key insight I took away from the two experiments was this: mysticism is a participatory sport. You're the one who has to transform yourself by endowing your surroundings with a new sense of meaningfulness. It's not enough to place yourself in an evocative space; what makes the difference is believing that what you're doing might actually work, or, better yet, knowing that it will work based on past experience. Even if it all begins with make-believe, even if it means becoming a child again, it will still work. I was reminded of the Biblical admonition found in Matthew 7: 7: "Ask, and it will be given to you; seek, and you will find; knock, and the door will be opened to you."

My most ambitious experiment occurred a year later. My wife and I were able to leave the children at the family cabin in the care of their grandparents and to take a short vacation by ourselves. Our goal was to visit Monument Valley, a national park situated on the Navajo reservation in northern Arizona, so we drove south from Colorado to Four Corners where the borders of Utah, Colorado, New Mexico, and Arizona intersect. When we arrived in the region, we registered at Goulding's Lodge, a tourist facility located close to the national park, and spent the rest of the afternoon driving through Monument Valley on a scenic dirt road. We marveled at the huge monoliths of smooth sandstone jutting straight up out of the desert floor, and when the road began to thread through a narrow canyon, we were equally awed by the tall, weather-worn columns of rock looming up on either side of the road like sentinels standing at attention. At twilight we drove back out of the park and returned to Goulding's Lodge. But while we were driving in the park, I'd realized that this was a once-in-a-lifetime opportunity to go on a more adventurous spiritual retreat. While my wife and I were eating dinner, I told her about my new idea: I wanted to spend the night wandering alone through Monument Valley. Would she help me do that? Would she drive me to the parking lot near the entrance, drop me off, then return early the next morning to pick me up? My wife was skeptical about the plan, and she didn't like the idea of spending the night alone in our room, but she was accustomed to me coming up with what she regarded as weird ideas.

That night she drove me to the tourist parking lot and dropped me off. She pointed out a sign that warned tourists that Monument Valley is owned by the Navaho nation and that it was illegal for anyone else to be in the park after dark. But I wanted desperately to do this—and I planned to be very discrete. I wouldn't attempt to do anything that would signal my presence and give me away. All I wanted was to be able to wander alone at night through that evocative landscape, opening myself to whatever inspirational experience might come my way. If there were spiritual powers lurking in the area, searching for signs of someone with an open heart, I'd be ready. If not, I'd experience what it felt like to spend a night surrounded by awesome beauty.

Luckily for me, there was a full moon that night. It was relatively easy for me to make my way along the dirt roads, and it was inspiring to look at the light of the moon reflecting off the huge monoliths of smooth, red sandstone. I felt proud to be following in the footsteps of famous mystics who set off on solitary retreats, not knowing where it all would lead. I hoped that by opening myself to whatever might happen, I'd increase the odds that something would indeed happen.

And what was it that I thought might happen?

Looking back, I think what I wanted to happen in Monument Valley was more or less the same thing I'd wanted when I was still a young boy living in a small farming town in Kansas. Back then I was already beginning to feel an urge to search for... to search for what? I suppose I was looking for some kind of response. Not a human response, and certainly not a response from God as He's portrayed in the Bible—I'd had enough experience with angry, arbitrary fathers—so I suppose I had an inchoate yearning for some kind of response from "The Beyond", from some unseen force that would turn out to be wholly different from anything we who live on earth would normally see, hear, or touch. I was searching for a response that would serve as a validation of my being, a response that would confirm my secret feeling that I must somehow be "special", and that, when the time was right, I would get a glimpse of my destiny, that I would learn what tasks lay ahead and what I could do to benefit fellow humans.

It was a fantasy shaped by stories I'd read about young men in Native American tribes who went out alone on vision quests. And it was also a fantasy stoked by the stories I heard in Sunday school about how Jesus went out into the wilderness alone and spent forty days and forty nights praying to God for guidance. I remember wondering, back then, what would happen if I were to do what Jesus did. When I was eight or maybe ten years old, I started to make regular forays to a hillock south of our little farming town where a big round, metal water tank sat perched on tall metal stilts. From that vantage I could turn one way and look over on the whole town, then turn the other way and look out at the gently rolling grasslands of the prairie that spread out in all directions and extended as far as the eye could see. Then I'd look up at the canopy of blue sky arching overhead and watch the puffy white clouds scuttering to the east in the stiff Kansas wind. I'd feel uplifted hearing the echo of a refrain from one of my favorite hymns, a hymn we sang in church about a different kind of father who was watching all of us and now watching over me. I stood beneath the water tank and took in the view: *This is my Father's world / And to my listening ears, / All nature sings and around me rings / The music of the spheres.* If what I'd learned Sunday school was true, God the Father was watching. He would see that I was here in this special place, and He would know what I felt.

Now, after the passage of so many years, walking along a dark dirt road in Monument Valley, I found myself once again in a place that seemed to be special—even more special than that hillock with the water tank, because this desert scene was so unusual and so spectacular. Now that I was an adult, I no longer expected to receive a message from the God of the Bible, but I did hope that I could awaken something inside me by walking alone amid the rock monoliths. It was exciting to hear the strange humming and whistling sounds as a strong wind ricocheted off the smooth rock walls. But after I'd walked for several hours, marveling at the beauty all around me, I was beginning to feel disappointed. I wasn't feeling anything stirring deep inside. No spiritual presence was making itself known.

I sensed what the problem was, but I did not know how to fix it: the problem was me, that I was unable to just let myself go. It wasn't hard to come up with good reasons for being extra cautious. I had to keep an eye out for rattlesnakes. A lot of them live here, and they're usually out hunting or looking for water late at night. Sometimes they slither out onto the roads to bask in the warmth of the sun that had baked in during the day. To make matters worse, I was not the only person traveling these roads at night. Several times I saw the headlights of a car begin to pierce the dark like spotlights, long before the cars got close to me. But even though they were still several miles away, I knew I had to hide, so I'd slip off the road and find some bush to crouch behind. I wouldn't be seen by the tribesmen heading back to their remote hogans, but I had to worry about stepping on top of a rattlesnake who might be hiding in the dark shadows beneath the bushes.

In the end, nothing happened. Despite being surrounded by the moonlit beauty all around me, I couldn't let myself go. I was always too alert, never able to commit myself emotionally in a manner that would have maximized the chances of my evoking some significant response from some spiritual presence, if indeed that was even a possibility. I was reminded of something Jesus said about finding spiritual release, a lesson he must have learned during one of his solitary quests in the Jordan wilderness. It was clear that this was an admonition that I hadn't been able to fulfill: "Consider the ravens; they neither toil nor reap, they have neither storehouse nor barn, and yet God feeds them. Of how much more value are you than the birds! And can any of you by worrying add a single hour to your span of life? If then you are not able to do so small a thing as that, why do you worry about the rest? (*Luke* 12: 24-26)."

The Irony of Ironies

Ah, those old memories... When I think of them now, it all seems so very long ago. It's not that those memories got lost— those memories of who I once was and what I once thought I wanted—but the old aspirations to go on a spiritual retreat and search for resonant meanings that are hidden from those of us who've chosen to ordinary lives, those old aspirations were long since retired, left to languish in some remote reservoir of memory. But now, as I recount these stories, the old memories are coming back to me, and here's the reason why I've decided to share them with you: before you read what's coming next, I want you to appreciate that there were times in my life, now long past, when you would have described me as a spiritual seeker—a cautious seeker, to be sure, someone inclined to hedge his bets by limiting himself to "manageable" experiments, but a seeker nonetheless. Knowing that about my early life, you'll appreciate the irony in the story I'm about to tell.

It was only after I'd given up those aspirations of having a mystical experience—only after I'd spent years in Boston, reintegrated with my normal life as a husband and father and professional medical writer—it was only then that I was suddenly, inadvertently, overwhelmed by a mystical experience that far surpassed anything I'd ever hoped for or even imagined in my younger days. It happened one night when I was lying in bed, waiting to fall asleep. A vision of bright, lightning-like flashes suddenly erupted, unbidden and unexpected. I was caught up in an ecstatic rapture so powerful that, even now, I shiver to think about it.

Not an Auspicious Night

It was four o'clock in the morning, and I was still wide awake. I never had problems with insomnia, so why now? Clearly something was off, but I didn't know what. Jet-lag? Maybe. I'd just flown across four time zones, and during my travels I'd only been able to sleep for four of the preceding thirty-six hours and had already accumulated a substantial sleep deficit; I shouldn't have any problem falling asleep. I was also feeling a bit depressed, but that's not all that unusual for me: I've been officially diagnosed with "atypical depression" secondary to "complex post-traumatic stress disorder", the kind of PTSD people acquire when they're still very young children. But while mood changes are a problem I often have to cope with, that's never interfered with my being able to fall asleep. I was feeling desperate for reasons that all parents will recognize: my wife and I had to get up at six o'clock, rouse our three young daughters out of their beds, cook them breakfast, drop them off at school, and then get to work ourselves.

I tried to relax by slouching down into our overstuffed couch, sipping a cup of warm, rum-laced milk, and listening to music playing loudly enough in my earphones to keep me from ruminating about what I should have said during the minor argument I'd had with my wife earlier that evening. Eventually I realized that this strategy wasn't going to work, so I gave up and went to bed anyway. Once there, I laid on my back, eyes closed, focusing all my attention on the dark void in front of me, listening to the sound of my breath flowing in and out—everything I'd learned to do in meditation classes. And my efforts were beginning to work. I was feeling more and more relaxed. All the distracting thoughts were gone, and I knew, based on experience, what would likely happen next. For me, this was a familiar routine, so I wasn't surprised when I saw the first vision of light appear.

The Visions Begin to Appear

The first vision was a thin black ring that swept into view from all sides of the visual field, as if it had just come from behind my head, then began shrinking in diameter so that it looked like it was moving away from me. But almost immediately after the black ring swept into the visual field, it was replaced by a bright green ring that suddenly effloresced where the black ring had been only an instant before. The green light-ring was also shrinking in diameter so that it looked like it was flying off into the dark void. Several green rings then began appearing, one after another, with clock-like regularity at five second intervals. Halfway through the shrinking trajectory—at precisely two seconds after the ring first appeared—the dark center region of each ring would fill with green light, converting the ring image to a disk. As usual, after I saw a set of three rings, they stopped automatically, as if a switch had been turned off somewhere in the brain.

Now another familiar vision arrived: a cloud of dark blue mist with porous textures and amorphous, ever-changing borders that coalesced at the center of the visual field. It looked like the photos of those beautiful, disk-shaped gas nebulae you see in books on astronomy. In a normal meditation session, I would spend a lot of time staring intently at the dark blue clouds whenever they appeared, watching to see if my trance was deep enough and intense enough to cause the cloud to develop a small disk of dark blue light at its center, a disk that was much brighter and much more opaque than the rest of the cloud surrounding it. On this night, I was surprised to see that I didn't have to wait and didn't have to concentrate all that much: shortly after the first dark blue cloud appeared, one of the small, brighter disks appeared, much earlier than would have usually happened, and this inner disk seemed to be much more "intense" than what I'd normally experienced in the past—as if it had some magnetic quality that riveted my attention. Shortly after it appeared, that bright inner disk began to undergo the transformations that make it so fascinating to watch, the transformations that turn it into an "eye-like" image. It starts when the light of the bright inner disk begins ebbing away from the center of that disk, opening up a tiny, dark space that looks like a "pupil".

That converts what used to be the disk into a thin, "iris-like" ring of bright light surrounding the dark inner "pupil", an image that I've often heard referred to as the "Third Eye". I've never been able to sustain that eye-image for very long; almost immediately after the dark "pupil" opens up, it fills back in as promontories of bright light from the "iris" begin shooting down into the dark space. It was entertaining, as always, to watch the eerie, ever-changing fluctuations, but on this occasion I wasn't interested in prolonging the vision of the dark blue cloud. Given that it was now past four o'clock in the morning, I just wanted to fall asleep. Then something happened that I'd never seen before.

Suddenly the dark blue cloud and the bright inner disk both condensed into a tiny dot of light that looked exactly like a "twinkling star". The "twinkling" effect was generated by a cluster of tiny filaments of white light that kept flashing in and out of existence at the very center of the visual field—like the bright, thin sparks flying away from one of those sparklers being waved about on the Fourth of July. This was a vision I'd never seen before, and it felt vaguely ominous. Like it might be blinking a warning. And, indeed, that's precisely what it was doing—blinking a warning.

Into the Dark "Tunnel"

Shortly after the twinkling star appeared, it suddenly vanished as a stream of black rings began pouring into the visual field, one after another, at a rate of two or three rings per second. These black rings had the same shapes and followed the same trajectories as the green light-rings that had appeared earlier, but this time the rings remained black as they "receded" into the dark visual field. Seeing so many black rings stream into the visual field at such a fast rate and then appear to fly away in a tight formation created the illusion of a dark, moving tunnel. The tunnel generated a powerful sensation of optic flow, a psychophysiological sensation that creates the illusion of movement even when the seer remains motionless. It felt like I was being pulled along with the receding rings, like all my attention was being sucked into the vortex of that dark tunnel.

The vision of a dark, moving tunnel was so compelling and so disorienting that I was about to put a stop to it—to open my eyes and look at something real. Then I remembered reading books by near-death survivors who said they saw visions of a dark, moving tunnel. They said the tunnel pulled them in, carried them off, and eventually deposited them in the midst of a bright, all-enveloping light where they were blessed with feelings of joy and bliss. That recollection made me pause. Was I seeing one of those dark tunnels? But why would that be? I certainly was not facing a near-death situation. Now I was more curious than concerned: What if I was seeing a version of that near-death tunnel that leads to a mystical rapture? That might well be what was happening. So maybe I should stick with this tunnel vision and wait for it to take me into the all-enveloping light and bring on those feelings of joy and bliss. I didn't want to bail out prematurely and miss that mystical experience.

The tunnel of black rings continued flying away for only a few more moments, then there was another sudden and dramatic change: the tunnel disappeared and in the same instant my visual field was filled with hundreds of tiny flecks of spark-like yellow lights. The sparks formed a spray that radiated out through the peripheral regions of the visual field toward my forehead. I felt an obscure compulsion to arch my back and push my head back against the pillow in response. The muscles of my face, toes, and fingertips also began to tremble ever so slightly. It was clear to me that the radiating sparks and the postural contortions were symptoms of some kind of paroxysmal event. I realized then that I'd let myself get distracted by the dark tunnel and the radiating spray and that I was letting everything get out of hand. But before I had a chance to extricate myself, I noticed a subtle change in the visual field. And, once again, I hesitated: I wanted to see what was going to happen next.

The Enveloping Light

Although the radiating spray was still streaming toward me, I sensed it was beginning to fade away as the entire visual field was now becoming brighter and bluer, brighter and bluer—like the light of dawn retiring the night sky. I couldn't tell if the fading away of the sparks was because the entire visual field had now become so bright or because the brain processes that were causing the sparks to appear were in the process of shutting down.

Now I found myself staring up into what looked like a cloudless sky, feeling comforted by a deep calm. Those near-death survivors had it right: they said the dark tunnel would pull me in, that it would carry me away, and then it would drop me off in the middle of an all-enveloping light. That's indeed what happened. But what about the feelings of joy and bliss? They had not yet arrived. Maybe that was still to come? I kept staring at the bright blue sky.

Nothing changed for a relatively long time. Up to this point, all of the changes had been occurring in rapid succession, so I expected that would keep happening. I was puzzled by the delay. But the near-death survivors hadn't provided much guidance about what would come after the all-enveloping light. Maybe all the usual changes had already occurred. I was starting to feel a bit bored with staring up at the bright blue visual field. Then I detected a subtle change. I could make out a faint smudge of white light in the upper right quadrant of the visual field. I say "smudge" because it looked like the bright, white light was still partially obscured by the sky-blue background. But then, as I peered in that direction, the white light brightened to become a figure shaped like a dome formed by walls of translucent white light. When my attention wavered ever-so-slightly, the rear of the bulb-shaped protrusion would dim and then fade away. That created the optical illusion of the bulb receding slightly into the blue background. Sometimes the bulb pulled so far back that it would disappear altogether, but if I kept staring at the spot where it vanished, the dome-shaped tip would brighten along with its posterior regions and then it looked like the bulb was protruding once again. Forward and back. Forward and back. That kept happening for what seemed like a relatively long time, but now I was not bored by the delay. I was confident that this vision of a bulbous protrusion was almost certainly being driven by some powerful excitation pulsating somewhere in the brain that was likely to trigger some new vision.

Suddenly the white bulb flared more brightly than before which made it look as if it had just thrust itself much farther forward. Then, in the same instant, the white bulb disappeared. The bright sky-blue background light filling the visual field also disappeared in that same instant. In the space that the white bulb had formerly occupied there was now a brace of three thin white rays silhouetted against the charcoal-gray background. The three rays were joined at the base to form a trident that stretched halfway up toward the outer rim of the visual field. My attention was immediately drawn to one of the rays—the one on the right—because it was very different from the other two. The upper tip of that ray on the right was bent left at a ninety-degree angle so that its tip pointed toward the other two rays. The image reminded me of the videos I'd seen in which cobra snakes were rearing up above their coils and pointing their heads towards some perceived threat. The image of those trident rays remained in my visual field for no more than one or two seconds, then suddenly the three rays were replaced by another ray image. Now there were six white rays instead of three and all six of those rays were long enough to reach all the way up to the outer rim of the visual field. One second later, the tips the six white rays slowly fanned farther apart. These transformations looked like the petals of a flower bulb opening in response to the warmth of the morning sun and then "wilting" farther apart. After the rays spread apart, they remained in that position and did not undergo any more changes.

I was surprised: this was a sudden shift away from the rapid changes leading up to this point—and the outstretched rays looked like they were heading somewhere. This delay might be a signal that something spectacular was about to happen. I started counted the passing seconds to see how long it would take. I just reached the count of twelve when the cataclysm began.

The Culminating Vision of Fiery Light

Flashes of lightning started erupting in my visual field. The flashes looked exactly like the flashes of sheet lightning that illuminate dark storm clouds from within. The flashes exploded first on one side of the visual field, then on the other, so it looked like lightning reverberating inside a cloud. I also heard strange sounds inside my head—a buzzing, sizzling sound, as if somewhere in my brain an electric circuit was in the process of shorting out. The muscles in my face and my arms and legs started to tremble uncontrollably. Once again I felt a compulsion to arch my back and push my head against the pillow but now with more exaggerated and more intense contortions than those triggered earlier by the vision of the radiating spray. My eyes rolled up toward the top of my head and my mouth dropped open in a slack-jaw position. But what really riveted my attention were the spasms in my bulbospongiosus muscle. It's a muscle that's located at the base of the scrotum in males and along either side of the vaginal opening in females. The bulbospongiosus muscle was clenching spasmodically, just like it does during sexual climax, and that sent waves of orgasmic sensations surging through my body. These erotic sensations were not localized in the genital region, so it felt less like I was experiencing a sexual orgasm and more like I was exploding with erotic energy and sending heat waves out in all directions. I was also caught up in a powerful surge of emotions—a mix of euphoria, ecstasy, awe, and fear.

And there were plenty of reasons to feel afraid: lightning-like flashes, buzzing sounds, postural contortions, muscle spasms, and a wave of orgasmic sensations all pointed toward this being some kind of seizure—an ecstatic seizure, but a seizure nonetheless. I didn't know what to do next. You'd expect a medical writer to know something about seizures, but I'd never been assigned to write a script on that subject, so I'd never done the relevant research. I did know that what was happening to me had to be some kind of "partial" seizure because I was still conscious, but that was not very reassuring because I knew that partial seizures can spread. If that happens—if the partial seizure "generalizes" by spreading throughout the brain—it triggers a seizure in which the victims lose consciousness, collapse, and sometimes begin convulsing. It was now clear that I'd let this mystical experience go on for far too long. I needed to put a stop to all this to avoid having it spread through the brain and become a generalized seizure.

But, once again, I hesitated. This was such an extraordinary event and one that might evolve to become something even more dramatic and transformative. But there would also be a cost incurred by backing away, so it seemed prudent at wait a bit longer. I kept giving myself excuses for why that was a good idea. I remember telling myself that this experience is too exciting and too euphoric to qualify as a "real" seizure. Maybe this is something that fits into a different category? Maybe it's very rare mystical phenomenon that occurs so infrequently and in such unpredictable circumstances that scientists have never had a chance to study the phenomenon in real time and discover that it's something different from a seizure. What if I decide to bail out now when I might be on the cusp of experiencing something truly momentous? What if I'm about to be granted some important new insights that reveal the true meaning of life? Isn't that what many mystics say about their visionary experiences?

But mixed in with the exhilaration of thinking I might experience some transcendent event I was also struggling with some importuning concerns. What if the ecstatic rapture doesn't stop? What if I get stuck in here and can't find a way to extract myself? What if there's no way back to my normal life? Ironically, that might well be the goal most sought by many religious mystics, but it was not one of my goals. I didn't want to change my life. I liked everything just the way it was: I liked living in Boston; I liked loving my darling wife; I liked helping my wife raise our three beautiful daughters; I liked working as a professional medical writer. I didn't want to lose any of that, even if it meant giving up the prospect of some spiritual transformation.

As these thoughts kept pushing through my mind, I decided that I needed to perform a test to see if I was still in control of what was happening. My first test was to stop fixating on the visual field and to open my eyes. All of the paroxysmal symptoms immediately stopped. I felt immensely relieved! I was still in control! If it had been a real seizure, I wouldn't have been able to stop it—or at least that's what I thought at the time. To continue the test, I tried closing my eyes again and fixating attention on the visual field. Whoosh! The whole conflagration erupted again. But now that I'd just proved to myself that I still was in control, I felt it would be okay to put aside my concerns and allow myself to enjoy being caught up in the ecstatic rapture.

But it turned out there were no more sudden, dramatic changes. Just more of the same—more trembling, more ecstatic emotions, and it didn't take long before the novelty and the excitement started to wear off. I began to feel bored. Yes, I know that sounds crazy: How is it possible that someone would feel bored during an ecstatic, mystical rapture? But that's how it felt, and that's why I decided that if nothing new was going to happen it was now time to bail out. So I opened my eyes. Everything stopped. I was left lying in bed, staring up at the ceiling, feeling stunned. I glanced toward the other side of the bed where I expected to see my wife having been startled awake by all the shaking, but she was still fast asleep. Did all those tremors and bodily contortions occur mostly in my mind? Hard to believe.

I was much too excited to have any chance of falling asleep. I glanced over at the alarm clock sitting on the table beside my wife and saw that it was now almost five o'clock—less than an hour from the time I went to bed and tried meditating to help me fall asleep. While I was caught up in the ecstatic rapture, it seemed go on for an eternity, but that was then—that was before I returned to the real world. I decided it was now time to get out of bed, get dressed, go downstairs, brew a cup of coffee, and head out for an early morning walk. I needed to take a walk. I needed to calm down.

The World Transformed

To my surprise, the walk turned out to be as much of a mystical experience as the vision itself. Once outside, it felt like I was walking through a magical landscape. The familiar neighborhood scenes were now dramatically transformed: the colors of the bushes and trees were intensely vivid; the empty spaces between objects appeared to be almost tangible. I stared up and out in every direction, awestruck.

My mind was flooded by importuning thoughts, the kind of thoughts I'd always dismissed as naïve clichés when I'd encountered them in books about mystical experiences—thoughts like, "The world is perfect just as it is, if only we humans were able to look at it afresh and see the reality," or "After enlightenment, everything changes, and everything also stays the same." Now I felt like these thoughts represented profound insights into the true nature of reality. I wondered why it had taken me so long to realize that.

As I walked on, it occurred to me that all of these perceptions seemed to be coated by a patina of "excess meaningfulness". Everything struck me as being so marvelous, so meaningful. It felt like I might be "imprinting" on my surroundings like a newborn duckling that breaks out of its shell and bonds with whatever happens to move first in its immediate proximity.

Usually what moves first is its mother; that's how the newborn duckling establishes the most important bond in its young life. Could something like that ever happen to human beings? Do they ever get primed to imprint on their surroundings?

Neurologists say something similar does indeed happen in cases of déjà vu: that's when people are confronted by a scene that strikes them as being intimately familiar and meaningful even though they've never encountered the scene before. People who've experienced déjà vu often try to come up with a confabulation, a made-up story about how they visited this place in a dream or in a former life. But neurologists have a different explanation, one that is simpler, more realistic, and more convincing. Neurologists propose that déjà vu occurs when neurons located in the emotional association centers of the limbic brain suddenly fire a burst of discharges for some unknown reason and then go quiet again. One effect of this anomalous discharge is that it releases extra neurotransmitter that then sloshes around in the synaptic clefts between the terminals of the axons and dendrite receptors of neurons in the emotional association centers of the brain. That excess neurotransmitter stimulates those neurons to add a strong emotional overlay to whatever visual signals happen to be about to surface in that person's brain—and that means whatever happens to be in front of the person's eyes at the time will get associated with feelings of intimate familiarity and profound meaning.

Now as I walked through the neighborhood, marveling at the seemingly miraculous transformation, I did indeed get the feeling that something had been stirred up deep inside, that excess neurotransmitter released in the emotional association centers of my brain must be coating my perceptions with "excess meaningfulness". I felt that, yes, I'd become one of those newborn ducklings who'd been primed to imprint on whatever moved first in my vicinity when I broke out of my shell, and now that's what was happening: I was imprinting on Mother Earth as if I were seeing the real Her for the first time.

In Dreams Begin Responsibilities

As I sat at my desk later that afternoon thinking about what happened earlier in the day, I could sense that, somehow, my life had just been transformed by what happened, but I couldn't find a way to put what I was feeling in words. Then I remembered reading a short story written by Delmore Schwartz that had an evocative title: "In Dreams Begin Responsibilities." That title has always resonated with me since I first encountered it, and now I realized that Schwartz's words expressed what I was feeling now. I'd been caught up in a dream that lifted me out of normal Time and Space, pulled me into a dark void, showered me with a spectacular explosion of lights, then dropped me unceremoniously back to earth and back into my normal life. Why did that happen? And what was I supposed to do now? I felt that somehow I must have become responsible for something. But responsible for what?

That was the moment I realized the true significance of what had just happened to me: I'd been granted the gift of seeing a rare type of vision—a vision that's only rarely seen by even the most accomplished mystics—so it would be rarer still, perhaps even unique, for someone like me, someone who'd given up on the possibility of having mystical experiences, someone who'd dedicated himself to a life focused on scientific understanding and to carrying out the myriad practical obligations of everyday life, to see the explosion of the fiery light and feel caught up in its ecstatic rapture. Now I realized that it had become my personal destiny to find a way to explain what just happened to me—and to find a way to communicate whatever I was able to discover to my fellow humans.

As tumultuous as the experience had been at the time, I remembered a lot of details about what happened during that vision. I'd watched my reactions to what I was seeing and feeling because I wanted to be able to remember what happened once it was all over. So now I'd been granted the unprecedented opportunity to combine my personal visionary experiences with my professional skills as a medical writer and to use that dual perspective when the time came to dig into the relevant scientific literature searching for the kinds of brain mechanisms that could potentially cause a person to see those visions of light. I felt confident that knowing the shapes, sizes, colors, movement patterns, timing intervals, and sequential order of those visions would likely enable me to match each of those characteristics with specific brainwaves. The visions of light would provide clues, not only to what happened in my brain, but what would have to happen in *any* human brain in order for the person to see what I'd just seen. So yes, it was true: I'd been given a rare opportunity, and now it was incumbent on me to accept the new responsibility that had been placed on my shoulders—to find out what happened and why. *In dreams begin responsibilities.*

CHAPTER 2

Fiery Lights and the Founders of World Religions

What the Founders Said They Saw

As I thought about the extraordinary events that had happened that night, I could better understand why seeing a vision like this, a vision that's so spectacular, so ecstatic, so awe-inspiring, would likely lead someone to believe that such a vision could only have come from God or from some other supernatural source. To begin, I needed to know more about people who reported having seen similar visions of bright, flashing lights and their descriptions of what they'd seen, so it seemed obvious that it would be useful to sort through the sacred texts of the world's major religions. When I immersed myself in that traditional literature, I found many accounts of religious mystics who described seeing ecstatic visions of bright, flashing lights that became the inspiration for launching their new careers as charismatic prophets. I also read articles by anthropologists who'd studied visionary experiences in remote tribes that still practice the shamanic arts. I kept a detailed list of all the names I encountered during this research along with the descriptions of what was seen. As that list got longer and longer, I discovered that many of those mystic seers described their visions in ways that were remarkably similar, not only to what the others had seen but also to what I'd seen. But I don't want you to have to take my word for this; I want you to be able to see that list of metaphors for yourself. Here are some of the ways that famous mystic seers described seeing visions of bright flashing lights that filled their visual fields:

Visions of Lightning Flashes

- "Fire and lightning flashing inside a dark cloud" (Ezekiel, *Ezekiel* 1: 4, 13)
- "Satan falling out of heaven like lightning" (Jesus of Nazareth, *Luke* 10: 18)
- "Almost blinded by a flash of lightning" (Muhammed, *Quran*, Sura 2: 20)
- "Flashes of lightning as short and brief as I could bear" (Mani, *Book of Giants*)
- "Flashes bright-like-lightning" (Indo-Aryan priests, *Rig Veda* 10.177.1; 8.48.6)
- "Lightning lights up the whole body" (Hindu priests, *Maitri Upanishad,* 7: 11)
- "Boundless light-manifestations" (The Buddha, *Majjhima-Nikaya* 128.3.161)
- "White *p'o*-spirits filling the inner space" (Lao Tzu, *Dao-de-jing,* verse 10)
- "A great vascillating brightness" (Anon., *3 Ways to Go Beyond the Heavenly Pass*)
- "Emperor One shines like a white sun" (Zhang Ling, *Book of Great Profundity*)

- "Waters of lunar efflorescence" (Yang Xi, *The Upper Scripture of Purple Texts*)
- "Lightning flashes" (Hildegard von Bingen, *Ecstatic Confessions*)
- "A wind raged, the earth shook, and a fire filled the sky" (Elijah, 1 *Kings* 19: 12)
- "Stars and lightnings were rushing me" (Enoch, 1 *Enoch* 8-15)
- "Lightning flashes" (Philo of Alexandria, *The Decalogue*, XI: 44)
- "They appear as if they were lightning" (Rabbi Askenazi in Anon., *Sefer Yesirah* 1: 8)
- "Soul sees… a lightning flash" (John of the Cross, *Ascent of Mt. Carmel* II: 24.5)
- "The flash of [Wisdom's] lightning" (Mansur al-Hallaj, *Kitab al-Tawasin*)
- "Flashes of lightning, quivering limbs" (Yahya Suhrawardi, *Treatise* VIII)
- "Lightning… continual flashes" (al-Qushayri, *The Qu-shaayriyyan Treatise*)
- "Lightning is the end of the road beginning with light" (Shankara, *Vedanta-Sutras*, II)
- "Flashes of lightning… molten light" (Paramahansa Yoga-nanda, 1993, p. 163)
- "Like lightning… a thousand-spoked wheel" (Abhinava-gupta, *Tantraloka*, 4: 133)

Visions of Fire

- "A blazing torch passing between pieces of a sacrifice" (Abraham, *Genesis* 15: 17)
- "A fire enveloping a bush but not burning it" (Moses, *Exodus* 3: 2)

- "A wind raged, the earth shook, and a fire filled the sky" (Elijah, 1 *Kings* 19: 12)
- "For YHWH your God is a devouring fire" (Anonymous, *Deuteronomy* 4: 24)
- "The Divine Presence… like scintillating flames" (Anonymous, *Sefer-ha-Hekhalot*)
- "There is a fire fiercer than fire" (Rabbi Shim'on in Matt DC, *The Zohar* 1: 50b)
- "A consuming fire… that provides ecstasy" (Abraham Abulfalia, *Shaarey Orah* 1)
- "A fire brighter in its whiteness than any other fire" (Eleazor ben Judah of Worms)
- "The seat of gold… the soul on fire" (Juan Yepes, *Dark Night of the Soul*, II: 20.5)
- "Immersed in light and fire" (Pseudo-Macarius, *The Homilies*, 15.10)
- "Clad in fire" (Abdisho' Hazzaya, *The Book of Questions and Answers*)
- "O, what swirlings of flame" (Symeon the New Theologian, *Hymns of Divine Love*)
- "The flames of fire are all around you" (Najmoddin Kubra, *Visio Smaragdina*)
- "The realm of Clear Light is a blazing mass of fire" (Jetsun Milarepa)
- "I was enveloped by lights" and it was like "burning alive" (Ibn al'Arabi)

Visions of a Bright Sun

- "A flash like the sun at daybreak" (Prophet Mohammed, *Bukhari's Hadith* 171-173)

- "Like the sun covered by a transparent veil" (Teresa of Avila, *Interior Castle* IX: 3)
- "Surpasses the splendor of the sun" (Angela of Foligno, *Memorial*)
- "A round, beautiful, illuminating light, like the sun" (Sofia von Kingnau, *SisterBook*)
- "A brilliant, dazzling light, a thousand suns coming out" (Ananda Ma, *Sayings*)
- "Out of the bliss-waves… arose a white paradise" (Yeshe Tsogyel, *Lotus Born*)
- "Like the light of sun in a crystal" (Rabbi Judah Halevi, *Sefer Ha-Kurazi*, IV: 3)
- "Zohar light… is like the light of the sun" (Moses de Leon, *Sefer ba Zohar*)
- "I became all eye" surrounded by "bright sun" (Gregory Palamas)
- "He appears as a sun, fiery and flaming" (Swedenborg, *Heaven and Its Wonders*)
- "A pillar of light… brighter than the sun" (Joseph Smith, Jr., *History of the Church*)

Visions of a Bright Light

- "A bright flash of light" (Paul of Tarsus, Acts 9: 1-9)
- "The messenger, Good Mind, wearing garments of light" (Zoroaster, *Yasna* 43: 16)
- "Out of the bliss-waves… arose a white paradise" (Yeshe Tsogyel, *Lotus Born*)
- "A white fluid… permeates the head" (Naropa, *The Six Yogas*, I: 143-6)
- "A white body… no visible members" (Ignatius of Loyola, *Autobiography*)

- "The vision of a dazzling white mountain" (A. Luria, reported by Hayyim Vital)
- "An ocean... luminous waves" (Ramakrishna, in Masson, *The Oceanic Feeling*)

Visions of Contemporary Mystics

- "The Sphere of Unmanifest Light found in the *sahasrara*... opened up and its light was released, and the brilliance of not one or two thousand, but millions of suns blazed all around" (Muktananda, *The Play of Consciousness,* 1988)
- "Bright light bathes me on all sides, as intense as the midday sun. Its dazzling brightness extends far behind my head and upper back" (James Austin, M.D., *Zen and the Brain,* 1998)
- "The emergent state has also featured a change in my experience of prayer. During deep states of quiet, when resting in point zero, a pulsating white light radiates around my head (Philip St. Romain, a Roman Catholic lay minister, *Kundalini Energy and Christian Spirituality,* 1994);"
- "God, he told us, had fired a beam of pink light directly at him, at his head, his eyes; Fat had been temporarily blinded and his head had ached for days. It was easy, he said, to describe the beam of pink light; exactly what you get as a phosphene after-image when a flashbulb has gone off in your face" (Philip K. Dick attributing a vision he saw himself to a character named "Fat" in his novel, *Valis,* 1991)
- "From my earliest experience of life, I have enjoyed a condition that I would call the 'bright'. As a baby I remember crawling around inquisitively with an incredible sense of joy, light, and freedom in the middle of my head that was bathed in energies moving freely down from above" (Cult

leader Franklin Jones, aka Da Free John, aka Adi Da, from his autobiography, *The Knee of Listening*, 1987)

- "Suddenly it felt like the bottom of my spine was plugged into a wall socket as I felt an enormous surge of energy rushing from the bottom of my spine up to the top of my head. All I could see was blazing white light" (Andrew Cohen, a New Age teacher, in *Autobiography of an Awakening*, 1992)

- "A being bathed in a white light hovered over the bed. / A blue glowing ball of energy came out of him and into me, and I was absolutely overcome by a feeling of ecstasy and joy... I consider it a real experience and a wake-up call" (Joseph P. Firmage, a Silicon Valley entrepreneur, describing a vision he saw in 1997 that convinced him he'd been contacted by an extra-terrestrial civilization that was urging him to sell his company to found a new religious organization, *Kairos*, that would be more open to technological advances than existing religions. Reported in *The Boston Globe*, 1/24/1999)

- "All at once I found myself crying out, 'If there is a God, let Him show himself! I am willing to do anything, anything!' Suddenly the room lit up with a great white light. I was caught up on an ecstasy which there are no words to describe. The surge of energy was so powerful that I even thought my body might explode." (Bill W., founder of AA, from his book, *Alcoholics Anonymous Comes of Age*, 1957)

- "Suddenly, with the roar of a waterfall, I felt a stream of liquid light entering my brain. The illumination grew brighter, the roaring louder, I experienced a rocking sensation and then felt myself slipping out of my body, entirely enveloped in a halo of light" (Gopi Krishna, *Kundalini: The Evolutionary Energy in Man*, 1971)

Now that you've read all of these descriptions of bright lights that fill the seers' visual fields, what do you think? Do you agree that these descriptions, while they're not exactly the same, appear to be remarkably similar? Or are you skeptical about that claim? It's clear that, at this stage in our investigation, you do not yet have enough information to answer that question. So what is the next step? How can we determine if the metaphors that were chosen by the founders and by the other influential mystics accurately characterize what they actually saw during their visionary experiences? To support a claim that the differences in metaphors do not relate to actual differences in the light sensations that appeared in their visual fields, I have to present evidence that will support two propositions: first, I have to demonstrate that when visions of bright, flashing lights cover the seer's entire visual field, this can only be generated by a certain set of brain mechanisms, no matter how the seer decides to describe that vision; and, second, I have to demonstrate that the neurophysiology of the specific brain mechanisms constrains the amount of variation that can occur.

CHAPTER 3

Fiery Lights and Limbic Seizures

The Role of the Hippocampi

In order for a person, any person, to see a vision of lighting-like flashes exploding in the visual field, neurons located at a critical junction in the visual pathways have to shift from firing in the normal, well-controlled, harmonic patterns to firing chaotic, paroxysmal bursts. In other words, a seizure must erupt. Because those seizure-generated flashes block the processing of other kinds of incoming visual signals, we can identify with more precision where in the brain the seizure is taking place: the paroxysmal discharges must be engulfing the two hippocampi, the terminal structures in the visual pathways. In normal perception, the feature extraction centers in in the visual cortices process incoming visual signals and relay them down to the two hippocampi, those tiny, seahorse-shaped structures. There's a hippocampus located on each side of the brain in the limbic region. The left hippocampus receives all of the visual signals that originated on the right sides of both retinae; the right hippocampus receives all of the signals that originated on the left sides. Paroxysmal discharges surging in the hippocampal terminals will produce maximal disruption because they prevent the hippocampi from processing of any other visual signals, so nothing other than the bright flashes will surface in the seer's visual field.

If a seizure remains confined within a hippocampus and does not spread into adjacent limbic and temporal regions, it's called a "simple partial seizure". During such seizures there are few, if any, symptoms that would alert an onlooker that the person was having a seizure. If the seizure spreads downstream into other limbic and temporal lobe regions and then also spreads through the corpus callosum to ignite the same limbic structures in the other side of the brain, this qualifies as a "complex partial seizure". People who experience complex partial seizures typically retain conscious awareness of what's happening to them, even though that consciousness might be temporarily impaired to some extent. Partial seizures are called "focal" seizures because they remain confined in the limbic and temporal lobe regions and do not "generalize" into other brain regions and trigger a loss of consciousness and physical collapse.

Once it became clear that the lightning-like flashes covering both sides of my visual field were caused by seizures erupting in both hippocampi, I started digging again in the scientific literature to find out what kinds of changes would have had to take place inside my brain in order to provoke seizures in both hippocampi. In Chapter 1, I described sequence of visions I saw leading up to the eruption of the fiery light. I mentioned there that I saw a small, white, bulbous glow that seemed to protrude in the sky-blue visual field—a figure that seemed to move forward, then pull back, then move forward again until suddenly it disappeared, along with the bright blue background. That was a very strange vision and one that clearly needed to become the next focus of the neurologically grounded, reverse-engineering analysis.

Ghost Images of the Hippocampus

Paging through anatomical drawings of the human hippocampus, I couldn't help noticing that the hippocampus has a very unusual and convoluted anatomy: it has an anterior "nose" region, a tubular extension with a rounded tip, that is bent back over the main body of the hippocampus. This anterior "nose" looks like the thumb on a human hand that bends over the palm to align itself with the other fingers on the hand. The tip of that anterior "nose" region that protrudes out and then bends back over the main body of the hippocampus is enveloped by a thin sheet of neurons that covers the dome-shaped tip. That thin sheet of neurons covering the anterior "nose" of the hippocampus turns out to be especially important for our analysis, because those neurons can be selectively stimulated much more intensely than hippocampal neurons located in the main body of the hippocampus.

When meditators are performing the usual techniques for inducing an empty-mind trance—when they've converged their eyes and fixated their attention on the visual field—these behaviors will selectively stimulate the neurons in that bulb-shaped sheet, augmenting other sources of excitation that are being directed down into the hippocampi at the same time. For example, in my case, the most important source of excitation converging on the hippocampi would be the intense barrage of powerful rhythmic pulses being generated by the onset of a "hyper-synchronous" seizure in the visual cortices that began with the visions of the dark tunnel followed by the spray of sparks. I'll have more to say about hyper-synchronous seizures and how they can be inadvertently triggered by unsuspecting meditators in Chapter 9; for present purposes, what's important to keep in mind is that this kind of high-amplitude synchronous excitation streams down from the visual cortices into the two hippocampi. That barrage will stimulate hippocampal neurons to discharge more frequently and more intensely, causing a diffuse brightening of the entire visual field. That's why, as I watched the visual field while the spray of sparks radiating out toward my forehead, I saw the visual field slowly change from the normal charcoal gray color to the bright blue of a summer sky. After that brightening occurred—and after it persisted a while without undergoing any more changes—I saw the vision of the small bulb formed by a brighter, whiter light that seemed to push forward into the upper right quadrant of the visual field.

The surfaces of the small, dome-shaped protrusion were formed by the glow of a translucent white light, and, when I was able to study the anatomical drawings of a human hippocampus, it was obvious that the protrusion had precisely the same shape as the tip of the anterior nose region of a hippocampus. Because I was meditating when this vision appeared, keeping my eyes converged and my attention fixated on the bulbous glow, I was selectively stimulating the neurons in that sheet that envelops the bulb-shaped nose of a hippocampus. That additional stimulation would cause those neurons to fire more vigorously than all of the other neurons located in that same hippocampus, and that extra stimulation would generate a glow that was brighter than the blue background being generated by the barrage of hypersynchronous excitation. Whenever I fixated my attention on that white, bulb-shaped protrusion, that sent more excitation pouring into that sheet of neurons surrounding the anterior nose region, stimulating more neurons in that sheet to fire at peak intensities, thereby generating the illusion that the white bulbous figure became longer, which made it seem that the figure moved forward.

I should point out that there's an obvious problem with the explanation as I've presented it so far: while it explains why I saw a bulbous protrusion shining in the upper right quadrant of the visual field, it does not explain why I saw only one image and not two. There are, after all, two hippocampi in the brain, so why did only one protrusion appear? Why wasn't there a similar image in the left side of the visual field? I'm not the only meditator who's reported seeing just one bulbous protrusion; all of the ancient mystical texts that describe this vision specify that there is only one image, so something else must be happening in the brain to explain why there's only a single image. If I speculate about what that additional factor might be, I suspect that it could be the result of some preexisting damage to inhibitory circuits in one hippocampus. That damage might allow more hypersynchronous excitation to pour into the anterior nose region of that hippo-campus than the one on the opposite side of the brain. And the damage to inhibitory circuits would also make that hippocampus vulnerable to a more rapid build-up of excitation in its nose region in response to the meditator's fixation of attention combined with the ongoing barrage of hypersynchronous activity arriving from the visual cortices. Many studies in the medical literature have found links between damage to hippocampal neurons and a personal history of chronic exposure to serious trauma. As our investigation proceeds, we will find that traumatic childhoods happen all too often in the lives of the founders and in the lives of the other mystics who've seen visions of fiery light.

This explanation might be relevant in my own case. I was exposed to chronic trauma-related stress as a very young child, which is why I've been diagnosed with atypical depression sec-ondary to complex PTSD. I've never taken any tests to see if those early experiences damaged neurons in my hippocampus, but if that damage does in fact exist, it would help explain why I saw only one bulbous protrusion, not two. And in my case, the fact that the bulbous glow appeared in the right side of the visual field suggests that preexisting damage to inhibitory neurons, if it did indeed exist, must have been most serious in the left hippocampus, which is where visual signals associated with the right half of the visual field get processed. As it happens, I'm left-handed, and the left side of my body is slightly smaller than the right. This might mean that my left hippocampus is slightly smaller and perhaps more vulnerable than the one on the right because of the difference in size.

Based on this analysis of the light visions that come right before the fiery light erupts, it would appear that in the same way meditators can "see" visions of slow-wave sleep rhythms, they can also "see" visions that constitute, in effect, ghost images of their hippocampi—first a ghost image of diffuse brightening generated by a build-up of hypersynchronous excitation in both hippocampi, then another ghost image of the anterior nose region of one hippocampus whose neurons are being selectively stimulated by more intense levels of excitation than neurons in the rest of that hippocampus. This is an extraordinary and wholly unexpected conclusion, but the neurologically grounded, reverse-engineering analysis of the bulbous white protrusion implies that this could happen.

Now we have one more light vision that still needs to be analyzed—the penultimate vision of the white rays. The white rays suddenly appeared in precisely the same location formerly occupied by the bulbous protrusion and at precisely the same time that the bulbous image and the bright blue background both disappeared. That timing suggests that the three changes were all linked to something new happening in the brain. That does indeed turn out to be the case. To generate the sudden brightening of the bulbous white protrusion, a sudden intensification in the barrage of hypersynchronous pulsations flowing down into the anterior "nose" region of the hippocampus would have been required. But then the hypersynchronous excitation must have been immediately terminated by something new happening in the brain. That would explain why the white bulbous protrusion suddenly brightened and immediately disappeared, and it would also explain why the bright blue background of the visual field generated by the hypersynchronous seizure disappeared. It's likely that the vision of the three thin white rays is related to that same event.

In the chapter on meditation-induced seizures that appears later in our investigation, I'll provide a more in-depth analysis that shows why the vision of thin white rays appeared. But for now I'll offer a provisional explanation, which is this: the three thin white rays were likely generated by the initial outbreak of a new kind of seizure, the outbreak of a "paroxysmal" seizure that erupted inside the anterior "nose" region of the hippocampus that had been generating the image of the white bulbous protrusion. It would appear that only three neurons in that anterior "nose" region fired paroxysmal discharges that sent waves of paroxysmal excitation flowing along the axons projecting out of those three neurons. That stimulated a few other hippocampal neurons to fire their own paroxysmal discharges, generating the shift from a vision in which the number of rays doubled and then the six rays spread apart. Once the stream of paroxysmal excitation spread out of the left hippocampus, that triggered paroxysmal discharges in the brain structures located downstream and on the other side of the brain. The result was a bilateral parietal seizure that manifested with bright, flashing lights, sensorimotor disturbances, and an ecstatic emotional aura.

Partial Seizures with Ecstatic Auras

When neurologists want to refer to the conscious experiences of epileptic patients during a seizure, they use the word *aura*. During their seizures, epileptic patients experience auras that almost always involve emotions that are intensely negative: feeling of disgust, fear, and other aversive reactions. Only about one-half of one percent of epileptic patients (0.5%) have reported auras with some pleasurable qualities. There are, however, rare reports of partial seizures in which the auras are so intensely pleasurable that they're called "ecstatic auras". The origins of ecstatic auras are the primary focus of our investigation into the phenomenon of religious visions of fiery light. I think it will be useful at the outset for us to review some of the cases that have been reported in the medical literature in which epileptic patients experienced ecstatic auras that involved visual symptoms in some way.

Naito and Matsui (1988) describe the case of a Japanese woman who kept voluminous, detailed diaries in which she described her paroxysmal experiences:

> At age 60, she experienced, while awake, a peculiar attack lasting several minutes, during which she said, "A halo appeared around god. Thank my god! Oh! Thank my god!" She then stared with motor arrest. She failed to respond to shouts from her family. Later, she was unable to recollect this experience… In April 1980, at her place of employment she suddenly cried out, "I saw my god!" and shed happy tears. She was then 61 and had no memory loss of the joyous experience and insisted even after that she felt extreme happiness, as if she had been in paradise. One early morning in May 1980, she watched the sun rising, and had a sudden complex yet pleasant experience. She related, "Triple halos appeared around the sun. Suddenly the sunlight became intense. I experienced a revelation of god and all creation glittering under the sun. The sun became bigger and engulfed me. My mind, my whole being was pervaded by a feeling of delight" (p. 123).

When this patient was tracked by twenty-four-hour electroencephalographic monitoring (EEG), the researchers found that she often experienced epileptic spikes in her temporal lobes while she was asleep—the same kinds of spikes that trigger complex partial seizures.

Another researcher describes a thirty-five-year-old man who had been prescribed anticonvulsive medications to control generalized seizures that woke him at night. He returned to the epilepsy clinic when the medications gradually stopped working. The patient reported that, in addition to the nocturnal seizures, he had now begun to experience a new type of seizure that occurred several times a day and felt "joyful and pleasurable":

A typical fit began suddenly with a feeling of irritation followed promptly by a sense of detachment. He would see a bright but not glaring light. He sensed that the light was the source of knowledge and understanding… At first the patient was frightened after these episodes but gradually came to see them as joyful and pleasurable. During the fit he felt at ease with himself and his environment. He sensed an ineffable contentment and fulfillment (Morgan H, 1990, p. 414).

In the neurological work-up of this patient, the CAT scan detected a tumor in the anterior temporal lobe of the right hemisphere. When that tumor was surgically removed along with the anterior hippocampus and amygdala, the pathologist found an epileptic lesion that confirmed the results of the CAT scan. This was the first case of an ecstatic aura where the physicians were able to document the exact site of the epileptogenic lesion.

In a study by Ketter et al. (1996), researchers simulated the effects of a limbic seizure by injecting a chemical called procaine into the anterior limbic regions of thirty-two volunteer subjects.

More than a quarter of the subjects (28%) reported seeing "unformed visual hallucinations (lights or colors reported as intense or very intense)". Almost all the subjects (90%) reported hearing auditory hallucinations they described as "unformed buzzing, ringing, or electronic sounds". More than a quarter (28%) of the subjects in this procaine study reported feelings of euphoria.

Limbic seizures often release endogenous opioids that can persist at elevated levels for up to two weeks. This happens because opioids are involved with routine neuronal signaling and synaptic reorganization that takes place inside a hippocampus. A hippocampal seizure will stimulate an abnormal release of these endogenous opioids (Bausch and Chavkin, 1997; Engels and Rocha, 1992).

A more recent study by Surbeck and colleagues (2013) adds new insights about the regions of the limbic brain that participate in the generation of sexual orgasms. The researchers report the case of a middle-aged woman with an epileptic disorder who usually experienced a variety of premonitory auras before her seizures began in earnest. Those auras manifested as flashing lights, feelings of déjà vu, or orgasmic sensations. While this woman was waiting for open-brain surgery to correct her condition, she gave the researchers permission to use depth electrodes to stimulate the brain structures that they suspected of being implicated in her seizures. When they stimulated the woman's left hippocampus, an after-discharge lasted eighteen seconds. When they stimulated the right hippocampus, the after-discharge lasted much longer—a full forty-five seconds. During these after-discharges, the woman experienced an "orgasmic ecstasy" (Ibid., pp. 62, 64). The after-discharges were recorded over several limbic structures that affect the processing of emotion, including the hippocampus, the temporal pole and the insula on the same side of the brain that had been stimulated.

This case suggests that a network of limbic structures have to be activated in order to generate an orgasmic aura.

The partial seizure with the ecstatic aura that I experienced when I saw the vision of fiery light is different from all the cases I just mentioned. The difference is that I don't have any kind of epileptic disorder. I know this because I consulted a neurologist to find out if my visions were being caused by some hidden epileptiform vulnerability that was only now beginning to emerge. He pointed out that I didn't meet all the criteria for a preliminary clinical diagnosis of epilepsy, and he ordered an EEG exam to test for the presence of any hidden epileptiform activity that might be responsible. He concluded that my paroxysmal episode was provoked by what I'd been doing just before it occurred, not by any underlying epileptic condition.

Ecstasy and Eroticism

During the hippocampal seizure that triggered my vision of fiery light, I experienced an ecstatic aura that included muscle spasms that usually occur only during sexual climax, along with orgasmic sensations coursing throughout my body. For hippocampal seizures to generate orgasmic sensations, the paroxysmal excitation must reach at least one of the limbic structures located downstream from the hippocampus. It has to reach the septum. An account of what happens when paroxysmal excitation flows into the limbic brain was revealed in a series of experiments performed by psychiatrist Robert G. Heath in which he used depth-electrodes to probe the limbic brains of epileptic patients who were waiting for open-brain surgery. Heath found that when he stimulated the limbic brain regions with low-amplitude currents, the patients reported pleasant auras. But when he applied high-amplitude stimulation to those same areas, the patients reported auras that were unpleasant and aversive. There was, however, one exception to this general rule: in one site in the limbic brain—in the septal region—the stimulation with high-amplitude excitation evoked auras that were intensely pleasurable. Heath's definition of the "septal region" included not only the septums but also the adjacent nucleus accumbens, the hippocampi, the amygdalae, the orbital cortex, and some nuclei dedicated to relay of sensory signals (Heath RG, ed., *The Role of Pleasure in Behavior*, 1964, pp. 219-243).

When Heath, later in life, wrote an article that gave an overview of what he'd learned from his many research projects studying brain regions involved with sexual pleasure, he noted:

> Studies in severely ill patients prepared with stereotaxically implanted deep and cortical brain electrodes... have invariably pointed to the septal region as the brain site most consistently implicated in the pleasure response. In some of the 60 patients studied thus far by these techniques, the pleasure response has been found to affect the septal region's main pathway of outflow (*The Journal of Nervous and Mental Disease*, 1972, pp. 3-17).

In this overview, Heath described the case of a twenty-four-year-old male patient who had depth electrodes implanted in several different limbic regions of his brain. When those electrodes were stimulated remotely by the researchers, the results turned out to be the same as Heath had reported in his earlier study: "He responded with pleasure only when electrical stimulation was applied to the septal region, responses to stimuli to other sites being neutral or aversive." This patient had also been given a three-button transistor device that enabled him to voluntarily stimulate three of the implanted electrodes. When that part of the experiment began, the researchers found that the man repeatedly stimulated the septal region of his brain as many as fifteen hundred times during the three hours he was permitted to use this device.

Heath also described another case, one that used a different kind of stimulation but then produced similar outcomes. In that case, the researchers stimulated the septal region of a thirty-four-year-old female patient by injecting the chemical acetylcholine into her septal region. That injection evoked a state of sexual arousal and repeated orgasms.

Heath's research is considered controversial. It's virtually certain that the design protocols he used would not be permitted today because researchers are now obliged to adhere to a much more rigorous set of ethical standards. But Heath's findings continue to influence contemporary researchers. Neurologist John Hughes cited the Heath studies when he proposed that the diagnosis of "ecstatic aura" ought to be restricted to only those seizures where septal involvement can be documented:

> The lateral septal nucleus (to and from the hippocampus) was… special. All other areas with a "pleasure-inducing" stimulation that "felt good" in these patients had an aversive effect with high currents, except one, the septal area. This area continued to be pleasure-inducing up to a maximum current of 12.5 mA (Hughes JR, "The idiosyncratic aspects of the epilepsy of Fyodor Dostoevsky," *Epilepsy & Behavior*, 2005; 7(3): 531-538).

Other cases of orgasmic auras have been reported in the medical literature: a study in which fifteen patients experienced "genital and sexual" paroxysms which registered as "spiking" in the scalp EEG; a study in which twelve female patients with temporal lobe epilepsy reported experiencing sexual sensations during partial seizures; and a study in which a patient experienced orgasmic epileptic auras when seizures erupted in the mesotemporal region on the right side of the brain. In a study by Hansen and Brodtkorb (2003), the authors report that eleven of their patients, all of whom had been diagnosed with temporolimbic epilepsy, experienced auras during their seizures. A third of the patients, including two men and two women, reported having auras with erotic sensations (4/11 = 36%), and half of the patients (6/11 = 54.5%) described their auras as a "dreamy state" that coexisted with their normal consciousness. Most of these patients enjoyed their auras, so much so that the researchers suspected that about half of the patients were occasionally self-inducing those seizures (5/11 = 45.5%).

The link between orgasmic sensations and the felt quality of mystical ecstasies has been recognized by many mystics who rely on erotic metaphors to convey a sense of how they felt during their ecstatic raptures. Here, for example, the Hindu poet, Princess Mirabai, implores the god, Krishna, to return to her side: "Dark One, / all I request is a portion of love. / Whatever my defects, / you are for me an ocean of raptures. / ... Mira says: Dark One—enter the penetralia, / you've taken this girl past the limits (*For Love of the Dark One*, 1993, p. 59)."

The links we've traced between ecstasy and eroticism and between hippocampal seizures and the initiation of septal seizures may play a much more important role in mystical experiences than has been previously been acknowledged. A sign of change occurred when two neurologists, Jeffrey Saver and John Rabin, published their article, "The Neural Bases of Religious Experience," in the prestigious *Journal of Neuropsychiatry and Clinical Neuroscience* (1997; 9(3): 498-510). In that article, Saver and Rabin propose that many mystical experiences can be explained by a "limbic marker hypothesis".

Limbic Involvement in Mystical Consciousness

In "The Neural Bases of Religious Experience", Saver and Rabin describe what they discovered when they reviewed all of the research articles they found in the medical literature that studied ecstatic seizures: "The few well-designed modern clinical cases of ecstatic seizures all appear to have had a temporo-limbic substrate," and they go on to add that the process that takes place in the brain leading up to the ecstatic seizure is typically a build-up of "hippocampal-septal hypersynchrony". Saver and Rabin don't specify how that build-up of hypersynchronous excitation begins or how it escalates to the point of triggering the outbreak of paroxysmal discharges. (That's an omission we'll be able to remedy later in our investigation with an analysis of the progression of meditation-induced light visions that lead to the eruption of the fiery light.)

Saver and Rabin go on to propose a "limbic marker hypothesis" that they regard as the most likely explanation for many of the anomalous experiences that are commonly regarded as "mystical". In their view, the contents of a person's perceptions, cognitions, and emotions can be suddenly and dramatically transformed by a momentary eruption of abnormal discharges in the temporolimbic regions of the brain. Those discharges "tag" the erstwhile ordinary experiences with a sense that, far from being ordinary, those experiences were exceptional, deeply meaningful, and emotionally transformative. These embellishments of everyday experience are then preserved in peoples' memories of the event and included when they tell others about their experiences. The Saver and Rabin limbic marker thesis proposes that many psychic symptoms described by mystics are linked with temporolimbic disturbances:

The core qualities of religious and mystical experience…
are the noetic and ineffable—the sense of having touched
the ultimate ground of reality and the sense of the unutter-
ability or incommunicability of the experience. Frequent
additional features are an experience of unity, an experience of timelessness and spacelessness, and a feeling
of positive affect, of peace and joy. We suggest that the
primary substrate for this experience is the limbic system.
Temporolimbic discharges can produce each of these
components in fragmentary or complete form: distancing
from apparent reality (depersonalization, derealization),
timelessness and spacelessness (autoscopy, time distortion),
or positive affect (ecstatic auras)… This limbic activity
underlies certain psychic seizure auras, near-death experiences, and religious and mystical experiences of normal
individuals (Saver and Rabin, 1997, p. 204).

Partial Seizures and Studies of Tibetan Monks

Before we move on from this investigation of meditation-induced
partial seizures and ecstatic auras, it's worth taking a closer look
at some contemporary experiments in which skilled meditators
are monitored by scalp EEGs. While these meditators are inducing their typical "peak experiences", the brainwave patterns
registering in their EEGs often resemble the patterns associated
with partial seizures. However, the researchers never consider
the possibility that they might actually be detecting seizures.

For example, in Lehmann et al. (2001), the researchers used
Low Resolution Electromagnetic Tomography (LORETA), a form
of computer-enhanced analysis of EEG brainwaves, to study a
Tibetan lama while he meditated in what the lama described as his
four different "modes", each having a different level of intensity.

During the meditation the monk described as the most intense and most spiritually elevated—his "self-dissolution" mode—the scalp EEG registered high levels of gamma band activity that formed a distinctive "tabletop" pattern at the very top of his head. During the "self-reconstruction" mode, which the monk designated as second in intensity and second in the degree of spiritual elevation, the EEG once again registered high-amplitude gamma surges with the tabletop but also registered surges over both ears. And in another LORETA study of a Tibetan lama by DeLuca and Daly (2003), when the monk signaled the researchers that he was having a "peak experience", they recorded an eruption of gamma surges with an "earmuff" pattern.

On first impression, nothing in these two studies would alert a reader that there might be some problems with the findings. But if we want to find out more about why expert meditators inducing their peak experiences produce these sudden, high-amplitude gamma surges that cluster in two distinctive patterns—around the top of the head in a tabletop pattern, and over both ears in an earmuff pattern—it is essential that we consult an important research paper published in *Epilepsia* in 1997.

In a paper entitled "Intracranial EEG Substrates of Scalp EEG Patterns from Temporal Lobe Foci," neurologists Steven Pacia and John Ebersole reported the results of a study in which their patients who were awaiting open-brain surgery for temporal lobe epilepsy gave them permission to implant depth-electrodes so they could compare the kinds of discharges that occurred deep in the limbic and temporal lobe regions with the brainwave patterns that appeared simultaneously in the patients' scalp EEGs. The study showed that when the seizures remained confined within the patient's hippocampus, the brainwaves that registered in the scalp EEG were high-amplitude, synchronous surges (100 µV) with theta frequencies of five to nine surges per second. These high-amplitude surges were localized over the temporal lobes, forming a distinctive earmuff pattern. The same earmuff pattern appeared when the partial seizure originated in the temporal cortex rather than in the hippocampal complex.

The researchers then identified another EEG pattern that was very different from the earmuff distribution. If the patient had a seizure that erupted first in a hippocampus and then spread downstream into related limbic and temporal lobe regions, which would qualify as a complex partial seizure, then the scalp EEGs registered surges of high-amplitude brainwaves arrayed in a tight cluster at very top of the skull in a tabletop pattern. Pacia and Ebersole point to an anatomical reason why seizures erupting in limbic and temporal lobe regions generate these two types of brainwave patterns: "The base of the temporal lobe represents a large cortical generator area, and it is oriented to produce maximal voltage fields at the vertex and base of the skull (op. cit., p. 652)."

In the LORETA studies mentioned earlier—the studies where Tibetan monks were asked to meditate and to induce their typical peak experiences while being monitored by scalp EEGs—the researchers detected brainwaves with the tabletop and earmuff patterns identified by Pacia and Ebersole as being associated with partial seizures. But the researchers studying those meditating monks did not cite the article by Pacia and Ebersole in their reference sections and did not discuss the possibility that those Tibetan monks might be experiencing partial seizures. This same oversight continues to surface in other studies.

In 2002, neuroscientist Richard Davidson, the founder and director of a multi-disciplinary research group in Wisconsin dedicated to studying healthy minds, used his personal relationship with the Dalai Lama to recruit a Tibetan monk named Mingyur Rinpoche to be the subject of an EEG study. The monk's flight to the U.S. took eighteen hours and crossed ten time zones, but that didn't stop the researchers from performing the first EEG test the day after he'd arrived. A net containing 256 EEG sensors was placed around Mingyur's head. He was instructed to spend one minute meditating on Universal Compassion, to take a thirty-second rest, and then to alternate between the two mindsets for four minutes. Davidson discussed the results of this experiment in an article he later wrote with psychologist David Goleman, the author of *Emotional Intelligence*. In their article, "How Meditation Changes Your Brain—and Your Life," Davidson and Goleman describe what surprised them about that first meditation session:

> Just as Mingyur began the meditation, there was a sudden, huge burst of electrical activity on the computer monitors displaying the signals from his brain. Everyone assumed this meant he had moved; such movement artifacts are a common problem in research with EEG, which registers as wave pattern readings of electrical activity at the top of the brain. Any motion that tugs the sensor—a leg shifting, a tilt of the head—gets amplified in those readings into a huge spike that looks like a brain wave but has to be filtered out for a clean analysis. Oddly, this burst seemed to last the entire period of the compassion meditation and so far as anyone could see Mingyur had not moved an iota. What's more, the giant spikes diminished but did not disappear as he went into the mental rest period, again with no visible shift in his body (*Lion's Roar*, May 7, 2018).

During all of the subsequent meditation sessions performed by Mingyur Rinpoche, similar bursts of high-amplitude brainwaves erupted. The researchers wanted to identify what was happening in the monk's brain to generate such high-amplitude brainwaves in the EEG, so they decided to administer a functional magnetic resonance imaging test (fMRI). The results of that test detected sudden surges of high-amplitude activity similar to what happened in the EEGs. The researchers realize that these results point to seizures, but they try to dismiss that conclusion:

> Mingyur's brain's circuitry for empathy (which typically fires a bit during this mental exercise) rose to an activity level 700 to 800 times greater than it had been during the rest period just before. Such an extreme increase befuddles science; the intensity with which those states were activated in Mingyur's brain exceeds any we have seen in studies of "normal" people. The closest resemblance is for epileptic seizures, but those episodes last brief seconds, not a full minute. And besides, brains are seized by seizures, in contrast to Mingyur's display of intentional control of his brain activity.

Two years after the Mingyur study, Davidson and a new team of researchers led by Antoine Lutz conducted yet another study of Tibetan monks (Lutz et. al., 2004). In this study, the researchers recorded high-amplitude gamma surges clustered at the top of the skull and also over the ears, the two distinctive tabletop and earmuff patterns identified by Pacia and Ebersole. But the researchers concluded, as they'd done in the other, earlier studies performed at the Wisconsin center, that the anomalous surges must have been generated by subtle muscle movements. Based on the assumption that these muscle movements distorted the data they'd recorded, the researchers decided to subtract the highest levels of that gamma activity from their data and then to reanalyze that altered data. After they made those deletions, they found that the remaining gamma waves produced by the Tibetan monks during their peak experiences were not only in the normal range but were also "balanced bilaterally" between the parieto-temporal and mid-frontal electrodes on both sides of the scalp. That led the researchers to propose, based on their reconstituted data, that Tibetan monks who engage in the life-long practice of meditation are able to condition their brains to produce healthier, more "balanced" brainwaves than occur in the brains of normal people.

Once again, as in the earlier study of Mingyur Rinpoche, the researchers did not cite the study by Pacia and Ebersole, and they did not otherwise acknowledge that there might be a connection between the EEG patterns they observed and the patterns associated with temporolimbic seizures by Pacia and Ebersole's research. But the problem with this study is not just that these researchers were unaware of—or ignoring—the relevance of the Pacia and Ebersole findings; it's that they also ignored some of their own data that pointed specifically to the temporal lobe region as the most likely source of the high-amplitude gamma wave surges that appeared in the scalp EEGs of the meditating monks.

In the online version of the article by Lutz and colleagues, the researchers include a "dipole source analysis" of the original data before it was reconstituted. In a dipole source analysis, algorithms analyze the brainwave patterns appearing in the scalp EEGs to calculate which regions of the brain are most likely responsible for generating those brainwave patterns. The dipole source analysis published by the researchers in their online version identified "two deep central dipoles and two shallow dipoles over the temporal lobes" as being the most likely sources of the activity registering in the scalp EEG. In other words, the high-amplitude gamma surges that produced the tabletop and earmuff patterns in the scalp EEGs were most likely generated by excitation originating in the limbic and temporal lobe regions. This is precisely what Pacia and Ebersole observed: "The base of the temporal lobe represents a large cortical generator area, and it is oriented to produce maximal voltage fields at the vertex and base of the skull."

Lutz and colleagues appear to be aware that there might be an alternative interpretation of the EEG patterns that appeared in their original data, because in their discussion of the results they acknowledge that "the high-amplitude gamma activity found in some of these practitioners is, to our knowledge, the highest reported in the literature in a nonpathological context." But they do not take the next step and consider the possibility that the peak experiences of the Tibetan monks might involve meditation-induced partial seizures.

Drawing on my own experience, I think I can explain why the Tibetan monks in these studies were able to rapidly induce these unusual EEG patterns. These monks almost certainly spent many years practicing the advanced meditation techniques known as "Highest Yoga Tantra", a practice known to generate a predictable sequence of light visions. That's the sequence of visions that's described by Naropa in his anthology, *The Epitome of the Six Yogas*, and it's also the sequence that I saw myself.

If a monk induces this sequence of visions repeatedly over a period of many years, and if he succeeds in triggering the paroxysmal vision of fiery light, these cumulative experiences will inevitably kindle changes in the firing thresholds of all the neurons that participate in generating that sequence of visions. As neurologists are fond of saying, "Neurons that fire together, wire together," and that's what would happen in these cases: the monks would acquire a conditioned response that enabled them, once they'd closed their eyes, fixated their attention on the visual field, and emptied their minds of distracting thoughts, to rapidly self-induce the same kind of hippocampal seizure that they'd induced so many times before. So it should not be surprising that monks who've acquired that kind of conditioned response would be able to quickly self-induce partial seizures during a scientific study.

CHAPTER 4

How Seers Become Saints: A Post-Seizure Syndrome

Residual Reactions, Mounting Concerns

The first changes I experienced after seeing the vision of fiery light were very subtle—so subtle that, at the time, I couldn't say what I was feeling. But there were other changes that were not at all subtle, changes that were impossible to ignore and deeply unsettling. Those changes revealed that the seizure erupted in the hippocampus and that it spread downstream into the limbic and temporal lobe regions, damaging some of the inhibitory neuron circuits along that pathway. If those inhibitory circuits were still wholly intact, the amount of excitation flowing from the visual pathways down into the hippocampus and then out into the limbic and temporal lobe structures would have been better contained. Let me explain.

For several nights after the seizure, when I got in bed, closed my eyes, and lay there waiting to fall asleep, I saw a faint smudge of dull white light glowing in the same spot where the bulbous white protrusion—the ghost image of the anterior tip of the left hippocampus—had appeared shortly before the seizure. At first the white glow was so faint that it looked like it was being partially obscured, but when I turned my attention in that direction, it took on a much brighter glow and then began to expand rapidly to fill the entire visual field with a white, fog-like light. The muscles in my face and fingers also began to twitch. That's when I realized what was going happen next and what I needed to do to put a stop to it. I quickly opened my eyes and sat up in bed, and the white light went away. When I put my head back on the pillow, I made a point of not focusing my attention on the visual field, and that was enough to prevent a repeat of the expanding glow. This white glow continued to surface for several nights, but only if I inadvertently stared at the portion of the visual field where so many of the paroxysmal visions had appeared. Fortunately, with each passing night, the white smudge phenomenon continued to dim until it disappeared altogether by the end of the week.

There were, however, other situations where it was apparent that I was taking in too much light energy. I remember one occasion when I was walking past the open field of a park covered with a white blanket of fresh snow. Breathing in the cool, clear air, feeling uplifted by the beauty all around me, I turned to gaze out over the field of snow. The bright sunlight reflecting off of that white expanse was more powerful than I'd anticipated. When I felt a faint stirring of tremors in my face and fingers and heard the telltale buzzing sound, I realized that my eyes were absorbing too much light, that they were sending an abnormal amount of excitation into the visual cortices, and that the excess light energy was flowing down into the hippocampi. I quickly looked away. The symptoms disappeared, but it was clear that something was wrong with my visual system.

This reaction to seeing the reflection of bright sunlight reminded me of stories I'd read about an esoteric Kabbalah ritual practiced by Jewish mystics during the Middle Ages. The mystics would fill large bowls with water and then cover the surface of the water with oil. They would then put the bowl in a strategic location where beams of bright sunlight would reflect off the oily surface and position themselves so the reflected light would stream directly into their eyes. The reflections of flashing light were said to give the Kabbalah mystics a foretaste of God's glory. Similarly, in a Christian context, there's the story of Jacob Boehme, a journeyman shoemaker who lived in Bohemia during the sixteenth century. Boehme reported that when he was "sitting one day in his room, his eye fell upon a burnished pewter dish which reflected the sunshine with such marvelous splendor that he fell into a deep inward ecstasy." He also had many other mystical visions and eventually sold his shoemaking shop in order to put himself forward as a religious prophet.

While looking at reflected sunlight continued to provoke a surprisingly strong response, I wasn't all that worried; it was easy, after all, to control that reaction by simply looking away. Then something happened that raised more concern. I was hiking along a mountain ridge in the Arizona desert. The sun was about to set behind the dark silhouette of the mountain ridges that formed the far horizon. So much dust was floating in the sky, especially along the horizon, that I thought it would be safe to take advantage of a rare opportunity to look directly at the sun's orange and red orb that was heavily obscured by the clouds of dust. But as I started looking at the sun, I began to feel strong stirrings of sexual arousal. There were tremors in the muscles of my face and extremities and also in the bulbospongiosus muscle near the pelvic floor that I've mentioned before, the muscle that usually becomes noticeably active only during sexual orgasm. I was astounded that an erotic reaction could be provoked by looking at the sun when its brightness was obscured by dust. I also felt an urge to "let myself go" and feel the ecstasy of merging into the natural beauty all around me, but this mystical experience also had an unpleasant "driven" quality.

This reaction to what seemed like a relatively weak stimulus—nothing more than the dull orange and red glow of the sun's disk obscured by clouds of dust—set off alarm bells in my mind. If I'd become this hyper-sensitive to light stimuli in the wake of my vision, clearly it would be prudent to set up an appointment with a neurologist. What if the paroxysmal vision damaged something in my brain? Or what if this was a sign of some hidden epileptic vulnerability that was slowly beginning to emerge?

When I returned to Boston and immersed myself once again in the usual routines, the memories of what happened up there on the mountain seemed less important and eventually faded away. I convinced myself that, no matter how startling and disconcerting the experience might have felt at the time, it was, after all, not dissimilar to the other episodes of hyper-sensitivity to reflections of bright sunlight. In all of those cases, it was easy to control my reaction by simply being more disciplined in recognizing the danger and turning away from the bright stimulus. The imperative of consulting a neurologist seemed less important, so I put off making an appointment. Several months passed without incident. Then came the tipping point.

I awoke in the middle of the night, half-conscious, fighting a nightmare: I was flying fast and low over the surface of a calm, blue ocean, skimming just above waves. I felt myself being pulled inexorably toward the distant horizon, where dark storm clouds were towering skyward. Lightning flashed inside the looming thunderheads, reverberating from one cloud to the next. This was obviously a reactivation of a memory fragment from the recent past, but now the sight was truly frightening because it felt I was no longer in control of what was about to happen. I had to find a way to stop my forward momentum. If I didn't act fast, I would crash into one of those billowing thunderheads and get sucked into the maelstrom. For someone just awaking from a dream, still half-conscious, it all felt very real, very imminent, and very frightening. I forced myself to open my eyes, to sit up in bed, to put both feet on the floor, and then I got up and walked up and down the hallway. It was a relief to see myself surrounded by the bedroom furniture and to feel the carpet beneath my feel. To make sure I wouldn't get pulled back into that nightmare, I walked downstairs, poured myself a glass of milk, sat beneath a lamp and spent a few minutes paging through an old magazine.

That nightmare vanished, as nightmares do, but its emotional residue remained. I'd been lucky this time around—I was able to escape—but what if that same nightmare were to return when I wasn't able to wake up in time to take remedial action? What if the nightmare came again, and I got sucked up into that dark cloud? Who can control their nightmares? Later that morning I called the neurologist's office and set up an appointment.

What the Neurologist Said

When I met with the neurologist, I handed him a page of notes summarizing what I'd been experiencing over the past several months. He read my notes, nodding his head but keeping his face so impassive that I couldn't assess his reaction. Then he looked up and asked if I'd written any other materials about this same subject. I said "yes" because, after all, I'm a writer, and what writer would pass up the challenge of writing about these experiences? But I was surprised by his question, so I asked why he wanted to know. "The kinds of experiences you've described are still not well understood," he responded, "These experiences are situated on the frontier between psychiatry and neurology." He then gave a brief description of a phenomenon called the "temporal lobe behavior syndrome". It tends to emerge in patients who have abnormal activity in the temporal or limbic regions of their brains, he explained, and while this syndrome is most often documented in patients who have recurring seizures, it has also occasionally surfaced in patients who have experienced only a single seizure. In rare cases it has appeared in patients who've never experienced an overt seizure but who are eventually discovered to have some covert, ongoing "epileptiform activity" that activates intermittently in the temporolimbic region of their brains without them becoming aware of it. Since it was clear that this issue had entered his mind because of the incidents I'd described—and because I'd recorded them in that page of notes—I asked if he would tell me more about the kinds of symptoms he was talking about. I hoped to find out what I'd written in my notes that made him think of the temporal lobe behavior syndrome.

There's a distinctive cluster of symptoms associated with this syndrome, he told me. One of the symptoms is "hyper-religiosity", which means the patients become preoccupied with religious and philosophical subjects. Hyper-religiosity usually occurs in conjunction with another symptom, "hypergraphia", so named because the patients feel compelled to write about their intensely personal religious experiences or about new religious ideas that keep intruding into their minds. They feel compelled to write even if they've never written much before. The symptom called "viscosity" involves losing the ability to recognize and respond to the subtle signals sent by a conversation partner who's trying to end the conversation. A related symptom, "circumstantiality", manifests when patients focus too much on telling minor details in a story and end up obscuring the main point they were trying to make. Sometimes patients become more irritable and prone to anger than they were before the seizures began. The last symptom the neurologist mentioned was "altered sexuality". It most often manifests as "hyposexuality", a dramatic loss of interest in sex. But it can also involve a change in the kinds of objects or situations that are regarded as sexually attractive. Sometimes this involves objects or situations that most people would regard as strange or bizarre.

I listened with rapt attention to the neurologist's brief overview of the subject. I would have liked him to continue, but it was obvious that he wasn't prepared to do that. This was neither the right time nor the right place for me to push him for more information. And, besides, given what he'd just said, it was obvious now why the temporal lobe behavior syndrome would have sprung into his head as soon as he read my sheet of notes. Was there evidence of hyper-religiosity? Check. Hypergraphia? Check. Hyposexuality? Well, about that I wasn't sure, but he said that the symptom could sometimes manifest not as a loss of libido per se, but rather as a change in what struck the person as being sexually attractive: I'd written a note about how I'd been sexually aroused by staring at the setting sun. That would definitely classify as a strange or bizarre sexual reaction, which was how it struck me when it happened. So. Hyposexuality? Check. It was there in the notes.

Clearly the neurologist had good reason to conclude that my symptoms were consistent with a temporal lobe behavior syndrome, but what about the seizure itself? Did I have to worry that I'd just experienced an *epileptic* seizure and that it might happen again? He told me that there are two criteria neurologists use to make a preliminary clinical diagnosis of epilepsy—that the seizures are "recurring" and they're "not being provoked" by the patient. Neither of these criteria would apply in my case: I had only experienced one seizure and there was reason to suspect that I was doing something that provoked the onset of that seizure. But the neurologist was concerned about the series of post-seizure incidents I'd described in my notes. He thought those symptoms might suggest the emergence of a temporal lobe behavior syndrome and recommended that it would be prudent for me to take an EEG test that might reveal some signs of hidden epileptiform activity.

I left his office with that appointment in hand and a determination to immediately track down everything I could find out about temporal lobe behavior syndromes. I walked to my car, slipped inside, and drove straight to Countway Library on the campus of the Harvard Medical School, the Mecca for all medical writers in the Boston area. I'd spent a lot of time in that library, so I knew right where to go to start digging into the scientific literature that would tell me what I wanted to know.

The Temporal Lobe Behavior Syndrome

The concept of the temporal lobe behavior syndrome was first identified by neurologist Norman Geschwind, chief of neurology at the Boston City Hospital. The process of discovery is described in a fascinating story narrated by Eva LaPlante in her book, *Seized: Temporal Lobe Epilepsy as a Medical, Historical and Artistic Phenomenon* (1993). LaPlante reports that Dr. Geschwind was presiding at one of the neurology grand rounds that helped doctors working at the hospital to keep current with new research and treatment breakthroughs. At this session, Geschwind shared his ideas about a new theory he was considering based on observations of his patients who had temporal lobe epilepsy. It was possible, he suggested, that the same brain lesions that caused the patients to suffer epileptic seizures might also, over time, cause changes in their personalities. As an example, he described some patients who felt compelled to write or draw, often about religious or philosophical subjects. He attributed this symptom of "hypergraphia" to seizure-induced changes leading to overstimulation of the limbic and temporal lobe regions. One of the doctors attending that grand round session, neurologist Steven Waxman, told LaPlante that he was skeptical about Geschwind's claim, but then something happened that changed his mind:

> Weeks later, a patient surprised him by mentioning during an interview that she recorded her seizures in a daily journal. The young doctor questioned her about the journal, and she offered to show it to him. She brought him several thick volumes, and since he seemed interested, she later brought more volumes. To his amazement, they were cross-referenced and organized by category into headache books, seizure books, and special event books. This patient, at least, exhibited Geschwind's hypergraphia 'in spades'. Waxman queried other patients about their writing, and many replied that they, too, wrote a great deal... A young man kept a meticulous, typed record of his life... A woman compulsively made lists... Another patient showed the doctor extensive written descriptions of all her religious feelings, each line of text in alternating colors, red and blue (*Seized*, p. 30).

As more and more examples emerged of dramatic changes taking place in the emotions and behavioral choices of their patients, Waxman and Geschwind collaborated to write the first scientific article in which they proposed that many patients with temporal lobe epilepsy would develop an "interictal behavior syndrome". The term, "ictus", is medical jargon for "seizure", so their choice of a label identifies this syndrome as something that emerges between seizures, not during the seizure itself. In their article, the authors define the basic concept: "A distinct syndrome of interictal behavior occurs in many patients with temporal lobe epilepsy. These changes include alterations in sexual behavior, religiosity, and a tendency toward extensive, and in some cases compulsive writing and drawing... The demonstration of interictal spike activity in temporal structures provides a pathophysiological basis for this syndrome (*Archives of General Psychiatry*, 1975, p. 1580)."

Physicians initially thought this syndrome was so unusual and so distinctive that it could be used to make preliminary diagnoses of temporal lobe epilepsy in cases that would otherwise be ambiguous. That would make the syndrome a very useful tool, as Geschwind pointed out in a later article: "Many of the patients we have seen have had only rather minor complex partial seizures, and many of the patients are, indeed, unaware that they are suffering from epilepsy... Furthermore, there are many cases in which this particular behavioral pattern has preceded the onset of the first clinical seizure (*Epilepsia*, 1983, p. 528)."

The initial hope that this syndrome might become a definitive diagnostic tool turned out to be too optimistic: while it was true that most patients with temporal lobe epilepsy reported some or all of these symptoms, it was also the case that similar symptom clusters were sometimes seen in patients who were suffering from other kinds of psychiatric disorders. The prospect of being able to diagnose temporal lobe epilepsy based solely on a patient presenting with the symptoms of the temporal lobe behavior syndrome had to be abandoned, but this didn't cause the concept to be discredited. Neurologists continue to use it today because it alerts them to the need for further investigation. Patients who've experienced only a single seizure, or no seizure at all, but who report some of the emotional and behavioral changes associated with the temporal lobe behavior syndrome need to be tested for the presence of hidden epileptiform activity.

The Bear-Fideo Inventory of Symptoms

As I combed through the scientific articles about the temporal lobe behavior syndrome, I came across a study by psychiatrist David Bear and his colleague, neuropsychologist Paul Fideo, that proved to be especially helpful because it provided examples that fleshed out the abstract medical terms. Bear had served an internship in neurology in which Geschwind was one of his supervisors, so he was intimately familiar with the concept. Bear recruited Fideo to help design a questionnaire that would enable them to gather more systematic information about how the symptoms of the syndrome actually manifested in the lives of patients. They administered the new questionnaire to a large number of temporal lobe patients and also to family members of those patients (Bear and Fideo, "Quantitative Analysis of Interictal Behavior in Temporal Lobe Epilepsy," *Archives of Neurology* 1977; 34: 454-466).

The results of the study were dramatic and revealing. One of the most widespread and important changes reported by the patients themselves and also by their family members was a new propensity to assign heightened emotional significance to objects and experiences that most people would regard as neutral or insignificant. This "superfusion of experience with emotional coloration" meant that the patient's "mood is maintained independently of, and often inappropriately for, a particular environment". The patient's "euphoria is projected into the environment and... serves to reorganize perceptual events, rather than being a reaction to these". These were changes that could have important consequences in the life of that person because "experiencing all objects and events as shot through with emotional significance engenders a mystically religious world view" and "an augmented sense of personal destiny".

When these symptoms of hyper-religiosity began to emerge, the patients often felt compelled to begin writing about their religious beliefs, filling up the pages of many notebooks. "Hyper-religiosity" often manifested in conjunction with the symptom of "hypergraphia". Bear and Fideo describe how patients often get immersed in the details of what they're trying to communicate. "Sensing emotional importance in even the smallest acts," the patient "performs these ritualistically and repetitively," and, because "the details bear the imprimatur of affective significance, many will be mentioned in lengthy, circumstantial speech or writing."

Bear and Fideo also found observable differences between patients depending on which side of the brain the temporal lobe abnormalities were located: "Right temporal foci led to external emotive or behavioral manifestations: anger, sadness, elation, circumstantiality, viscosity and hyper-moralism. By contrast, left hemisphere patients had ruminative, intellectual tendencies: religiosity, philosophical interests, and a sense of personal destiny."

Another symptom that usually emerged in their sample was "altered sexuality". Most often this involved "hyposexuality", a loss of interest in sex. I found detailed descriptions of hyposexuality symptoms in an article published by researchers in India (Shukla et al., "Sexual Disturbances in Temporal Lobe Epilepsy: A Controlled Study" *British Journal of Psychiatry* 1979, 134, pp. 288-92). Shukla and colleagues report that the male patients in their study "had a global loss of interest in sex, did not have erections or nocturnal emissions, never had fantasies or dreams of a sexual nature and abandoned sexual intercourse altogether". The symptom of hyposexuality also affected women: the female patients "took part in sexual relations only on repeated requests from their husbands, remained totally passive and did not reach orgasm". The authors of the study were particularly surprised to find that, during their in-person interviews, none of the patients mentioned their newly acquired lack of interest in sex until the researchers specifically asked about that symptom, and even then, none of the patients expressed any concern about this dramatic change that had taken place in their lives.

Bear and Fideo concluded their study by proposing a new theory about what happens to patients with temporal lobe epilepsy: "The effect of a temporal focus may be to establish new functional connections between neocortical and limbic structures or to disrupt mechanisms that normally inhibit fortuitous sensory-limbic associations." In a later article, Bear discussed the personality changes experienced by Fyodor Dostoevsky, the famous Russian author, as an example of sensory-limbic hyper-connections created by temporal lobe seizures: "And while he suffered repeated temporal lobe seizures which formed the basis of his many literary descriptions, his interictal personality took on well-known characteristics: deep emotionality, impulsive aggressivity, recurrent depression, mystical religiosity, a sense of enhanced personal destiny, heightened moralistic concern over the problem of good and evil, ritualistic obsessionalism culminating in compulsive gambling, and—fortunately in his case—the strong desire to write at length (David Bear, 'Temporal Lobe Epilepsy—A Syndrome of Sensory Limbic Hyper-Connection.' *Cortex*, 1979, 15: 358)."

Recent Examples of the Temporal Lobe Behavior Syndrome

Paulo Trevisol-Bittencourt and Andre Troiano describe the case of a thirty-five-year-old Brazilian man diagnosed with complex partial epilepsy who displayed several symptoms of the temporal lobe behavior syndrome. His seizures could be controlled by meditation but the behavioral symptoms continued unabated.

This patient was a talented artist who felt compelled to draw and paint buildings and houses in an effort to communicate what he was seeing and feeling, a symptom analogous to the compulsive writing associated with hypergraphia. He also displayed the symptoms of hyper-religiosity and hyposexuality. The physicians performed an MRI test that detected damage in the patient's medial temporal region that could be triggering intermittent epileptiform discharges—the kind that can activate a temporal lobe behavior syndrome (*Arquivos de neuro-psiquiatria*, 2000).

A study of hyper-religiosity in patients with partial epilepsy by Rima Dolgoff-Kaspar and colleagues was published in *Epilepsia* in 2011. The researchers wanted to explore the relationship between what the patients see in their auras and what kind of spirituality they chose to pursue. They compared thirty-eight adult patients with a reference group of sixteen college students and measured five different factors. One of the two main categories they used to classify the responses was the "numinous aura". They defined this aura by drawing on the descriptions of mystic experiences found in the Saver and Rabin article we discussed in Chapter 3. Those mystical experiences included dreamy states, feelings of detachment and leaving the body, derealization, bodily distortion, time distortion, and ecstatic pleasure. The goal of the study was to compare and contrast reports of these kinds of "numinous auras" with reports of more detached experiences that had a conventional or intellectualized quality and were classified under the headings of "religiousness" that could manifest as a "cognitive orientation toward spirituality" or as a basic sense of "existential well-being". When they analyzed their data, the researchers found that twelve patients reported experiencing a high frequency of numinous auras compared to the twenty-four patients who fell into the low-frequency group. People in the high-frequency group reported experiencing from six to sixteen numinous auras, whereas people in the low-frequency group reported a number that ranged from zero to four auras. The high-frequency group also scored significantly higher in the subcategories the researchers associated with numinous auras: experiential spirituality and paranormal beliefs. By contrast, for patients in the low-frequency group, the scores in these two subcategories were not significantly different from the scores of the students in the comparison group who had not been diagnosed with epileptic disorders. The researchers concluded that "epilepsy patients with frequent numinous-like auras have greater ictal and interictal spirituality of an experiential, personalized and atypical form, which may be distinct from culturally based religiosity. This form of spirituality may be better described by the term *cosmic spirituality* than hyper-religiosity."

Another case study of a temporal lobe behavior syndrome giving rise to the symptom of hyper-religiosity is described by writer Eve LaPlante: she describes a woman whom she calls "Jill" who was a director of personnel for a large corporation in Boston. Jill developed temporal lobe epilepsy during her thirties. Her doctors prescribed drugs, but the drugs did not control her seizures. Jill told LaPlante that, while she wouldn't describe herself as a religious person, her temporal lobe epilepsy "made me realize there's a whole other realm out there… My nice seizures—the colors and floating sensations—are the closest to religious or spiritual feelings that I've ever had, and they've made me understand for the first time how people can think they've discovered God (*Seized*, p. 69)."

LaPlante also describes the case of Karen Armstrong, a prolific and well-known author of religious books including *A History of God, Muhammed: A Prophet for Our Time, Buddha*, and *The Battle for God: Fundamentalism in Judaism, Christianity, and Islam*. When Armstrong was young, she wanted to become a nun. When she was eighteen years old, she entered a Roman Catholic convent as a new postulant. Three years later she was accepted into the

Society of the Holy Child Jesus as a full-fledged nun. Her superiors recognized that Armstrong was someone with intellectual gifts, so they offered to sponsor her studies at St. Anne's College, Oxford. When Armstrong writes about this period of her life in her autobiography, she describes her ongoing struggles with anorexia and other health issues. She also recalls having felt a "terrible dislocation" between her daytime experiences studying at a secular university where she was encouraged to question everything and then going back to the convent where she was subjected to a regimen of absolute obedience. While she was still studying at St. Anne's College, Armstrong decided she had to withdraw from her holy orders. Several years later, she was diagnosed with temporal lobe epilepsy. Armstrong told LaPlante what happened during her seizures: "Suddenly everything comes together in a moment—everything adds up, and you're flooded with a sense of joy, and you're just about to grasp it, and then you lose it and you crawl into an attack… It's easy to see how, in a prescientific age, an epileptic or any temporal lobe fringe experience like that could be thought to be God Himself (*Seized*, p. 114)."

LaPlante also cites the names of many other famous writers who are suspected of having temporal lobe epilepsy and experiencing the emergence of a temporal lobe behavior syndrome, including the poet Alfred Lord Tennyson; Jonathan Swift, author of *Gulliver's Travels*; Charles Dodgson, also known as Lewis Carroll, author of *Alice's Adventures in Wonderland* and *Through the Looking Glass*; Philip K. Dick, author of the science fiction novel *Valis*; and Walter Percy, author of *The Thanatos Syndrome* and *The Second Coming.*

What I Saw that I Hadn't Seen Before

Bear's theory that temporal lobe seizures can lead to "sensory-limbic hyper-connections" can explain some of the changes that I experienced after I saw the vision of fiery light. I've described how, immediately after the ecstatic seizure, as I was lying in bed waiting to fall asleep I would see a smudge of white light at the same spot in the visual field where the bulbous white protrusion appeared just before the vision of fiery light. If I looked up at that glow, it would rapidly expand to fill the visual field with a white fog-like light. I've also described occasions when I looked out over a snowy field reflecting the sun's bright rays and then felt my muscles begin to tremble ever so slightly along with an urge to "let myself go" to enjoy the surge of upwelling emotions that I knew would soon arrive. In these situations, it was clear that too much light energy was being allowed to flow into the visual system and down into the hippocampal terminals, then on the limbic and temporal lobe structures located downstream. These reactions revealed that the seizure that generated the vision of fiery light must have damaged some of the inhibitory neuron circuits that would have controlled the excitation flowing through these pathways. In other words, there was a seizure-driven sensory-limbic hyper-connection which, in my case, was a "visual-limbic hyper-connection". This change would also explain why, when I was hiking along that mountain ridge in Arizona and stared at the sun's orange orb through clouds of dust, I experienced that strange erotic arousal: it happened because seizure-related damage to inhibitory neurons in the visual pathways allowed abnormal amounts of excitation to flow through a conduit of hyper-connected neuron circuits that stimulated my septal neurons. Bear's theory also explains why, when I was walking around my neighborhood after the seizure,

I felt such a strong emotional reaction to surroundings that would normally strike me as uninteresting—the concept of a visual-limbic hyper-connection causing an overstimulation of the limbic emotional association centers helps make sense of that deep sense of meaningfulness that seemed to be coating everything I was looking at, the same kind of reaction that occurs during déjà vu. Bear and Fideo would identify this reaction as an example of the symptom of "hyper-emotionality" that results in a "superfusion of experience with emotional coloration" where a person's "mood is maintained independently of, and often inappropriately for, a particular environment".

All of the changes I've just mentioned were dramatic enough that I recognized they had to be connected to the paroxysmal vision of fiery light. But after consulting the neurologist and learning more about the temporal lobe behavior syndrome, I began to wonder if some other strange experiences, ones that I have not yet mentioned, might also have been associated with the emergence of a temporal lobe behavior syndrome. Even now, I'm sure if these changes I'm about to describe were actually evoked by a temporal lobe behavior syndrome or if they represent ideas that only came mind in retrospect because I have a very suggestible imagination. While I don't know for sure, I do think it's important for me to describe these experiences because they involve emotions and behaviors that would be very advantageous if they were to happen to mystic seers who nurtured aspirations of becoming charismatic religious prophets.

After the vision of fiery light, I lost all tolerance for watching movies or television programs that depicted violent episodes, especially those involving gratuitous violence. I stopped going to almost all cinema movies. That sensitivity has not diminished with the passing of time—even now I'm only willing to see a movie if it's perfectly clear that there won't be any violence. This is a change that strikes me as being consistent with Bear's symptom of hyper-emotionality. But, then again, it might just be a symptom of becoming older.

Another change, one that was short-lived but impressive while it lasted, was a tendency to indulge in the "aestheticization" of situations. By "aestheticization", I mean something akin to that kind of "aesthetic arrest" that people sometimes feel when they're introduced to a new work of art that rivets their attention or with the kind of aesthetic appreciation that occurs when people become fascinated watching cloud formations passing overhead and being roiled by the wind into strange new forms. This kind of "aesthetic arrest" began to occur in situations that would never have evoked that reaction in normal circumstances.

I first noticed this new propensity when I was out for my usual early morning walk and happened to cross paths with an attractive woman who lived in the neighborhood. We stopped for a brief chat, as we'd done many times before, but now, as we talked, I noticed that there weren't the usual faint stirrings of attraction. Instead, I noticed that I became fascinated by the creases lining the woman's forehead or by some gesture she kept using while she talked. It felt strange to find myself becoming absorbed by perceptions that were completely irrelevant to the woman's presence and to our ongoing conversation.

This new propensity to relate to other people with what I've described as this detached, "aesthetic" sensibility also occurred in a more disturbing setting. I noticed that I'd begun to feel a new sense of emotional distance from my wife and from my children. It wasn't that I no longer loved them, but it seemed that I was now loving them in a different way. What I noticed, to my distress, was that my feelings felt detached from them as the loved ones with whom I'd shared a long and intimate emotional relationship and for whom I usually felt that fierce, atavistic love that men feel for their wives and children. Now I loved them as representative humans who belonged to the greater human family in which every person deserves love. I found this reaction to be quite distressing, because it suggested that my love for my family was no different from my loving feelings for everyone in the world, and I knew that was not really true. I was reminded of all those people I've known or read about who chose to dedicate their lives exclusively to helping other people and then, because they took up that mission so strenuously, they ended up neglecting or even mistreating their own family members. The Hindu saint, Mahatma Gandhi, comes to mind as an example of one someone who was diligent in practicing an extreme version of the Hindu religious principle of renunciation and someone who was also a master at mobilizing political forces. But he was a man who often neglected the needs of his wife and child even when he was living with his family. Personally, I was pleased when this tendency to slip into an "aesthetic" distancing stance during my interactions with my loved ones disappeared after a few weeks. That's also when my normal sex drive returned, and I suspect that it was not just a coincidence that these two restorations occurred at about the same time.

What's interesting about these observations is this: if a person, after experiencing a single seizure, abstains from inducing more paroxysmal visions, and if the person does not experience any other kinds of recurring seizures, then it would appear that the human body has an innate capacity to slowly repair at least some of the damage to inhibitory neuron circuits damaged by the sensory-limbic hyper-connection. This observation provides some insight about why some religious traditions have recommended the opposite course of action. For example, there are Hindu mystical traditions in which meditators who've succeeded in inducing their first vision of fiery light are advised to keep doing whatever they were doing, to keep inducing their visions of fiery light until they see that light flashing continually and experience the constant presence of the ecstatic rapture that accompanies that vision. I'm not sure that this outcome is even possible, but if meditators do keep trying to induce paroxysmal visionary experiences, it's likely that they will also develop the symptoms associated with the temporal lobe behavior syndrome. That outcome could turn out to be very helpful for someone who aspires to become a charismatic spiritual leader with a cult of followers. The symptom of hyposexuality might prove to be especially valuable because it decreases the chances of succumbing to the sexual temptation that has resulted in many leaders of cults being deposed from their positions. There have been a number of notorious cases in the United States where spiritual teachers whose claims of spiritual authority were based in part on their visions of light have been forced to give up their leadership positions after reports of improprieties surfaced in the news media. These leaders had initiated sexual relationships with some of their followers who felt unable to refuse because they were enthralled by their leader's elevated spirituality. What I suspect is that these gurus found it easy to remain celibate for as long as they kept inducing their trademark visionary experiences in order to demonstrate their spiritual transcendence. But then, once they'd succeeded in attracting a large group of followers—and once they'd recruited a Mother Superior who could relieve them of the responsibility of managing the followers who were appointed to carry out the daily chores of the new community—those spiritual leaders might well have been tempted to stop burdening themselves with ascetic regimens and with the cataclysmic experiences triggered by the paroxysmal visions. If they stopped inducing those visions, the "sensory-limbic hyper-connections" that were powering their temporal lobe behavior syndromes would no longer be continually reinforced by the recurring seizures. The brain could then begin reactivating the normal neuron circuits that had once been dedicated to inhibiting the amount of excitation flowing into the limbic regions, thereby weakening the effects produced in the brain by the sensory-limbic hyperconnection. This recovery of normal function was something I experienced myself: I described how I experienced some unusual and disturbing symptoms of hyposexuality that began to fade rapidly in the wake of my paroxysmal vision as normal neuron circuits began to reconnect. If spiritual leaders who are being worshipped by their followers choose to abandon the practice of self-inducing real seizures and shift instead to just simulating their ecstatic raptures when they need to impress the followers, their normal sexual urges would likely return. But their followers won't be aware of that change—and that makes it easy for those leaders to arrange private meetings with attractive, awestruck followers who feel they can't turn away from the prospect of experiencing what might be a "transcendent" sexual relationship with their guru.

The Changes in Seers Match the Virtues of Saints

A remarkable overlap exists between the behavioral changes experienced by mystic seers and the cluster of virtues that pious people in all religions expect to see modeled by their saints. When seers see the vision of fiery light and experience the emergence of the temporal lobe behavior syndrome, they are likely to perceive the ordinary, uninteresting, and uninspiring aspects of daily life with a sense of wonder. Many religious saints possess a similar talent. Mystic seers, like religious saints, share their unusual emotional reactions in a way that attracts the attention, admiration, and gratitude of their listeners. The seers are also able to inspire people by preaching a new message that gives listeners new hope for a better life. The symptom of hyposexuality also allows a seer to live a life of spiritual purity, uncomplicated by sexual improprieties that shatter the image of sanctity. And the mystic seers, like the saints, can testify that an invisible spiritual realm exists because they've experienced it themselves. They've seen the incomparable, otherworldly radiance that God grants to those who learn how to see.

CHAPTER 5

Epileptic Seizures and Visions of Fiery Light

Ecstatic Seizures: What's Epileptic and What's Not?

Many religious mystics report seeing visions of bright flashes filling the visual field which would appear to be consistent with the eruption of a partial seizure. Earlier we discussed the two criteria that neurologists use in their offices to make a preliminary diagnosis that a seizure is epileptic: they want to know if there has been more than one seizure and if the seizures erupted spontaneously or were "provoked". When I began analyzing the reports of visionary experiences described in the mystical literatures of the world's major religions using these two criteria, I found that there were very few religious mystics who saw visions erupt spontaneously. Most of the mystics while they were engaged in practices we'll discuss in Chapter 6, practices that are known to "provoke" seizures—performing rituals that incorporated extreme stimulus overload or adopting extreme ascetic regimens that combined long meditation vigils and loss of sleep.

Before we begin to examine the evidence about visionary experiences documented in the traditional sources, I want to make clear that our objective is not to detract from the innovative ideas proposed by the various mystic seers on the grounds that their ideas occurred during or after the eruption of seizures. To criticize a new religious idea on the grounds that it was ignited by an epileptic seizure or after the seizure by the emergence of a temporal lobe behavior syndrome is to make a logical mistake that psychologist William James, author of the famous treatise, *The Varieties of Religious Experience,* called the "genetic fallacy". James points out that "In the natural sciences and industrial arts it never occurs to anyone to try to refute opinions by showing up their author's neurotic constitution. Opinions here are invariably tested by logic and by experiment, and it should not be otherwise with religious opinions (1961, pp. 32-33)." The more appropriate standard, according to James, is the "empiricist criterion" which involves a pragmatic assessment of whether the idea has the potential to help humans live better lives. Please keep this qualification in mind as we study the visionary experiences of four influential religious mystics for whom there is credible evidence that they experienced epileptic seizures. Our goal to determine what appeared in their visual fields and what caused it to appear.

The Life and Visions of Paul of Tarsus

Paul of Tarsus, a Jew who lived during the 1st century of the Common Era, is the man whose ideas decisively shaped Jesus' teachings into the version of Christianity that prevails today. Paul's innovative ideas about Jesus being a "Kristos", a divine Savior who offered eternal life to all humans who believed in him, were significantly different from the ideas being taught by Jesus' original disciples. The disciples organized a Jesus

Movement that they conceived as a branch of traditional Judaism where adherents would be obliged to accept traditional Jewish practices like circumcision and strict dietary regimens. In their view, the crucified Jesus was resurrected from the grave and he was living in heaven and waiting for the right time to return to earth as the long-awaited Jewish Messiah who would defeat the enemies of Israel and establish God's kingdom throughout the land. Although Paul initially joined the nascent Jesus Movement, he would later be moved to challenge the ideas of the original disciples, claiming that he possessed a divinely inspired authority equal to theirs because Jesus had appeared to him personally in a vision of bright light. After seeing his vision, Paul left Israel and spent three years traveling in Arabia. There is no record of where he went or why, but it was during this journey that he came to believe his visionary experiences revealed that the true meaning of Jesus' teachings was that eternal salvation was now available to all humans, Jews and Gentiles alike, provided they believed in the divinity of Jesus and obeyed his teachings.

To find out more about Paul's visionary experiences, we'll consult two sources in the *New Testament*. The first source will be the book of *Acts*, an account of Paul's life written thirty years after his death. The authors of the *New Testament* attribute the book of *Acts* to the work of a man named Luke who is said to have accompanied Paul on many missions, but the consensus view of current scholars is that the actual author is anonymous. We'll also want to study excerpts from two letters that Paul wrote to Christian congregations he'd founded when he learned, many years later, that they were questioning whether some of his teachings were correct.

According to Luke, Paul was born in Tarsus, a major commercial center located on the southern coast of the land we now know as Turkey. The culture of that city was primarily Hellenic, a legacy of the Greek hegemony that once prevailed throughout the Mediterranean region but had by now long since given way to Roman domination. His family were Jews who owned a tent-making business. The family was prominent enough to have been awarded Roman citizenship. When Paul was a young man, he traveled to Jerusalem to study Jewish law with a famous teacher named Gamaliel. After finishing his studies, Paul joined the Pharisee sect and began calling himself Saul, a name that was traditionally Aramaic. He then convinced the Temple authorities in Jerusalem to assign him to a team of enforcers charged with traveling to the city of Damascus to arrest Jews in the local synagogues who'd joined the Jesus Movement (*Acts* 9: 1). Paul would not have been hesitant about taking on this task: he'd watched with approval as a mob of angry Jews seized Stephen, one of Jesus' original disciples and a leader of the Jesus Movement, dragged him outside the city gates, and stoned him to death (*Acts* 7: 54, 8: 2).

When Paul and his fellow enforcers were on the road to Damascus, they were startled by a strange and disturbing event: Paul suddenly cried out and collapsed. When his companions helped him to his feet, Paul realized he was blind. Luke gives his readers three different accounts of what happened during this vision. Here's the first version:

> Now as he was going along and approaching Damascus, suddenly a light from heaven flashed around him. He fell to the ground and heard a voice saying to him, "Saul, Saul, why do you persecute me?" He asked, "Who are you, Lord?" The reply came, "I am Jesus of Nazareth whom you are persecuting. But get up and enter the city, and you will be told what to do." The men who were traveling with him were speechless, because they heard the voice but saw no one. Saul got up from the ground, and though his eyes were open, he could see nothing; so they led him

by the hand and brought him into Damascus. For three days he was without sight, and neither ate nor drank (Acts 9: 1-9, *The New Oxford Annotated Bible*, 1991).

In a second account describing the same event, Luke claims that Paul's companions also saw the light but did not hear the disembodied voice (*Acts* 22: 3). Then he also presents a third account in which he states that Paul and all of his companions saw that vision of bright light and that all of them fell to the ground (*Acts* 26: 14). In the third version, Luke includes a more detailed description of the message that Jesus wants Paul to begin preaching:

> I am Jesus whom you are persecuting. But get up and stand on your feet; for I have appeared to you for this purpose, to appoint you to serve and testify to the things in which you have seen me and to those in which I will appear to you. I will rescue you from your people and from the Gentiles—to whom I am sending you to open their eyes so that they may turn from darkness to light and from the power of Satan to God, so that they may receive forgiveness of sins and a place among those who are sanctified by faith in me (Acts 26: 14, *The New Oxford Annotated Bible*, 1991).

Why did Luke feel obliged to present three different and contradictory versions of Paul's vision on the road to Damascus? And what can we reasonably infer about the actual content of Paul's vision based on the allegations contained in Luke's accounts? We'll take up those questions as soon as we've finished the traditional story about what happened next.

Luke writes that Paul's companions led him into the city by hand and hired a room where he could rest and recover his sight. After dropping him off, the other men proceeded to carry out the assigned mission of persecuting Jews in the local synagogues who'd joined the local Jesus Movement. While Paul was languishing in the room where his companions left him, another unexpected event occurred. A man named Ananias, an elder in the local synagogue who was also a member of the local Jesus Movement, knocked on Paul's door. For Ananias, this visit was a dangerous undertaking; he knew that Paul was one of the enforcers who'd come to Damascus to arrest people like him. But Luke claims that Jesus appeared to Ananias in a vision and commanded him to make the visit: "Go, for he is an instrument whom I have chosen to bring my name before the Gentiles and kings and before the people of Israel (*Acts* 9: 14)." Paul let the unexpected visitor into his room. Ananias reported that he'd been sent by Jesus and that he had been empowered to cure Paul's blindness by laying his hands on Paul's head. When Paul allowed himself to be touched, "immediately something like scales fell from his eyes, and his sight was restored. Then he got up and was baptized… (*Acts* 9: 17-18)."

After converting to the Jesus Movement, Paul stopped calling himself Saul and agreed to speak about his experiences in the local synagogues, telling everyone about the powerful vision that led him to see the error of his ways and to accept the truth of Jesus' teachings (*Acts* 9: 19-20). But soon after his conversion, Paul decided to leave Damascus and to travel to "Arabia" where he remained out of circulation for three years. When he returned to Damascus, he brought with him many new ideas that he'd come to believe about the true significance of Jesus' life and death, ideas that were radically different from the teachings of the original disciples and the Jesus Movement. He began preaching to all who would listen, heedless of the controversy that he was provoking with leaders of the Jesus Movement.

Now that we've reviewed the main features of Luke's story about Paul's life, let's focus our attention on the question of what actually happened when Paul saw that vision while he was on the road to Damascus. Given the obvious contradictions and the implausible claims put forward in Luke's accounts, the most reasonable hypothesis is that Paul was the only person who saw a flash of light and heard a voice. In that case, it's reasonable to infer, based on what we've discussed in previous chapters, that Paul's vision of bright light was triggered by the eruption of a partial seizure that then generalized throughout Paul's brain, causing him to lose consciousness and fall to the ground. In this view, Luke's rationale for claiming that Paul's companions experienced some of the same symptoms was most likely to prove to his readers that the flash of bright light and the disembodied voice were objective events, not the product of a seizure erupting inside Paul's head.

Why did Luke decide to include three different versions of Paul's vision despite the fact that there were obvious contradictions. Perhaps Paul gave slightly different accounts of his vision to different audiences, adding new details as his own theological ideas evolved, and when Acts was written thirty years after Paul's death, different congregations had different recollections of what Paul told them and they wanted their version to be incorporated in Luke's writings.

We can learn more about Paul's visionary experiences by focusing on letters Paul wrote to some Christian congregations he'd founded during his early travels. Paul wrote these letters to respond to rumors that his congregations had been visited by missionaries from the Jesus Movement in Jerusalem who criticized his teachings. For example, in a letter Paul wrote to a Christian congregation in the Greek city of Corinth, he says he's writing "to deny an opportunity to those who want… to be recognized as our equals in what they boast about. For such boasters are false apostles, deceitful workers, disguising themselves as apostles of Christ (2 *Corinthians* 11: 12-15)." He reminds the congregation about the "exceptional nature of the revelations" he'd received directly from Jesus in Heaven, revelations that endowed him with a spiritual authority that far surpassed whatever the newcomers might claim. In this letter, Paul also mentions that he suffers from "a thorn in his flesh", a physical issue that keeps him from becoming too "conceited" because was chosen to become Jesus' prophet:

> If I must boast, I will boast of things that show my weakness… I will go on to visions and revelations of the Lord. I know a person in Christ who fourteen years ago was caught up to the third heaven—whether in body or out of the body, I do not know, but God knows. And I know that such a person… was caught up into Paradise and heard things which are not to be told, that no mortal is permitted to repeat. On behalf of such a one I will boast, but on my own behalf I will not boast, except of my weaknesses. But if I wish to boast, I will not be a fool, for I will be speaking the truth. But I refrain from it, so that no one may think better of me than what is seen in me or heard from me, even considering the exceptional nature of the revelations. Therefore, to keep me from being conceited, I was given a thorn in my flesh, a messenger from Satan, to torment me, to keep me from being too elated… Three times I pleaded with the Lord to take it away from me. But he said to me, "My grace is sufficient for you, for my power is made perfect in weakness." Therefore, I will boast all the more gladly about my weaknesses… That is why, for Christ's sake, I delight in weaknesses, in insults, in hardships, in persecutions, in difficulties. For when I am weak, then I am strong (2 *Corinthians* 11: 30, 12: 1-7, in *The New Oxford Annotated Bible*).

This letter does not provide any details about what Paul means when he says he has "a thorn in my flesh", but there are some clues in another letter, a letter written at about the same time and sent to a Christian congregation in Galatia. Paul thanks the congregation for treating him kindly despite the dread they felt when they saw him suddenly lose consciousness and collapse while standing in front of them preaching his sermon. He urges the congregation to not let his "physical infirmity" cause them to reject his teachings about Jesus being a personal Christ, which the missionaries from the Jesus Movement were advising them to do:

> I am afraid that my work for you may have been wasted. Friends, I beg you, become as I am, for I also have become as you are. You have done me no wrong. You know that it was because of a physical infirmity that [when] I first announced the gospel to you; although my condition put you to the test, you did not scorn or despise me, but welcomed me as an angel of God, as Christ Jesus. What has become of the goodwill you felt? For I testify that, had it been possible, you would have torn out your eyes and given them to me. Have I now become your enemy by telling you the truth? They make much of you, but they want to exclude you… Listen! I, Paul, am telling you that if you let yourselves be circumcised, Christ will be of no benefit to you… For in Christ Jesus neither circumcision nor uncircumcision counts for anything; the only thing that counts is faith working through love (*Galatians* 4: 8-17, 5: 2-6).

It's reasonable to infer that the "physical infirmity" that the congregation witnessed was an epileptic seizure based on the words Paul used when he thanked the Galatians for "not scorning or despising him". In some translations of the *New Testament*, this particular phrase is rendered as "not spurning or rejecting me". Dr. David Landsborough, a British physician and a Presbyterian missionary, explains what can reasonably be inferred from the fact that Paul chose to use this specific phrase to describe what happened in this incident:

> Paul acknowledges the magnanimity of the Galatians for not rejecting him on account of some humiliating disease which he exhibited on a former visit. To "spurn" or "reject" is the translation of a verb in the original which literally means "to spit out at," hence "you did not spit out at me." Epilepsy was sometimes called morbus qui sputatur. Spitting was the superstitious reaction of a witness to an attack of epilepsy—although it was not necessarily specific to that disease (Landsborough, "St. Paul and temporal lobe epilepsy," *The Journal of Neurology, Neurosurgery, and Psychiatry* 1987; 50: 660)."

Landsborough suggests that Paul's references to being "in the body or out of the body—that I do not know; God knows" are consistent with his having experienced an aura of depersonalization during a partial seizure. He also points out that "Paul also 'heard sacred secrets which no lips can repeat' suggesting an intensely esoteric, rapturous state associated with an elaborate auditory sensation whose details cannot be recollected (p. 660)." Landsborough concludes that, all things considered, there is enough evidence in the Biblical record to support a diagnosis of temporal lobe epilepsy for Paul:

> The diagnosis of TLE in Paul's case is suggested [by some commentators] on the basis of his recorded subjective experience of a single attack. Were this an isolated event without recurrences it would be difficult to sustain the diagnosis. But Paul experienced other "visions." His historian Luke writes that in one vision he saw a Macedonian standing before him appealing to him to cross over from

Troy to Macedonia to help (Acts 18: 9); in another, while praying in Jerusalem, he fell into a trance (Greek: ekstasia) and saw Jesus (Acts 22: 17-21). In other writings Paul does not provide details of his "visions and revelations," but it is suggested that some were ictal in origin, and that the one detailed description he gives was not of an isolated event (p. 661)."

Another important observation, one not mentioned by Landsborough, is that Paul clearly exhibits the symptoms of the kinds of temporal lobe behavior symptoms that emerge after a limbic seizure: an emotional deepening that enabled him to attribute new meanings to events that wouldn't attract the attention of most normal people; an unshakeable conviction that he'd been divinely endowed with an enhanced personal destiny; an intense hyper-religiosity combined with the hypergraphia exemplified by the many years he spent preaching and writing letters that exhorted his followers to seek salvation by believing in Jesus as Christ; and the symptom of hypo-sexuality can also be inferred from the fact that Paul never married and never faced any accusations of sexual impropriety during his long career.

While it seems likely that Paul suffered from some kind of epileptic disorder which triggered recurring seizures that erupted spontaneously, it's important to remember that having a "thorn in the flesh" did not prevent Paul from becoming a prodigious innovator of new religious ideas that ended up changing the course of human history. Paul's teachings resonated with the needs and aspirations of many different people who lived in many different countries and in many different historical eras. He certainly deserves admiration for his accomplishments and for his unique interpretation of Jesus' life and death that led him to be recognized as a co-founder with Jesus, the Jewish rabbi, of a new Christian religion.

The Visions of Mani, the Apostle of Light

The second founder of a new world religion who reported seeing spontaneous, recurring visions is Mani, the founder of the Manichaean religion. The Manichaeans competed vigorously—and often successfully—with early Christian missionaries proselytizing in the Mediterranean region. The influential Christian theologian, Augustine of Hippo, was a Manichean living in North Africa before he converted to Christianity and moved to Italy.

Mani was born in the city of Babylonia in the third century of the Common Era. When he was only five years old, his life was dramatically disrupted when his father abandoned the family to join a heretical Jewish cult and took his young son, Mani, with him. The father wanted to be sure that his son would grow up as a member of that same cult. When Mani was twelve years old, he started seeing visions of a bright, flashing light. He called these visions his *Syzygos*, which means his "Divine Twin" or "Light Twin". He continued to see these same visions throughout his life. When he was asked to describe what he saw, he said the visions "sometimes looked like lightning" and they were as "short and very brief such as I could bear". Sometimes the visions caused him to collapse onto the ground (Gardner and Lieu, 2004, pp. 47-48).

Mani was moved by his visionary experiences to anoint himself as the "Apostle of Light". He synthesized an eclectic mix of ideas that he'd gleaned from diverse sources—from his father's exotic cult, from the Zoroastrian religion of the Persian Empire, and from early Christian communities—and proclaimed the birth of a new Manichaean religion. In the case of Mani, as in the case of Paul, there's evidence that his visionary experiences would satisfy the two criteria physicians use to make a preliminary clinical diagnosis of epilepsy: he experienced many visions of a fiery light he called the *Syzygos*, those recurring seizures erupted spontaneously, and sometimes the visions caused him to collapse to the ground.

The Visions of Emanuel Swedenborg

Our third case study involves a mystic seer who founded a new sect within the Christian tradition. Emanuel Swedenborg was born into a wealthy family with royal connections—his father was the court chaplain and also a professor of theology at Upsala University. Emanuel's mother died when he was only eight years old. Little is known about his early upbringing, but once he matured, he received a cosmopolitan education, studying science and math at Upsala University. After graduation he engaged in a diverse range of activities: he traveled extensively throughout Europe; he designed new inventions; and he helped organize Sweden's first scientific society. In recognition of his talents, Swedenborg was appointed to be the Extraordinary Assessor in the Royal College of Mines when he was only twenty-eight years old. But all the while that he was so actively engaged in worldly affairs, Swedenborg was also preoccupied with the challenge of identifying where the soul resided in the human body.

One day when Swedenborg was traveling in Europe, he was overwhelmed by a major spiritual crisis. It began with vivid nightmares and trembling muscles that peaked at two o'clock in the morning. He reported that he was awakened by a "strong shuddering from head to foot, with a thundering noise as if many winds beat together; which shook me; it was indescribable and prostrated me on my face… At that moment I sat in his bosom, and saw him face to face (Fanning, *Mystics of the Christian Tradition*, 2001, pp. 146-7)." Reeling in the wake of this visionary experience, Swedenborg abandoned his scientific work and began studying how to be a medium who was empowered to channel spirits from other dimensions of reality. And he kept on seeing visions. They would typically appear during the night or during the early morning hours when he would be roused from a dream to find he was already in a trance and watching a vision unfold. Two quotations from Swedenborg's writings make it clear that he saw a bright light that looked like a fiery sun or a calm white moon and that felt he was seeing visions of God:

> That the Lord actually appears in heaven as a sun, has not only been told me by the angels, but has also been given me occasionally to see. What, therefore, I have heard and seen concerning the Lord as a sun, I will here briefly record; ... To those who receive Him in the good of love, He appears as a sun, fiery and flaming according to reception. These are in his celestial kingdom. But to those who receive Him in the good of faith, He appears as a moon, white and shining according to reception. (Swedenborg, *Heaven and Its Wonders and Hell from Things Heard and Seen*, Lippincott, 1890, pp. 77-78).

> There is light in the heavens cannot be comprehended by those who think only from nature; when yet the light there is so great, as to exceed by many degrees the mid-day light of the world. I have often seen it... Its whiteness and brilliancy surpass all description. The things seen by me in the heavens, were seen in that light... The light of heaven is not natural, like that of the sun, but spiritual (p. 83).

Drawing on his visionary experiences and also on the emotional changes associated with his temporal lobe behavior syndrome, Swedenborg became a prolific author, writing thirty books about his revelations. His enhanced sense of his personal destiny led him to become a charismatic religious leader who rejected many of the key teachings of the dominant Lutheran Church. He saw no need for concepts like the Trinity, the Devil, and the Resurrection. Instead he argued that a mystical attunement of heaven and earth was already latent in the human body where it awaited activation by the body's owner. The Lutheran authorities were preparing to charge Swedenborg with heresy, but he died before they could assemble an ecclesiastical court. After the founder's death, his followers organized a new Christian sect called the Swedenborgian Church which continues to flourish.

PART II.

The Self-Induction of Light Visions

CHAPTER 6

Rituals of Extreme Stimulus Overload

The Ritual Induction of Light Visions

Our primary focus in this investigation is on the visions of light that can be induced by the practice of empty-mind meditation, but there is another approach that can also be used to induce these visions—participating in rituals that provoke visions by inflicting some kind of extreme stimulus overload. The techniques used to induce this kind of overload include fasting, self-infliction of pain, sacrificing sleep, exerting oneself to the point of physical exhaustion, and then allowing oneself to slip into trance states. Often the rituals combine all of these techniques. The goal of extreme stimulus overload rituals is to force the sympathetic nervous system to mount a vigorous fight-or-flight response that builds to the point that the participant is hovering on the cusp of physical and psychological exhaustion. That kind of arousal mobilizes the body's autonomic nervous system to intervene in order to restore a more normal physiological homeostasis. It does this by forcing a sudden, dramatic termination of the sympathetic nervous system arousal that leaves the parasympathetic nervous system in charge. When the parasympathetic nervous system takes over, the brain begins firing synchronous slow waves similar to those that govern the nightly transition from waking to sleep. It also stimulates the release of endogenous opiates. Michael Winkelman, a psychologist and anthropologist who specializes in the study of shamanic practices, has described some of the important physiological changes activated by the shift to parasympathetic dominance:

> Shamanistic practices also release endogenous opiates through a variety of stressors (e.g., pain, fasting, water restriction, strenuous exercise, hyperstress of emotions, etc.)… Opiates directly affect the hypothalamus, producing slow wave activity… particularly a rapid increase in delta/theta brain waves and a reduction of fast frequencies… Endorphin levels are highest at night… a typical time for shamanistic activities. Austerities such as flagellation, self-inflicted wounds, exposure to temperature extremes, and feats of endurance all result in the release of endogenous opiates (Winkleman, *Shamanism: The Neural Ecology of Consciousness and Healing*, 2000, pp. 150-1).

Let's review some examples of ritual religious ceremonies that use the techniques of extreme stimulus overload to trigger visions of a fiery light. We'll begin with the *n/um* dance of the San Bushman tribes of South Africa, then discuss the Sun Dance of the Native American Sioux, the *Soma* ritual of the ancient Indo-Aryan tribes, and the *Haoma* ritual practiced by the Indo-Iranian tribes who were distant relatives of the Indo-Aryans.

The San Bushman of South Africa

The San Bushmen have the oldest genetic profile of all anatomically modern humans. They lived as bands of hunter-gatherers in the remote regions of the Kalahari Desert and remained relatively isolated from foreign influences until well into the modern era. They speak *Khoisan*, the oldest of all known languages (Cavalli-Sforza, 2006, 2000; Underhill et al., 2000).

The myths of the San Bushmen emphasize the process of change that continually transforms everything about the world they inhabit and the life they live. They believe in a supreme spiritual power they call *G//aoan* that is undergoing constant change: it sometimes manifests as the Sky God, sometimes as the Trickster. It can take over the spirit of an animal or deceased ancestor, and it can also enter into the body of a living person—someone in the tribe who is recognized as a skilled spiritual healer (Keeley, 2003, p. 145-146; Katz, 2005, pp. 425-442; Guenther, 1999, pp. 3-6).

The primary ritual of the San people, the medium through which they express their spiritual understanding of the universe, is a ritual dance designed to activate a potent healing energy called *n/um*. When the dance begins, members of the band gather around a raging fire to watch, clap, and sing while the men who perform the dance that night begin to shuffle around the central campfire, contorting their postures and focusing their attention inward. These ritual dances can go on for hours and often last throughout the night. After the dancers exerted themselves for a relatively long time, some begin to feel the first stirrings of the n/um energy. It manifests as abdominal spasms, trembling limbs, and as sensations of an intense "boiling" heat. Those dancers who begin to experience the n/um make an effort to keep calm and to keep their attention focused within, because these are said to be the prerequisites for moving forward and entering into the altered state of consciousness called *!kia*. Dancers who attain the !kia state of consciousness are said to acquire special spiritual powers that they can use to help others in the tribe. Once dancers get caught up in the state of !kia, they begin moving around the circle of onlookers, touching those who want a blessing or who need to be healed.

While in the state of !kia, many dancers report that they see a vision of white light. In a recent collection of interviews with San healers, ten of the twenty interviewed (50 percent) reported that the way they know they've entered the state of !kia and have the power to heal is that they see a vision of a white light while they're experiencing boiling sensations and muscle spasms:

First I get filled with pain, then the light comes. It takes away all the pain. … When the light comes… it knocks me out. I fall down and must be brought back to consciousness by others (Testimony of Rasimane, in Keeley, 1999, p. 47).

When the power comes to me and changes me, I see the light coming into my face. The light shows me that there is truth in the dance (Testimony of Ngwaga Osele, Ibid, p. 93).

In the dance, the light that comes to me is like a flashlight beam. … It makes you shiver and causes your body to shake and tremble (Testimony of Komtsas Xau, Ibid, p. 105).

As the steam is pumped into my head, my eyes start changing. One way to describe this is to say that the front of my eyes drop away and a second set of eyes behind them become opened. These second eyes are like seeing from the back of the eyeballs. With this second sight I still see even when I close my eyes… / If the power inside me is strong enough, I will see a special light. Bushmen doctors see different kinds of light. It may be a cloud of light in front of them or a light hovering over the entire community of dancers. When you're very strong you will see lines or strings of light that go up to the sky... When they go up to the sky, they are white in color or shiny like silver metal (Testimony of Bo, in Keeley, 2003, p. 38).

For the San Bushmen, the n/um energy—and the white light of !kia that many of the dancers see when the n/um is present—represent spiritual potentials that are latent in nature and waiting to be activated by those members of the tribe who have the requisite personal qualities, the spiritual prowess, and the willingness to exert themselves for the benefit of the tribe.

The Sun Dance of the Native American Sioux

The Lakota Sioux tribes were nomadic hunter-gatherers and pastoralists living on the Great Plains of western United States and Canada when European explorers first made contact. The traditional Sioux religion honors the spiritual process that is said to underpin nature and all other phenomena. This invisible energy is the "Great Spirit" or the "Great Mystery" (*Wakantanka*). Members of the tribes who face difficulties beyond what they can accomplish using their own resources can beg the Great Spirit to take pity and come to their aid. They hope to receive a vision themselves or to have the Great Spirit send a message to a tribal shaman who will pass it on to the petitioner (Powers, 1982 [1977], pp. 45-47). The Sioux believe in the existence of many other spirits and sacred beings, but, like many other hunter-gatherer bands, such as the San Bushmen, they have not erected an elaborate, systematic mythology. The prayers they send to the spirit world usually address practical problems—seeking help from the spirits to assure a good hunting season, to heal the sick, and to prevail in wars with other tribes.

The primary religious ritual of the Lakota Sioux is the annual Sun Dance. As I described in Chapter 1, the dance takes place inside a circular wooden frame with leafy branches piled on top to provide cover from the hot summer sun. A tall pole is placed at the center of that sacred space. Thin rawhide ropes drape down from the top of the pole, ropes that will assume an important role in the piercing ceremony that takes place on the fourth and final day. The men who've chosen to participate in the piercing ceremony prepare themselves by adopting a regimen of extreme austerities for three days leading up to the final ceremony—they fast, drinking only limited amounts of water, lose a lot of sleep, spend a lot of time praying in the hot, steam-filled sweat lodge that's been erected onsite, and venture out many times during the day and night to perform a ritual dance. On the fourth and final day, those exhausted tribesmen are ready to begin the piercing ritual. As fellow members of the tribe watch from beneath the leafy shelter, the dancers enter the sacred circle. Tribal shamans move from man to man, piercing the pectoral muscles on either side of each man's chest with eagle talons that they then hook to the rawhide ropes hanging from the central pole. When the drums begin to beat and the chorus of singers begins to chant in their high-pitched, falsetto voices, the dancers shuffle back and forth, swaying to the beat of the drums while keeping the ropes that bind them to the central pole stretched taut. They blow on sacred whistles worn around their necks and stare up at the bright sun overhead, keeping their eyes diverted slightly to the side of the sun's bright orb but close enough that they see a bright, red-dish light filling up the entire visual field. One informant who participated in many Sun Dances reported that "as we stare into the sun and dance and pray, the glare and the reflection build until something, the power, hits you like a fire bolt. If you watch carefully, you will see that all the dancers seem to be hypnotized (Mails, *Sundancing at Rosebud & Pine Ridge*, 1978, p. 144)."

The climax begins when the first dancer throws himself on his back. The eagle talons tear out of his chest, and bits of flesh fly out in all directions. The pain, which was already excruciating, becomes even worse. Other dancers follow his lead. As they lie on the ground, some of them lose consciousness for brief intervals. Others slip into a deep trance state as they continue to stare off to one side of the sun and beg Wakantanka to grant them a vision.

In *Black Elk: The Sacred Ways of a Lakota* (1991), a contemporary Sioux medicine man, Wallace H. Black Elk, describes what it was like for him to participate in a Sun Dance ritual when he was one of the piercers who'd just thrown himself on his back:

My heart stopped, and I stopped breathing. I couldn't blink my eyes. I couldn't move. I lay there frozen, like I was petrified, but I was conscious. / Then I looked in the direction of the sun. It appeared really huge and bright. Then the sun became a black polka dot, and it dilated. Different colors began to appear—blue, green, orange, red, and like that. Each time a different color appeared until there was a complete rainbow that appeared around the sun, a circular rainbow. Then as I looked up into the blue sky, a hole appeared in the sky like a big window. Then a man appeared in the window. ... Then out of nowhere a cloud of vapor formed, like dust and smoke. It started getting thicker, and I could see lightning and hear thunder. Then a bolt of lightning that was rapidly moving up and down began to slowly descend to the ground. Then that man started walking down the bolt of lightning and landed right beside me (Ibid., pp. 132-133).

The Sioux Sun Dance is another example of using extreme stimulus overload to induce visions. In this ritual, as in the n/um dance of the San Bushmen, the goal is to see a vision of light that bestows special spiritual powers. The two ancient rituals we'll consider next pursue that same goal, but they both use different techniques to induce an extreme stimulus overload. The Indo-Aryan Soma ritual and the Indo-Iranian Haoma ritual are similar because these rituals were practiced by nomadic tribes that are believed to descend from common ancestors and who formerly lived in close proximity on the Central Asian steppes. Both tribal groups migrated out of their original home in the steppes. The Indo-Aryans moved south into the Indian subcontinent, probably about two thousand years before the Common Era. At about the same time, their cousins, the Indo-Iranian tribes, moved south and east into the territories would later become known as Persia and, more recently, as Iran. The religious rituals of both tribal groups involved drinking a drug that contained an exhilarant and staying awake all night while they chanted hymns to their gods. Then just before dawn, the celebrants initiated a dramatic change: they stopped chanting and let themselves slip into a deep meditative trance while they waited to receive the visions they hoped to receive from the gods who'd sent visions to their ancestors.

The Indo-Aryan *Soma* Ritual

When the nomadic Indo-Aryan tribes left their ancestral homelands in the steppes of Central Asia and migrated into the Indian subcontinent sometime between 1500 and 1200 BCE, they brought with them their sacred *Soma* ritual. We know a lot about this Soma ritual because it is described in the ritual hymns they chanted to the gods—hymns that were eventually compiled to compose the *Rig Veda* (RV), the world's oldest written scripture. The *Rig Veda* became one of the foundations of the Hindu religion of India. The hymns of the Soma ritual described in that ancient text provide detailed descriptions of the light visions said to have been seen by the tribe's ancient ancestors, the visions that other participants in this same ritual could now expect to see.

To prepare for this ritual, the tribal priests gathered the stalks and leaves of a plant that they called *soma* to honor the god, Soma, who was the patron of the ritual because he was the god who had endowed this plant with powerful magic. The priests soaked the stalks and leaves in water to make a beverage, also called *soma*. Scholars used to speculate that the soma plant might have been some kind of hallucinogenic mushroom, but the weight of scholarly opinion today is that the psychotropic element in soma was most likely ephedrine, an adrenaline-like stimulant that can be extracted from the ephedra plants that grow in abundance in the regions where the Indo-Aryan tribes lived.

The theory that I've proposed in my earlier publications is that participants in the Soma ritual drank an exhilarant, not a hallucinogenic drug, and that, as a result, the celebrants saw visions of pure light, not the kinds of dream-like visions containing hallucinations of people, places, or things as some commentators have claimed. (Readers interested in learning more about these technical details are invited to read my article, "The Soma Code: Luminous Visions in the Rig Veda, Parts I-III," published in *The Electronic Journal of Vedic Studies* 2002; 8(3): 31-92. That article is posted on two websites, www.Academia.edu and www.ResearchGate.net. The most detailed and comprehensive version of my theory appears in my book, *Meditation & Light Visions: A Neurological Analysis* (2009), which is available from Amazon. Readers can also match the descriptions of visions in the hymns of the ancient *Rig Veda* with computer-generated video animations of light visions posted on my website, www.religiousvisionsoflight.com.)

When the tribal priests drank soma, they became exhilarated and then stayed up all night, drinking soma and chanting ritual hymns in which they begged the gods to send them the same visions they'd sent to the tribe's ancestors. The hypnotic effect of the exhilaration and the chanting, plus losing a night of sleep, combined to produce the kind of extreme stimulus overload in which the sympathetic nervous system drove an ever-higher state of high arousal to the cusp of triggering a parasympathetic collapse. Then just before dawn the priests stopped chanting and put themselves into a deep meditative trance that, according to their traditions, would prepare them to receive the visions that would sent by the gods. It's not clear if this shift was triggered because of the arousal of their sympathetic nervous systems became so intense that it triggered a parasympathetic collapse or if it was because this change from chanting to meditation was a deliberate tactic known to have worked in the past.

The hymns of the *Rig Veda* give us detailed descriptions of the light visions that the god Soma would send to the worshippers. This sequence of light visions described in the hymns was handed down from one generation to the next, which means the descriptions were tested again and again and found to be accurate. The same sequence of light visions described in the ancient texts is celebrated today as a progression that's generated when meditators activate a reservoir of spiritual energy called *kundalini* stored near the pelvic region. Once that "kundalini" energy is kindled, it rises up through a "sheath of subtle energy centers" called *chakras* or *cakras*. In the Sanskrit language, "cakra" has several relevant meanings: it is a word for *wheel,* but it is also the word used to refer to a spiritual faculty, an "inner eye" that enables meditators to see visions of light, and a word used to refer to "subtle energy centers" that compose a spiritual conduit that's said to be aligned with the human body. All of those meanings are usually present when meditators use that word: the seers say they activate the cakras that constitute their spiritual faculty of inner vision which enables them to see the visions of inner light, and the visions they see, which are sometimes shaped like wheels, can also take on other forms as the kundalini energy rises up through the hierarchy of subtle energy centers. When the kundalini energy reaches one of those energy centers, it activates a vision of inner light that manifests with a color and a shape that are characteristic for that cakra.

What follows is a list of abbreviated descriptions of each light vision in the hierarchical sequence that skilled meditators use to pull themselves up a spiritual ladder, rung by rung, until they achieve the culminating vision of fiery light:

Rung #1. The hymns of the *Rig Veda* describe the first visions to appear as visions of "radiant wheels" that "move away from the seer" and then "traverse the firmament without horses, without reins" (*Rig Veda* 4.36.1-2). These wheel-shaped lights are said to be "chariots", but that's not because these visions incorporate dream-like images of a real chariot; rather, it's because the *function* of this initial set of visions is to pull the seer forward toward the next vision in the sequence. Professor Jan Gonda, a preeminent Dutch scholar who's written the most influential book on this subject, *The Vision of the Vedic Poets* (1963), explains that the Indo-Aryan priests were not simply the passive recipients of these visions called *dhitayah:* "… the man to whom *dhitayah* come is not idle," Gonda writes. "It is on the contrary expressly stated that he must fashion them, give them a definite form. This activity is compared to the carpenter or cartwright (p. 184)." The priests taught that these *dhitayah* represented "a breaking through of a stream of the great and fundamental power called *rta*, of a sudden influx of sacredness, of an extraordinary insight into the reality beyond the phenomena of this world (p. 172)." To obtain this vision, the priests knew they would have to look inward and apply the mental effort required: "The poets are said to make the god favorably disposed merely by means of their faculty of sight," Gonda explains, "The image used is that of the felly [i.e., wheel-rim] which is bent; they 'see' this felly with their inner 'eye' and thereby they bend it, i.e. they exert their influence upon the god (*nemim namanti caksasa*) (p. 33)." According to the hymns of the *Rig Veda*, these visions of these green light-rings are the visions that appear first in the Soma ritual.

Rung #2. After the "radiant wheels", the hymns describe visions of "flame-arrows" that are "many-colored", "smoke-like" in texture, and formed into round shapes like "streams of water funneling down into holes" (RV 10.25.4). These descriptions match my visions, which manifest as dark blue or purple clouds with porous textures and amorphous, ever-changing borders.

Rungs #3 and 4. The hymns of the *Rig Veda* do not mention the tunnel-like vision of black rings nor the vision of a spray of radiating sparks that comes after black rings. The omission of the vision of black rings may have been because those rings are often barely perceptible such that they manifest only as a sensation of optic flow—as a sensation of movement. Or the vision of black rings may have been omitted because it doesn't fit the Indo-Aryan metaphysical paradigm in which a series of bright radiances are supposed to appear, the bright radiances that are emanations of the primordial light of *Rta*, the energy of Cosmic Truth and Order. The vision that comes immediately after the tunnel-like vision of black rings—the vision of a spray of sparks—is also not mentioned in the hymns of the *Rig Veda*, but it is described in the *Upanishads*, the commentaries written by later generations of priests to explain the original Vedas. In those later commentaries, the spray of sparks is described as the auspicious vision of "fireflies" that constitutes one of the "preliminary forms which produce the manifestation of Brahman in Yoga (*Svetasvatara Up.*, II: 11)." The spray of sparks is also described in Patañjali's famous text, the *Yogasutras*, the first instruction manual for meditators, where he warns meditators to not turn their eyes away from the vision of a spray of sparks radiating out toward the seer: "Those countless speckles striking—they have a purpose," he writes in verse 4: 24. The purpose is to move them along the path that leads to Brahman.

In a Tantric Hindu text composed many centuries later, there's an obscure reference stating that the meditators will get caught up in a "churning… [that] must be performed with whirling force". I interpret this to be a reference to what the meditators experience when they feel the sensation of optic flow that gives them the feeling of moving through a dark space, and, indeed, that same verse in the Tantric text adds that this churning sensation will continue "until there appear the dazzling sparks (*Shivasutravimarshini*, quoted in Silburn, 1988, p. 43)."

Rung #5. Next "the conscious dawns… the purple dawn appeared (RV 4.1.11-17)." This is a reference to the inner visions with dawn-like characteristics that appear *before* the advent of the natural dawn, to visions of "days that dawned before the sun… Our ancestors discovered the hidden light and created the Dawn (RV 7.76.2)."

Rung #6. As meditators stare into the blue light of the inner dawn, they see the god Soma begin to manifest: first the god appears in the "vision of newborn Soma". The "newborn" has a bulbous shape that looks like "a cow's udder swollen with milk", and it has a white color "like a boll of white wool". The bulb of "newborn Soma" appears to push forward and pull back, which is why the hymns describe the vision as being "like a bull's horn [being scratched forward and back against a tree]", or like a "penis" that's moving in and out.

Rung #5. When the newborn Soma frees itself from the white bulbous protrusion, it becomes three rays of white light silhouetted against background that has suddenly gone dark: "In jets, the pressed Soma is clarified" so that "its juice becomes three-fold". Then those jets of Soma juice become more numerous, changing into a "dazzling mesh spread afar", and as those rays spread farther apart, they create the impression that they've just lowered themselves in the visual field, creating an effect that looks like a hawk "alighting on its nest". Now the god Soma has done his part: he's brought the participants in the Soma ritual who've invoked all of those earlier visions to the final destination they all yearn to reach: Soma has brought them to the point where they will see the sudden intrusion in which another god takes over. They see bolts of lightning hurled into their minds by Indra, the god of thunderstorms. The priests explain this sudden explosion of lightning-like flashes by teaching that while the humans were celebrating the Soma ritual, in the heavenly realm the god Indra was also celebrating a similar ritual in which he drank immense amounts of the heavenly version of soma. After his night of drinking and losing sleep, Indra became so exhilarated that he started hurling the lightning bolts that illuminate the minds of the humans with visions of the "inspired thought that is bright-like-lightning (RV 10.177.2)", visions in which the seer "clothes himself in the fire-bursts of the sun (RV 9.71.9)".

Zoroaster and the Indo-Iranian *Haoma* Ritual

The Indo-Iranian tribes who were distant cousins of the Indo-Aryans shared many common religious practices, including a *Haoma* ritual which, as its name suggests, follows the pattern of the Soma ritual. The Indo-Iranians also collected their hymns and compiled them in a sacred scripture called the *Avesta*. During the Haoma ritual, the Avestan priests prepared a beverage called *haoma* in honor of the patron god, a beverage that almost certainly would have contained the ephedrine exhilarant used by the Indo-Aryans. The priests drank haoma, stayed up all night chanting hymns, and ended up falling into deep trance states. Two scholars, who studied the ancient Avestan texts to find what they revealed about the effects of drinking haoma, state that this practice "brought about a condition outwardly resembling sleep (i.e., *stard*) in which targeted visions of what is believed to be a spirit existence were seen (Flattery and Schwartz, 1989, p. 23)". Note that the word *stard* cited here can be translated as "stunned", "dazed", or "sprawled". All of these adjectives would be appropriate descriptions of what happened at the end of the ritual if, like the Indo-Aryans, the Indo-Iranian priests pushed their bodies and minds to the point of triggering a parasympathetic collapse equivalent to a meditative trance or made a deliberate shift into a meditative trance state.

Zoroaster was an Avestan priest who lived in a small village in the northwest region of the territory we now call Iran. His ancestors had given up the old ways of wandering and raiding to settle in a permanent village where they continued to herd cattle but also took up agriculture. Zoroaster was officiating at the Haoma ritual in his native village when he saw a vision of fiery light that transformed his life and launched him on a new career as a charismatic prophet. It happened just before dawn when Zoroaster, like the other priests, had just spent the entire night in a state of exhilaration, drinking haoma and chanting the traditional hymns. Because he was one of the officiants in charge of the ceremony, he noticed that water was needed in order for the priests to keep making more haoma. Zoroaster picked up some empty buckets and waded into the river located nearby. He filled the containers and was wading back to shore when he suddenly saw the vision of a bright, flashing light. He described that vision as an encounter with *Vohu Manah,* a name which can mean "Good Mind", "Good Thought", or "Good Purpose".

In the traditional sources, it's said that his vision of "Good Mind" manifested as a "being with the shape of a man" who was wearing a garment "which was like light itself". Zoroaster is said to have been transported by "Good Mind" into the presence of the "Immortals", an assembly consisting of all the *Amesha Spentas* of the Avestan religion. They all were shining with lights so bright that Zoroaster "no longer saw his shadow on the ground (*Zadspram*, Chapters 20-21; from Boyce, 1984, p. 75)".

While these passages in the *Zadspram* scriptures describe Zoroaster's first vision, which was "like light itself" as having "the shape of a man", that's the only reference to his having seen a human-like figure. All of Zoroaster's other descriptions are consistent with his having seen flashes of bright light. The fact that he calls that first vision "Good Mind" or "Good Thought" would appear, based on the superficial meaning, to refer to a state of consciousness and not to the vision of a human-like being. And he adds that this "Good Mind" was "clothed in a garment that looked like light itself", which suggests that what Zoroaster actually saw was a vision of a pure light unlike any light he'd seen in nature.

He then goes on to say that during this same encounter he saw more visions. These visions are described in the traditional sources as "the assembly of the Immortals", but what Zoroaster actually describes is seeing flashes of "lights so bright that he no longer saw his shadow on the ground". Given how ambiguous the descriptions in the traditional account would appear, and given what we know from our neurologically grounded analysis of the vision of fiery light, what most likely happened to Zoroaster that morning just before dawn as he waded back to shore was that he suddenly saw an eruption of bright flashes—a vision of fiery light accompanied by an ecstasy that well deserved the name he gave it, the name "Good Mind".

This interpretation also matches what we know about the culminating vision of the Indo-Aryan Soma ritual that manifests as a light "bright-like-lightning". This comparison is relevant because the Soma ritual involved essentially the same combination of extreme stimulus overload, drug use, and sleep loss that Zoroaster had just put himself through. From this perspective, the phrase claiming that what Zoroaster saw was a "being in the shape of a man" has all the earmarks of being something that was inserted when the scribes who wrote the traditional account felt they had to give their readers something comprehensible.

Zoroaster saw other visions in addition to the one he saw during that fateful Haoma ritual. A good example is a prayer that was incorporated in the official Zoroastrian scriptures that makes it clear that the prophet taught his followers that their god, Haoma, would appear to them as a green light. The prayer begins by urging worshippers to welcome "Haoma, the Green One," because that god has the power to lead meditators along a path that will end with them seeing the vision of light seen by Zoroaster himself. The prayer reads: "Reverence to Haoma!... O Green One! I call down your intoxication, your strength, victory, health, healing, furtherance, power for the whole body, ecstasy of all kinds. ... This first boon I ask of you, O invincible Haoma! The Paradise of the Just and Light that encompasses all happiness (*Yasna* 9, 3.2.1)." Note that the prayer ends by referring to "the Light that encompasses all happiness" which was also the goal of the Soma ritual practiced by the Indo-Aryans. The sequences of light visions described by the two different cultures follow a similar progression: the first visions to appear in both cultures are green lights, and those visions of green light can be propitiated so that they launch the seer on a path that culminates in flashes of bright white light. When the Indo-Aryan meditators saw those flashes described in the *Rig Veda* as being "bright-like-lightning" they told themselves that "we have become immortal; we have gone to the light; we have found the gods (RV 8.48.3; Doniger / O'Flaherty, *The Rig Veda*, 1971)." Similarly, when Indo-Iranian meditators saw the visions of green light, they knew they were on the path to see the vision the prayer in the *Yasna* describes as "the Light that encompasses all happiness".

After Zoroaster saw the initial visions of "Good Mind" and the "Immortals", he began to see visions in which he said he was able to communicate directly with the supreme god of the Avestan tradition, a god known as *Ahura Mazda* or as *Ohrmadz*. Zoroaster reported he saw Ahura Mazda manifesting as pure Light, and that's the concept that got incorporated in the Zoroastrian sacred scriptures. There it's written that the supreme god lives in a realm of endless light: "For boundless time He was ever in the light. That light is the space and place of Ohrmazd. Some call it Endless Light (*Zadspram* 2.3: 47-49, in Boyce, *Textual Sources for the Study of Zoroaster*, 1984, p. 45)." That primordial light was used by Ohrmadz to create the world that's known to humans: "Ohrmadz fashioned forth the form of his creatures from His own self, from the substance of light—in the form of fire, bright, white, round and visible afar (2.3: 47-9)." And he also used some of that Endless Light when He "created Fire, whose radiance is from the Endless Light, the place of Ohrmadz (*Zadspram* 3: 7)." When humans kindle fires, these fires are considered to be a blessing conferred by Ohrmadz and a symbol pointing to his existence. This concept that a supreme god would manifest to humans in a fire would eventually spread far beyond the Zoroastrian religion.

It took a long time for Zoroaster to gather followers and even longer for him to attract the support of someone with wealth and influence. Once he found a sponsor, a king who ruled a small kingdom in eastern Iran, Zoroaster's religious ideas and practices began to spread rapidly throughout the local region and then eventually extended farther east into the kingdoms of the fertile crescent, including the kingdom of Babylonia. When Cyrus the Great conquered Babylonia and incorporated that city as the capital of the First Persian Empire, he proclaimed Zoroastrianism to be the official religion of his Empire.

Michael Witzel, a professor of Sanskrit and Indian Studies at Harvard University and author of *The Origins of the World's Mythologies* (2012), traces how Zoroaster's teachings began with his personal interpretation of ideas he'd originally adopted from the Indo-Iranian Avestan religion but then merged with newer ideas evoked by his own visionary experiences. When Zoroaster's synthesis of old and the new ideas became the dominant religion of the Persian Empire, Zoroastrian ideas influenced the Hebrew priests and scribes who'd been exiled from Judea and forced to live in Babylon where Zoroastrianism was the official religion. Later, when those priests and scribes returned to Judea and were commissioned to write the early books of the Hebrew *Torah*, they imported some of the Zoroastrian ideas. Professor Witzel cites several examples:

He [Zoroaster] started out from the old Indo-Iranian concept of the renewal of time and society at year's end, but he transposed it to the final period of one's own life and that of the world. He stressed the inevitability of the choice during the fight of two opposing forces at year's end that was commonly made at this critical time: one had to choose between righteousness (*asha*, Vedic *rta*) and evil (*druj*, Vedic *druh*)… In Zoroaster's new worldview, the choice is to be made "now," in every human's life; the outcome would lead one, via the *Cintuuant* bridge, to *Ahuramazda's* Heaven—or to "hell"—"falling from the bridge into the molten metal". This is the ultimate origin of the Christian and millenarian American ideas of heaven and hell, conceived about a thousand years before Jesus—an idea that, due to path dependency, still is extremely powerful in the modern West, especially in America (Witzel, *The Origins of the World's Mythologies*, 2012, pp. 89-90).

Zoroastrianism and the Early Hebrew Bible

When the king of Babylon, Nebuchadnezzar II, invaded the Hebrew kingdom of Judea and destroyed its capital, Jerusalem, in 597 BCE, he forced Judean elites—the rulers, the high priests, and other privileged groups—to become exiles in Babylonia so he could keep better control over them. In Jewish history, this period is remembered as the Babylonian Captivity. But then the kingdom of Babylonia was taken over by another conqueror, Cyrus the Great, who incorporated it into his Achaemenid Empire, also known as the First Persian Empire. Cyrus reversed Nebuchadnezzar's policy of requiring the Judean exiles to live as exiles in Babylon, but even though the exiles were now free to return to their native land, many of them decided to remain in Babylon. They'd become accustomed to living in a rich urban and cosmopolitan environment. But there were exiles who did choose to return, and once they got back to Judea, they quickly wrested control from those who'd never been exiled who were mostly peasants living in the countryside and poor city-dwellers.

One of the top priorities of the new rulers of Judea was to legitimize their right to rule. They commissioned priests and scribes to prepare scrolls that would document the existence of a straight line of descent from legendary times when the Hebrew kingdoms of Judea and Israel were said to have been part of one United Kingdom ruled over by divinely anointed kings like David and Solomon. But as the priests and scribes gathered all the old oral traditions and other miscellaneous materials they could find, hoping that would enable them to reconstruct a chronology of Hebrew origins, they encountered a lot of gaps. They were forced to confront many uncertainties and thus to fill in the missing pieces as best they could, never forgetting that they'd been assigned to come up with stories that would support the claims of the current rulers to be direct descendants of David and Solomon. Faced with these challenges, it seems highly likely that the priests and scribes would have had to insert some creative fictions to close gaps in the traditional stories. One strategy they used, consciously or unconsciously, was to incorporate their own versions of Zoroastrian ideas they'd been exposed to during the Babylonian Captivity, ideas they probably thought had been left far behind. But they'd seen how the Cyrus the Great established Zoroastrianism as the official religion of Babylon, and they would have associated that religion with the fact that Babylon was by far the most powerful and prosperous kingdom in the region. So while those Judean priests and scribes wrote the scrolls that would become the books of a new Hebrew *Torah*, it would have been difficult for them to put out of mind the values of that more powerful, more prosperous culture they'd been exposed to for so many years.

Weston La Barre, a psychoanalytic anthropologist, describes the psychological effects evoked by this kind of culture crisis. He writes that when confusion that arises among members of a traditional society who are being threatened by a more powerful, more technologically sophisticated culture, the members of that weaker, more traditional culture are forced to ask themselves: "Shall the models for my behavior be the old ambivalently loved persons of my tribe?—or the new ambivalently hated persons of a more powerful alien tribe? (La Barre, *The Ghost Dance: The Origins of Religion*, 1970, p. 338)." This aphorism is particularly apt for helping us understand why the Judean priests and scribes who'd returned from the Babylonian Captivity and who were tasked with writing a new genealogy of the Hebrew people might end up adopting some Zoroastrian religious ideas. Among the ideas that scholars point to as having been absorbed from the Zoroastrian model are the following:

1. There is only one God, and that supreme God lives in a world of Light;

2. God is continually striving to win a cosmic struggle between the forces of Light and Good and the forces of Dark and Evil;

3. Each human being has to choose which side to support: the forces of Light and Good, or the forces of Darkness and Evil, and each human soul, after death, has to face a Day of Judgment. For the Zoroastrian, this moment came when it was time to cross a bridge called *Cintuuant* and to find out if the soul's fate was to fall into the hellish reservoir of molten metal below or to make it across and into a paradise of light; and,

4. God created Fire in his own likeness and gave Fire to humans as a symbol of His presence, so if He manifests to humans, he manifests as Fire.

The idea that the Hebrew God, Yahweh, manifests His presence with a vision of a mighty Fire appears again and again in the Hebrew Bible, not only in the first five books of the Torah but also in the works attributed to various prophets. The patriarchs who founded the Hebrew religion—Abraham, Moses, Elijah, and Ezekiel—are all said to have seen visions of Fire when God wanted to contact them to issue His new commands. We'll want to return to this topic in Chapter 10 to take a closer look at the visionary experiences attributed to the Hebrew patriarchs and to assess what those stories reveal about what really happened.

CHAPTER 7

Slow Wave Sleep and Visions of Green Rings

Sleep: The Meditator's Secret Portal

The idea that sleep is involved when meditating yogis are in a deep trance is not new: yoga meditation texts from ancient times report that meditators experience an altered state of consciousness that exists somewhere between the usual states of waking and sleeping. That trance state is called *turiya* by Hindus and *dhyana* by Buddhists. In an article entitled "Training attention for conscious non-REM sleep: The yogic practice of yoga-nidrâ and its implications for neuroscience research", author Stephen Parker recommends that neuroscientists revisit the findings of an EEG study initiated in the late 1960s by Elmer and Alyce Green, two researchers at the Menninger Foundation. The subject of the study was a Hindu yogi named Swami Rama who induced his deepest trance state while the researchers monitored his brainwaves using a scalp EEG. They discovered that he was generating brainwaves with the delta band frequencies that are usually associated with the deepest stage of NREM sleep:

Their studies of the conscious control of involuntary processes drew on collaboration with an Indian master of yoga meditation, Swāmī Rāma of the Himālayas, which opened a number of intriguing possibilities, which have yet to be followed up in detail with the most recent research tools and methodologies. Among these is the ability to enter the deepest, non-REM delta wave sleep while maintaining awareness both internally and of one's surroundings (*yoga-nidrā*). The particular interest in this ability lies not only in the benefits that accrue from especially deep relaxation and an especially pure experience of mindful awareness, but also from the yogi's description of this as a way to gradually learn to enter the deepest states of meditation (*samādhi*) and remain there even when otherwise active in the world (*turīya*) (Parker, *Progress in Brain Research* 2019; 244: 255-272).

I should have suspected that there might be a link between meditation and sleep based on my own personal experiences. Whenever I meditate, I see visions of green light-rings that seem to fly off into the dark void, but those same green light-rings sometimes appear spontaneously when I'm not meditating but am feeling very relaxed—if I'm lying in bed waiting to fall asleep, or during the last few minutes of a deep tissue massage. But it was only after I inadvertently triggered the partial seizure by meditating at four o'clock in the morning while suffering from a substantial sleep deficit that I recognized the critical importance of learning more about how synchronous brainwaves associated with sleep onset interact with synchronous brainwaves generated by meditation.

How Meditators "See" Sleep

When I'm meditating, the very first vision to enter my visual field is not actually a green light-ring; rather, it's something with a similar shape and a similar movement that quickly turns into a green light-ring. Here's what I see first: a thin black ring sweeps in from all sides of the visual field, as if it had just come from behind my head, then begins shrinking steadily in diameter. The black ring is barely perceptible against the dark, charcoal gray of the visual field, so its appearance might not be detected by all meditators. But even if meditators don't notice that black ring, they're still likely to experience a sensation of optic flow as the ring begins shrinking in diameter. Immediately after the black ring enters the visual field, it disappears, eclipsed by the sudden efflorescence of a bright green ring that occupies the space just behind it. That new green ring (and the invisible black ring situated just in front of it) continue to shrink steadily in diameter, so it looks like there's a green light-ring flying away toward the center of the dark void. I've watched this phenomenon unfold on many different occasions and it always features the same clock-like timing: a new green light-ring flashes into view every five seconds and continues shrinking steadily in diameter for precisely four seconds, then it suddenly disappears. Halfway through the ring's concentric trajectory—when it's been in view for precisely two seconds—the center of the ring suddenly fills with more green light and becomes a green disk.

The color of the light that filled in the center of the green ring changed after I'd been practicing meditation on a regular basis: the center of the light-ring began filling in, not with more green light but with a dark blue color. This created an image that looked very much like the iridescent green and dark blue "eye" that decorates the tip of a peacock's feather.

Visions of green light-rings are described in the mystical literatures of many religious traditions—in the Hindu *Rig Veda* and the *Upanishads* commentaries, in Naropa's Tibetan Buddhist anthology, *The Epitome of the Six Yogas*, and in some early Daoist texts. Those visions are also described by famous mystics in Western religious traditions—by Ezekiel, by Evagrius, and by the Prophet Muhammed, to name only a few. We'll take a closer look at many accounts of visionary experiences later in this chapter, but first it's important to learn more about what has to happen in the brain in order for these visions to appear.

My neurologically grounded, reverse-engineering analysis of the green light-rings that I've seen myself reveals that those light-rings are generated by the same brainwaves that govern the nightly transition from waking to sleep. The first stage of the transition to sleep is designated as "stage 1" non-rapid-eye-movement sleep, or NREMS. During this first stage, people begin to feel drowsy and become progressively more detached from what's happening in their environments and from their inner thoughts and feelings. This initial stage of the transition, "Stage 1" NREM sleep, begins when large networks of cortical neurons begin spontaneously firing synchronous bursts at a very slow rate of less than one burst per second (< 1 Hz). What some meditators are able to see during Stage 1 sleep are tiny blobs of green light with amorphous, ever-changing shapes that bubble up in the visual field and quickly disappear. Meanwhile, the cortical slow waves flow down through the neural circuits that extend all the way to the brainstem. Once those waves arrive in the brainstem, they initiate physiological changes that build up until they reach a threshold value. When that happens, the brainstem's sleep rhythm oscillators begin firing their own synchronous bursts which are much more powerful than the cortical slow waves that triggered them. The synchronous bursts fired by the sleep rhythm oscillators are called "spindle bursts" because they register in a scalp EEG as tracings with a waxing and waning pattern that has the shape of an old-fashioned spindle of wool. The spindle bursts fired by the sleep rhythm oscillators create "spindle waves" that flow back up the neuron circuits toward the cortical regions. When those spindle waves arrive at their destination, they force cortical neurons to join in firing synchronous bursts with the same rhythmical pattern. This entrainment of cortical neurons blocks them from processing the incoming sensory signals. That's the moment when people "fall asleep" because they lose consciousness. And it's also the signal that "Stage 2 NREM sleep" has begun.

But if that's the case—if people normally lose consciousness when Stage 2 NREM sleep begins—how is it possible for some expert meditators to retain enough conscious awareness to "see" visions of light generated by the spindle waves arriving in the visual cortices? Why don't those meditators fall asleep like everyone else? A study published by Vernon Mountcastle and colleagues found that if humans keep their eyes converged inward and their attention fixated on the visual field, the excitability of the neurons in their visual cortices can increase by as much as 350 percent (*The Journal of Neuroscience*, 1981; 1(11): 1218-1235). Once in that hyperexcitable state, neurons in the visual cortices are able to resist being entrained by the rhythmic pulsations flowing up from the brainstem; instead, those neurons retain the ability to register the arrival of synchronous spindle waves as if those waves were normal visual signals that originated in the meditators' eyes. What these meditators see first when a synchronous spindle wave arrives in their visual cortices is the vision of a thin black ring that sweeps in from all sides of the visual field, and what they see next is the sudden efflorescence of a bright ring of green light that's assumes its position close behind the black ring.

These ring-like shapes get imposed on spindle waves when they interact with an anatomic structure located midway between the brainstem and the visual cortices. That structure, called the "lateral geniculate nucleus (LGN)", contains neurons that specialize in receiving the vision-related signals coming in from a person's eyes and firing a corresponding set of vision-related signals that then get transmitted through the axons of the LGN neurons that project all the way up to target neurons located in the visual cortices. There are two LGNs: the one located on the right side of the brain processes all incoming visual signals that originated in left sides of the seer's retinae; the one on the left processes all incoming visual signals from the right sides of the retinae. During normal perception, the vision-related signals that originate in a person's retinae stream into the LGNs where they trigger vision-relay neurons to fire in a pattern that encodes the patterns of the signals arriving from the retinae. But before the signals fired by the vision-relay neurons can be transmitted out of the LGN, they have to pass through a thin sheet of inhibitory neurons that stretches over the outer surface of both LGNs. This sheet of inhibitory neurons is called the "thalamic reticular nucleus (RTN)". The interactions of these RTN inhibitory neurons and the LGN vision-relay neurons they're attached to are responsible for generating the visions of both the black rings and the green rings that meditators see when brainstem starts firing the spindle bursts of Stage 2 NREM sleep.

The ring shapes of the meditation-induced visions is a function of the shapes of the LGNs. Researchers who study primate LGNs have published 3-dimensional drawings of how six sheets of vision-relay neurons are layered together to create this anatomical structure, and they show that the top layer, when it's removed from the stack, is shaped like a dome that's been split in half vertically (Le Gros Clark, *Journal of Anatomy*, 1940-41; 75: 419-433). If the top-layers from the right and left LGNs, each shaped like a half dome, were to be aligned together, they would approximate the shape of a full dome. That's a finding that will become critically important when we discuss how the LGNs generate ring-shaped light visions. Researchers have also constructed a visuotopic map of the upper layer of a primate LGN that shows where vision-relay neurons responsible for generating light sensations in different regions of a person's visual field are positioned (Connolly and Van Essen, *Journal of Comparative Neurology*, 1984, 226: 544-564). The visuotopic map shows that the top half of the upper layer of the LGN is taken up by just those vision-relay neurons that represent central vision. In other words, almost half of that LGN layer contains neurons that send signals that only appear within a 10-degree circle at the center of the visual field. This anatomical information helps explain why spindle waves flowing up through the two RTN/LGN complexes can generate images shaped like rings.

When a spindle wave from the brainstem reaches the bottom of the thin sheet of LGN/RTN complex, it activates vision-relay neurons in the LGN but also activates neurons in the RTN sheet covering the outside of the LGN which inhibits the protruding axons of those vision-relay neurons, preventing them from relaying their vision-relevant signals. Because these bottom level vision-relay neurons innervate the most peripheral regions of the visual field, the RTN inhibition cuts off all light-related signals that would normally appear along the peripheral rim of the visual field. That thin band of inhibition cuts off even the random signals from the retinae that generate the normal charcoal gray background of the visual field. What meditators see is a thin black band, darker than the charcoal gray background, that extends all around the outer rim of the peripheral visual field. Then as the spindle wave begins to move higher up the sides of the two RTN/LGN complexes—the one on the right and the one on the left—the wave activates the vision-relay neurons located a bit farther up in the LGN while the same wave moving up through the RTN matrix inhibits the axons of those very same vision-relay neurons. The spindle waves flow up the sides of both LGN/RTN complexes simultaneously, and that means that the two sets of signals being forwarded from those two complexes will get fused together to generate the perception of integrated images appearing in a unified visual field. So a thin spindle wave flowing up the sides of the two LGN/RTN complexes, each shaped like a half dome, will generate the image of a thin band appearing along the bottom rim of a dark dome and then moving up toward the top of the dome, shrinking in diameter the wave rises and the dome wall slopes inward. The RTN inhibition of the LGN vision-relay neurons will send signals to the visual cortices that will fuse to form the image of a thin black band all along that rim, but then as the spindle wave rises and its band of inhibition moves higher up the dome-shaped layers of the RTN/LGN complexes, the image of the thin black ring seen by meditators will shrink in diameter and seem to be flying away into the dark void.

A simple thought experiment might make this process easier to envision. Imagine that you're sitting in planetarium, looking up at the dark dome overhead. Your tour guide points out that the spectacle you are about to see requires the input of two projectors, one that projects light onto the left side of the dome while the other projects light onto the right side. As the show begins, you look up at the dome above and see that the first signals the two projectors sent to the dome: those signals have fused to form a thin black band stretched around the rim of the planetarium's dark dome. As you watch, the thin black ring begins shrinking in diameter so it looks like it's moving away from you into the dark void. This is a close analogy of what happens when spindle waves flow simultaneously up the sides of the RTN/LGN complexes. In effect, the rising spindle wave generates a visual image that is a "moving shadow" of itself.

Meditators catch only a brief glimpse of the black ring because its presence is suddenly eclipsed by a bright ring of green light that's tucked just behind the black ring. The vision of the bright green light-ring is stimulated by the same spindle waves that generate the black ring. As the wave of inhibition imposed by the spindle wave keeps moving higher up the sides of the two RTN/LGN complexes, this releases the inhibition imposed on the axons of the vision-relay neurons that innervate peripheral vision. As soon as those vision-relay neurons along the lower edge of the RTN/LGN complexes get released from inhibition, they all fire a burst of "rebound spikes." The wave of rebound spikes fired by vision-relay neurons generates a thin band of light-bearing signals that is a mirror image of the thin band of no-light signals that preceded it. When this happens, what meditators see is a ring of signals containing no light information whatsoever—the signals generated by the spindle wave inhibition that generate the image of a black ring—followed immediately by a ring of green light generated by the wave of rebound spikes fired by the disinhibited LGN vision-relay neurons. The tandem rings—the black ring and the green light-ring—keep shrinking in diameter at a steady rate as the spindle wave keeps moving ever higher up the sides of the LGN/RTN complexes. Two seconds into the shrinking trajectory of the ring images, the center of the green light-ring will fill in with more green light to form a disk. That happens when the spindle wave reaches into the upper regions of the RTN/LGN complexes that contains the vision-relay neurons that innervate central vision.

To return to the planetarium analogy, imagine that while you're looking up at the dark dome overhead you see a thin black ring appear that then begins to move in from the outer rim as it shrinks in diameter. But then you see a flash of bright green light that forms a ring occupying the same space as the black ring you were watching only moments before. Actually, the black ring is still there and still shrinking in diameter, but it's very hard to see because of the bright green ring is so distracting.

Then, as you watch, you see the empty center of the green ring suddenly fill in with more green light to form a disk. That green disk then keeps shrinking in diameter for two more seconds, compacting into the middle of the visual field, when it suddenly disappears. You're left staring up at the planetarium's dark, empty dome waiting for something else to happen. What you imagined yourself seeing in that thought experiment is analogous to what meditators see when spindle waves start flowing up the sides of the LGN/RTN complexes.

Scientific studies of what happens in the brain during the transition from waking to sleep reveal that when the brainstem shifts to firing the synchronous spindle bursts that inaugurate "stage 2" non-rapid-eye-movement sleep, those spindle bursts are fired with clocklike regularity at a rate of one burst every three to ten seconds (0.3 to 0.1 Hz). That's consistent with the timing of the green light rings that I see while I'm counting the passing seconds ("1001, 1002, etc."): I see one green ring enter the visual field every five seconds, a rate of 0.2 Hertz.

Other scientific studies show that when spindle bursts are fired in the brain stem, the number of spikes fired during a single discharge waxes and wanes over an interval that can range from one to three seconds. That timing is consistent with my observation that each green light-ring remains visible in the visual field for precisely four seconds. That extra second is probably an artifact of the time required for visual signals generated in the LGN/RTN complexes to flow up to the visual cortices.

Scientific studies also show that the number of spindle waves required to put a person to sleep can range from as few as three waves to as many as six—and that the number of spindle waves needed to put a particular person to sleep is usually the same on most nights (Uchida et. al., *Brain Research Bulletin*, 1994; 33: 351-355).

It's also important to note that scientific studies of sleep have not found any evidence of there being another kind of brainwave that exhibits the same clock-timing as the spindle bursts associated with stage 2 NREMS and that sends its waves through the LGN/RTN complexes.

Now it's time to move beyond the analysis of brain mechanisms and to begin exploring how mystics from many different religions and many different historical eras have used meditation to induce visions of green light-rings—and how those mystics used those visions to create myths that took on important roles in their respective religious traditions.

Visions of Green Light-Rings in World Religions

The Egyptian Eye of Horus

When a pharaoh died in ancient Egypt, his mummified body would be placed in a tomb located deep inside the pharaoh's pyramid. Then the high priest would enter the tomb dressed in a ceremonial leopard skin accompanied by fellow priests to begin performing the "Opening of the Mouth" ceremony. The high priest would chant sacred spells as he used a ceremonial adze to pry open the rigid jaws of the dead pharaoh. Then he would use green and black paint to draw the outline of an eye-shaped oval with a tiny tail on the pharaoh's forehead. This oval was a symbol of the *Wadjet,* the "Eye of Horus", also known as the "Lord of Malachite" and "The Green One (*w3t*)." The Wadjet was an ancient Egyptian symbol of royalty and protection. The goal of this ritual was to induce the real "Eye of Horus" to fly out of the Underworld, to retrieve the soul of the dead pharaoh, then to fly the soul back into the Underworld where it would face a Day of Judgment before the supreme god, Osiris.

I wanted to explore how the Egyptian priests might have come up with this myth, and my research led me to an article entitled "Mysticism in Pharaonic Egypt?" published in 1982 in the *The Journal of Near Eastern Studies* by Egyptologist Edward Wente. In that article Wente analyzed two ancient texts, *The Book of the Underworld* and *The Book of Gates*, and he discovered many passages where Egyptian priests claimed they could see visions of light once they entered the "netherworld". In *The Book of Gates*, a priest claims that "The ones who offer to gods on earth are the ones who perceive light in the netherworld (p. 172)." Another passage in that same text states that these priests actually take on the form of light: "The one who gives the gods their offering gifts is among those whose linen is light-colored in the netherworld (p. 173)." These entries help explain why some of the Egyptian High Priests commissioned hieroglyphic carvings in which they claimed to be "Chiefs of Seers". That hieroglyphic includes the symbols, *wr m3*, a combination of the symbol for "to see" (*m3*) and the symbol for "secrets" (*wr*).

These passages show that Egyptian priests knew how to use meditation to enter into deep trance states where they saw visions of colored light. Their visions would have reminded them of the bright rings they'd seen in the eyes of falcons and hawks: the eyes of falcons are surrounded by a thin ring of brightly colored skin called a "cere". In the eyes of hawks, it's the iris of the eye that forms a bright ring on the surface of the eyeball. In both of these raptor species, the rings in or around the eye are usually a bright yellow color, not green like the Eye of Horus, but notwithstanding that difference in color, the resemblance of the rings decorating the eyes of the raptors to the rings of green light in a meditation-induced vision sequence is unmistakable. Later generations of priests who knew how to use meditation to enter into the realm of spirits could see for themselves that the ancient myth of the Eye of Horus, "The Green One", was true:

they could see the vision of the Eye of Horus at work as they watched the rings of green light flying away from them carrying the soul of the dead pharaoh into the Netherworld.

Ezekiel and the Fiery Ophanim

Ezekiel was a Hebrew priest who lived in ancient Judea. When that nation was conquered by Assyrian invaders in 598 BCE, Ezekiel and many other high-ranking members of Judea were forced to move to Babylon and live there as exiles. Ezekiel began to attract attention as a priest who could see visions and as a prophet who was predicting that Judea would be attacked once again because the people living there were continuing to live in sin. Ezekiel's reputation as a divinely inspired prophet was sealed in 586 BCE when an army sent by a new monarch who'd taken over in Babylonia—a king called Nebuchadnezzer II—breached the gates of Jerusalem, laid waste to the city, destroyed the Temple, and forced a second wave of Judean elites to move to Babylonia.

Several years after Ezekiel was exiled in Babylonia, he began practicing a ritual in which he'd sit on the banks of the Chedar River and pray to the Hebrew God, Yahweh. It was during one of these sessions that he was overwhelmed by a powerful vision that caused him to collapse and lose consciousness. When Ezekiel recovered consciousness, he was unable to speak for seven days (Ezekiel 1: 28). In that vision, Ezekiel saw many different images, including visions he described as looking like wheels:

> The appearance of the wheels and their workmanship was like sparkling beryl, and all four of them had the same form, their appearance or workmanship being as if one wheel were within another. When they went, they went

upon their four sides, and they did not turn aside when they went (Ezekiel 1: 15-21, *The New Oxford Annotated Bible*).

There are several important details in his description that need to be pointed out because they are easy to overlook. Ezekiel says there were four wheels. That's important, because it means the number of wheels he saw matches what we know about the number of green light-ring visions that can appear during meditation-induced sequences. Ezekiel also claims that these wheel visions had a "sparkling beryl color". Beryl is a mineral that often has a pale green color, so that detail is also consistent with his having seen visions of green light-rings. Ezekiel goes on to say that this vision looked "as if one wheel were within another". Notice the use of "as if", which suggests that he isn't sure what he's seeing—and that suggests that he's not seeing the image of one large wheel with several smaller wheels nestled inside of it. In ancient documents the phrase, "one within another", often refers to the serial order in which images appear, which in this case would mean that Ezekiel is saying that the wheel-shaped images appeared "one after another". He also specifies that when these wheel visions disappeared from view, they did not roll off to one side in the way that wheels normally move; he states that these wheel visions flew away from him "upon their four sides, and they did not turn aside." This suggests that Ezekiel wants to point out that the wheel visions moved straight away from him rather than rolling toward one side of the visual field. These many similarities between Ezekiel's description of his wheel visions and the visions of green light-rings that appear first in a meditation-induced sequence make it reasonable to infer that while Ezekiel was sitting on the banks of the Chebar River, he used meditation to induce a deep, empty-mind trance. In the Biblical account of this vision, Ezekiel doesn't mention seeing the wheel visions until after he's described many other visions, but based on our analysis of the brain mechanisms that generate meditation-induced visions of light—and based on descriptions of visionary experiences preserved in the ancient meditation texts of other religious traditions—it's likely that Ezekiel's visions of green light-rings were the first visions to appear.

Another Hebrew mystic famous for seeing visions of green wheels is Rabbi Nehuniah ben Hakana who lived in Palestine during the second century CE. Rabbi Nehuniah was an early exponent of a Jewish mystical practice known as *Kabbalah*. He described visionary experiences that can appear to devout seekers who learn a meditation technique he called *Merkabah*, "The Way of the Chariot". According to Rabbi Nehuniah, these meditators enter into an altered state of consciousness that enables them to begin ascending mentally through a hierarchy of mystical spaces. He taught that each space in that mystical hierarchy was associated with a different kind of vision. The penultimate station in this hierarchy is the "Seventh Chamber" in which the seeker sees visions of "the flaming eyes of the Chayot, highly vibrating beings composed of pure energy, and the wheel-shaped Ofanim, winged eyes that glitter with the inherent brilliance of God's presence, the Shekhinah (Epstein P, *Kabbalah: The Way of the Jewish Mystic*, 1988, p. 43)."

The Circling Yang in Early Daoist Texts

In the *Taiping-jing*, "*The Scripture of Great Peace*", a Daoist text written sometime before the third century CE, there is a description of a meditation technique known as *Shou-i*, "Preserving the Light of the One":

With prolonged practice... you will be able to see within your body. The physical body will become lighter, the

essence more brilliant, and the light more concentrated…
/ To practice guarding the light of the One, when you
have not yet attained concentration, just sit quietly with
your eyes closed. There is no light seen in the inner eye.
/ Practice guarding the One like this for a long time and
a brilliant light will arise (Kohn, 1993, pp. 194-5).

This meditation technique, which is clearly a form of empty-mind meditation, is said to induce visions of inner light, and
another Daoist text gives a more detailed description of the first
visions to appear during the practice of Shou-i:

When guarding the light of the One, you may see a pure
green light of lesser Yang… When the splendor of Yang
starts to shine and spreads its light, … its breath [*chi*]
turns and circles like the wheels of a chariot (Robinet,
1993, p. 110).

Visions of Khidr in Islamic Mysticism

Khidr, "The Green One", is celebrated in Islamic mystical circles
as a spiritual being who serves as a "teacher to the prophets" but
also as a "hidden guide" who will "come to the aid of those seekers
who don't have earthly teachers (Hirtenstein, *Ibn al'Arabi, Spanish
Sufi Mystic*, 1999)". This concept of a hidden guide originally
appeared in the verses of the *Quran* where it is said that Moses
once met a mysterious messenger, a "servant of God". Moses
asked if he could accompany this servant of God and observe
what he did in order to learn the true nature of the experiences
they would encounter (Surah 18: 65-82). The messenger voiced
doubts that Moses had enough patience to learn from a mentor,
but since he also recognized that there were many things that

Moses did not understand, he agreed to let Moses travel with him. While on their journey, the mysterious guide committed some acts that Moses believed to be immoral—for example, the guide killed a young man for what seemed to be no apparent purpose. Moses objected, but the guide told him that there were many things that would happen in the world for which Moses would never be able to understand the true nature of what took place—that some events that might seem evil based on a superficial impression might actually be merciful.

The *Quran* does not assign any name to this mysterious guide, so it's interesting to ask how he came to be called *Khidr*, "The Green One", and also to ask why Khidr came to be celebrated by Muslim mystics as a patron saint "who will come to the aid of those seekers who don't have earthly teachers". One possibility is that Muslim meditators who'd seen visions of green light appear during their prayer vigils hit on a name that clearly alluded to seeing a green light without them having to take the risk of making it explicit that they were seeing an inner light. In the Arabic language, the word for green is *"akhdar"*, and if you drop that initial letter "a", what's left is *Khdar*. In Arabic, this word sounds about the same as *Khidr*, and that remarkable similarity suggests that Muslim meditators who'd learned how to induce visions of green light made a connection between the visions that appeared to them early in their meditation and the anonymous messenger mentioned in the *Quran*. Making that connection with a Quranic reference would enable them to talk safely with each other about visionary experiences that might otherwise get them in trouble. And as I've mentioned before, it is relatively easy for someone to learn how to induce visions of green light, even without any instruction, so it would be likely that many Muslim seekers who did not have experienced teachers as their guides might inadvertently induce a vision of Khidr, "The Green One", by putting themselves in a deep trance state.

A famous Muslim mystic named Ibn al-Arabi gave Khidr credit for having come to his aid when he couldn't find an earthly teacher who would take him on as a disciple and teach him how to perform *dhikr,* the practice of "invocation" prescribed by Muslim mystical traditions. Al-Arabi's obsession with spiritual matters began he was only twelve years old. He became seriously ill and fell into a coma. When his father, a Muslim warrior, was finally able to return home, his son has been comatose so long that his father decided it was time to recite the Muslim funeral rite. That was when al-Arabi suddenly woke up. But he was no longer the same carefree boy he'd been before this all happened: feeling compelled to search for spiritual insight, he began wandering in a nearby cemetery because he felt a sense of kinship with people who'd already departed life. When he discovered an empty tomb, he decided to camp inside for several days and nights. It might have been during that vigil in the empty tomb that al-Arabi put himself in the kind of deep meditative trance that would enable him to see visions of Khidr, "The Green One", but it's not clear from his writings when he was introduced to the spirit who comes to the aid of seekers who don't have earthly teachers. By the time he emerged from the tomb, al-Arabi knew he had to leave home and to begin a search for a spiritual teacher who would take him on as a disciple. But his search was not successful, and eventually al-Arabi accepted the fact that he would have to acquire the spiritual insights he yearned for by means of his own efforts.

In addition to his visions of Khidr, Al-Arabi reported seeing other visions of green light. He had to be especially careful when he described these visions because he was, in effect, claiming to have seen visions similar to those seen by the Prophet Muhammed himself. Al-Arabi said that, like the Prophet, he saw visions of "the green Litters of the people of Paradise" described in the *Quran* (55: 76). This was a bold move because he'd used the same words used by the Prophet himself, but al-Arabi made a point of adding that he only saw those "green Litters" from afar and that he was not able to enter into Paradise himself and see them up close like the way the Prophet Muhammed had done. Al-Arabi also claimed he'd seen another vision seen by the Prophet Muhammed—the vision of the "Lote-Tree beyond which none may pass, / Near it is the Garden of the Abode (*Quran* 53: 14-15)." Here again, while he uses the same phrases used by the Prophet himself, he makes a point of adding that his own vision was merely a mental experience which did not involve a physical ascent like the experience claimed by the Prophet Muhammed in his miraculous "Night Journey (Surah 17: 1)".

Al-Arabi reported that his visions of green light gave him "knowledge of entering and circularity". This odd description suggests, first, that his visions of green light had a ring shape, hence his recognition of the importance of "circularity", and it also suggests that when he says the green lights convey "knowledge of entering" he is hinting that, like the Prophet Muhammed, he has seen visions of green light-rings fly away from the seer and then keep disappearing precisely the same time and same place in the visual field, as if each ring had just passed beyond human understanding. Al-Arabi's "knowledge of entering" mirrors the Prophet Muhammed's visions of the "Lote Tree marking the boundary of the Garden of the Abode," visions that suddenly disappeared at the same time and place. It's said that this happens when they cross into the divine realm where Allah resides and no human eye can follow. (We'll want to take a closer look at the visions of the Prophet Muhammed, but that will happen in later in Chapter 11.)

Halos of Five Lights in Buddhist Tibet

A Buddhist teacher named Naropa, who lived in northern India, compiled an anthology of yoga meditation techniques he adapted from Tantric Hindu sources. That anthology, *The Epitome of the Six Yogas*, was translated into the Tibetan language by Marpa, one of Naropa's Tibetan disciples. When Marpa returned to Tibet as a Buddhist missionary, he used the *Six Yogas* as a resource to help him and his fellow missionaries found a new and uniquely Tibetan version of Buddhism which incorporated some religious practices from the native *Bon* culture. This new Tibetan Buddhist sect was called *Vajrayana*, "The Vehicle of the Thunder-Bolt" or "The Diamond Vehicle". The name embodies the Tibetan Buddhist belief that it is possible for an accomplished meditator to achieve Enlightenment in a single lifetime by slashing through all the karmic burdens of the seeker. Enlightenment is said to arrive like a bolt of lightning so powerful it could split a rock in half or like a diamond that can slice into even the hardest substances.

The foundation of the Tibetan *Vajrayana* tradition is a type of advanced meditation practice called *maha-anuttara-yoga*, "Highest Yoga Tantra". This practice is known as "The Path with Forms" because it emphasizes cultivation of meditation-induced light visions all the way up the Indo-Tibetan vision ladder until the meditators see flashes of fiery light. When that happens, the meditators are said to have achieved the "Final Realization" in which they come to realize that Ultimate Reality manifests as a primordial radiance that is always changing and that remains inherently "empty" because it never embodies permanent thoughts, objects, or images. Those mysterious visions of light induced by the practice of "Highest Yoga Tantra", the same visions of light that enable Tibetan Buddhist meditators to attain Enlightenment in a single lifetime, are ultimately revealed to be just another apparitional reality: "When illusory forms contact the Formless… one gains understanding of the Pervading and the Real. And mastery of the Very Bright and of the Enduring, and of the Siddhi of Transformation ('The Yoga of Clear Light' 4: 35-36, in Naropa's anthology, *The Epitome of the Six Yogas*)."

When Tibetan monks begin to practice the techniques of Highest Yoga Tantra, setting out on the journey they hope will end in Enlightenment, they are taught that the first light visions they should expect to see will be shaped like wheels. In Naropa's *Six Yogas*, meditators who read "The Yoga of the Psychic Heat" are told to "Meditate upon the four wheels, / Each shaped like an umbrella, / Or like the wheel of a chariot (1: 66)." The reason why this vision is said to resemble an "umbrella" is that the rim of the wheel collapses in diameter in the same way that the rim of an umbrella collapses as it's being closed after a rain. Another influential Tibetan Buddhist text, Nagabodhi's *Elucidation*, reports that one of the original founders of *Vajrayana* Buddhist tradition, Marpa the Translator, gave this description of the vision of green light-rings: "First one experiences the hallucination-like sign / That arises with the halo of five lights (Mullin, 1996, p. 167)." Marpa's specification that there will be five "halos" is consistent with our neurological analysis showing that the number of spindle bursts fired during the onset of Stage 2 NREM sleep can range from three bursts to six. And in a Tibetan text entitled *The Natural Liberation of Seeing: Experiential Instructions on the Transitional Process of Reality-Itself* by Lama Karma Lingpa, the first light visions to appear in a meditation-induced sequence are described as "lamps of pristine absolute space". Meditators who've induced light visions on many occasions see a change in the color that fills in when the green light-rings are halfway through their inward trajectory. Karma Lingpa writes that those ring-shaped "lamps" fill in with a dark blue light that makes them look like "the eye of a peacock feather (Chagmé, 2000)".

Visions of Eskimo Shamans in Alaska and Siberia

A prerequisite for becoming a shaman among the Iglulik Eskimos of Alaska is learning how to generate the *angákoq*, an inner "illumination" which is said to be "a mysterious light which the shaman suddenly feels in his body, inside his head, within the brain, an inexplicable searchlight, a luminous fire (Rasmussen, 1930, p. 111)." Another anthropologist reported that the Eskimo shaman he observed "gets his visions sitting or lying in deep concentration at the back of the sleeping platform, behind a curtain or covered with a skin. The drum is not used in this connection (Holtved, 1967, p. 47)." Eskimo shamans in Siberia commemorate their journeys to the spirit world by making face masks that they then paint with symbolic images of the visions they've seen during their meditative trance. The paintings on many of these masks depict a set of concentric circles, a symbol that suggests those shamans saw visions of green light-rings.

CHAPTER 8

Sleep Rhythms, Blue Clouds, and the "Third Eye"

Stage 3 NREM Sleep and Visions of Dark Blue Clouds

When the brain stem stops firing the Stage 2 spindle bursts that generate the visions of green light-rings, the cortical regions of the brain shift back to the firing pattern that initiated the transition from waking to sleep—to the cortical slow waves fired at a rate of less than one per second (< 1 Hz). This signals the shift from Stage 2 to Stage 3 NREM sleep. As each cortical slow wave ripples out through the networks of cortical neurons, waves of excitation are transmitted back down into the LGNs. Those waves stimulate vision-relay neurons to fire in patterns that mirror the patterns of the cortical slow waves, then those waves from the LGNs flow back up to target neurons in the visual cortices. This oscillation intensifies the waves moving back and forth between the cortical regions and the LGNs. Those waves are formed when groups of neurons fire synchronized bursts that erupt at unpredictable locations and unpredictable intervals. Those unpredictable bursts send ripples radiating out through the relevant neuron networks in an "expanding wave" that spreads out in unpredictable, asymmetric patterns. (More details about the neurological processes involved can be found in my book, *Meditation & Light Visions: A Neurological Analysis*.)

While stage 3 sleep rhythms are active, meditators see cloud-like visions of dark blue lights with amorphous ever-changing boundaries and porous, mist-like textures. The clouds appear at unpredictable intervals and cluster around the center of the visual field. The dark blue clouds surround the center of the visual field because the vision-related neurons that encode color signals are most densely packed in those areas of the visual system that innervate "central vision". In the retina of each human eye, the area dedicated to central vision has a radius that extends out twenty degrees out from the very center of the visual field, which means it covers only about a fifth of the total area of the retinae and of the meditator's visual field. The visions of dark blue clouds remain confined within that region. When stage 3 sleep rhythms are active, a scalp EEG registers brainwaves with slow, delta band frequencies that range from one wave every two seconds (0.5 Hz) to as many as four waves appearing within each second (4.0 Hz).

How Dark Blue Clouds Develop a "Third Eye"

The relative densities of color-sensitive neurons can also explain why meditators who induce visions of dark blue clouds often see a tiny disk of very bright blue light coalesce at the center of the dark blue cloud. That bright inner disk has a more opaque, solid-looking surface that contrasts with the porous textures of the dark blue cloud that surrounds it, and it has a radius that extends only about five degrees from the center of the visual field, a significantly smaller radius than the twenty degrees associated with central vision. The intense brightness and saturation occurs because the color-sensitive neurons that innervate that inner region of central vision are much more densely packed than color-sensitive neurons in the rest of central vision.

As the expanding waves generated by stage 3 sleep rhythms keep restimulating the densely packed neurons in that small inner region, meditators see the tiny disk of brighter, more opaque light begin to shine. They also see that disk begin to change in ways that make it look like a disembodied "Third Eye" staring back at the seer. This happens when some light ebbs away ever so slightly from the center of the visual field to open up a tiny black hole at the center of the bright inner disk which is at the center of the dark blue cloud. That tiny black spot looks "pupil-like" because it's surrounded by an "iris-like" ring of bright blue light which is itself surrounded by the dark blue cloud which also has a ring shape. The opening up of that tiny black spot reveals that there is a miniscule area at the very center of each retina that is devoid of light receptors because it's where the optic nerve attaches to each retina. Normally the brain hides that tiny dark space, covering it over with whatever other light sensations happen to present in the visual field, but meditators who keep their attention fixated intently on the bright blue disk can see the effects produced in the visual field when that tiny space at the very center of each retina that does not have any light receptors becomes visible. Almost as soon the light of the bright inner disk ebbs back to reveal the black, "pupil-like" space, that space begins filling back in with fingers of bright blue light that jut down into the dark space from the "iris-like" ring that surrounds it. Those fingers of light twist around and expand to quickly fill in the "pupil-like" space, restoring the disk shape of the bright blue light at center of the dark blue cloud.

Meditators who see this image say it looks like a "Third Eye" hovering in the visual field, staring back at viewer. In Indo-Tibetan mystical traditions this vision is called the "Eye of Wisdom" (*Ajña cakra*) and its appearance is considered to be a sign that the meditators are far along the path that ultimately leads to "Self-Realization" or "Enlightenment". Meditators in many other religions have also seen visions of the dark blue clouds with the brighter disks within, and they also used these visions to create myths that take on important roles in their respective religious traditions.

Visions of Dark Blue Clouds and "Third Eyes" in World Religions

Agni's Fire-Arrows in Ancient India

The hymns of the *Rig Veda* contain many references to visions of "flame-arrows" sent by Agni, the god of fire. The hymns describe these flame-arrows as being "many-colored (RV 10.91.5)", as "smoke-like (RV 1.27.11; 5.11.3; 7.2.1; 1.3.3)", as having rounded shapes that look like they're flowing up out of "a hole in the ground abounding in water (RV 1.67.7; 3.10.5)", or that look like the funnels created by the "streams of water assembling into holes (RV 10.25.4) (Gonda, 1963, p. 173)." Descriptions of similar images appear in the *Upanishads* where commentators write about visions that look like "fog" or "smoke" (*Svetasvartara Upanisad* II: 11) or like "bubbles rising in heated butter (*Maitri Upanishad*, 7: 11)". A verse in the *Chandogya Upanishad* emphasizes that meditators should pay special attention to these visions of dark blue clouds that look like lotus flowers because the small dark space at the centers of these flowers can open a path that leads to Brahman: "In the city of *Brahman* there is an abode, a small lotus flower; within it is a small space. What is within, that should be sought, for that, assuredly, is what one should desire to understand (8: 1.1, Radhakrishnan, 1992, p. 491)."

In the esoteric Hindu tradition called Tantras, a teacher named Abhinavagupta calls the visions of dark blue clouds the *Bhru-madya,* or "Brow-drink". He advises meditators to pay attention to the transformations taking place at the very center of that vision: "In *bhru…* rests a cognitive energy subtler than the 100th part of a tip of a hair… [and there] dwells the dot, *bindu* (Silburn, *Kundalini: The Energy of the Depths.* 1988, p. 129)." That bright *bindu* will lead a meditator to the vision of fiery light.

Another influential Tantric guru named Goraksanath adds another new detail: he writes that this bright dot of light at the center of the visual field is a sign that the meditator's cognitive energy has been concentrated into its most intense and purified form, which is why it looks like a tiny, shimmering "star". He adds that this "star" can explode and send tiny splinters of light radiating out in all directions (Goraksanath, *Amaraughasanana,* in Silburn, p. 128). This last description matches the vision that I saw after the vision of the black rings forming a dark, moving tunnel: when that "tunnel" suddenly disappeared, it was replaced by streams of tiny sparks radiating out through the periphery of my visual field.

Dark Blue Visions in Early Israel

When Moses and the Hebrew tribes were camped at the foot of Mt. Sinai after having escaped from captivity in Egypt, Moses climbed up the mountain to negotiate with the God, Yahweh. This was the same God that sent Moses the vision of the Burning Bush and that ordered him to return to Egypt to rescue the

Hebrew tribes. Moses and Yahweh negotiated a new covenant in which the Hebrew tribes promised to worship Yahweh "above all other gods" and Yahweh promised to recognize the tribes of Israel as His "Chosen People". To celebrate, the Hebrew tribes organized a "Feast of the Covenant", and the Biblical account claims that during this celebration, "Moses and Aaron, Nadab, and Abihu, and seventy of the elders of Israel went up, and they saw the God of Israel. Under his feet there was something like a pavement of a sapphire stone, like the very heaven for clearness (Exodus 24: 9-10)." On first impression, this seems to be a strange claim; it's not likely that Moses and seventy old men would all experience a mystical ascent while a tribal feast was underway, but there's more to learn from this account.

Whoever wrote this story about the ascent of the elders must somehow have known that it was possible for humans to induce visions of light with shapes that are "something like paving stones", visions that are translucent and "like the very heaven for clearness", and shapes that have a "sapphire" color. But in the traditional account there is no reference to any of the celebrants having engaged in some type of meditation practice or empty-mind prayer vigil that would be consistent with them beginning to see visions with the characteristics of the early meditation-induced visions. Nor is there any reference to them having seen the visions of the green light-rings that usually appear before the dark blue clouds. These omissions suggest that the authors of the story are not describing the actual visionary experiences of Moses or the elders; rather, it seems more likely that the Hebrew priests and scribes who were commissioned to write the first books of the *Torah* inserted this account of visionary experiences based on what they knew about meditation-induced visionary experiences from other sources. That's a subject we'll want to take up in Chapter 10 when we take a close look at the visionary experiences of the original Hebrew patriarchs—Abraham, Moses, and Elijah.

There's another Hebrew mystic—the prophet Ezekiel—who is also said to have seen visions of dark blue light. His descriptions are ambiguous and difficult to decipher which suggests he was confused about what it was that he was really seeing or that he was at a loss about how to describe what he'd seen in words that his contemporaries might understand. That's why Ezekiel keeps resorting to the phrase, "something like" as when he describes "something like a throne" and "something like a human form". Here is Ezekiel's description of a vision that included lights with a "sapphire" color:

> Over the heads of the living creatures there was something like a dome, shining like crystal, spread out about their heads… And above the dome over their heads there was something like a throne, in appearance like sapphire, and seated above the likeness of a throne was something which seemed like a human form… and there was a splendor all around. Like the bow in a cloud on a rainy day, such was the appearance of the splendor all around. This was the appearance of the glory of the Lord… When I saw it, I fell on my face (Ezekiel 1: 22-18, *The New Oxford Annotated Bible*).

There are several details in Ezekiel's account are worth noting because they're consistent with his having seen a meditation-in-duced vision of dark blue clouds. First, he says he saw "something like a dome" which implies that he saw a disk of dark blue with a dark space at its center that made it look like the center of the disk was higher than the rim. When he says that "above the dome" he saw "something like a throne", it's possible that he was referring to a disk of brighter light that appeared at the center of the dark blue cloud. The most important detail in this passage is Ezekiel's specification that the "throne" image had a dark blue "sapphire" color. This small image that looked "something like a throne" was associated with "something which seemed like a human form". That might be a reference to his having seen the small bright disk at the center of the dark blue cloud open a dark, "pupil-like" space which then promptly filled back in as fingers of bright light began jutting down into the black space from the bright ring surrounding it. Those fingers of light jutting down into the black space typically twist and turn which does indeed make it look like they could be alive. But perhaps the best evidence for the claim that Ezekiel saw visions of dark blue clouds is that he also saw the kinds of visions that appear just before the dark blue clouds—the visions of "wheels within wheels". That detail clearly points to his knowing how to put himself in an empty-mind trance and how to induce meditation-induced visions of light.

Visions of Hesychia and Katastasis

Evagrius Ponticus was a Christian monk lived during the fourth century of the Common Era. He was a citizen of Byzantium who'd been elevated to the rank of archdeacon in the official church hierarchy. But then he got involved in a romantic imbroglio. Even though none of his peers knew that anything untoward had happened, Evagrius suffered a crisis of conscience and felt compelled to abandon his career in the official church. He became a solitary seeker searching for spiritual renewal and set out for Jerusalem where he took up residence as a penitent in one of the local monasteries. Before he could immerse himself in the spiritual quest, Evagrius contracted a major illness that lasted for a very long time. When he recovered, he felt even more compelled to find some kind of spiritual solace. He decided to become a monk. He also decided to travel to Egypt where he knew there were many monastic colonies known for imposing the kinds of extreme ascetic regimens that were designed to induce a state of stillness that was highly prized in Byzantine Christianity—a state of stillness called *katastasis*. The ascetic regimen adopted by Evagrius is described by author Columba Stewart in a book she wrote about another monk named Cassian who followed a similar path:

> While he was living in the Egyptian monasteries, Evagrius went to ascetic extremes: he only ate once a day, renounced eating meat, fresh fruits and vegetables, recommended drinking as little water as possible, wore a sackcloth, did not bathe, allowed himself to sleep for only a third of the night and devoted the rest of that time to prayer and meditation. He was occasionally known to stand naked in a well during a winter night (*Cassian the Monk*, p. 72).

Eventually Evagrius began writing books about the virtues of extreme ascesis and about how this practice enabled him to have many mystical experiences. Based on his writing, he developed a reputation as one of the leading authorities on *hesychia*, the practice of silence that enables a person to reach the state of *katastasis*. In *The Praktikos: Chapters on Prayer*, Evagrius describes *katastasis* in a way that reveals its similarity to the kind of empty-mind meditative trance state we've been discussing in our investigation—the kind of empty-mind trance state in which visions of pure light appear in the visual field. Evagrius reports that "… the spirit begins to see its own light; when it remains in a state of tranquility in the presence of the images it has during sleep, it maintains its calm as it beholds the affairs of life (Bamberger, *Evagrius Ponticus*, 1970, p. 64)." In another passage that is revealed to him as a vision of dark blue light:

> Then he will see that his own state at the time of prayer resembles that of a sapphire; it is as clear and bright as

the very sky. The Scriptures refer to this experience as the place of God which was seen by our ancestors, the elders, at Mount Sinai (Evagrius, Fragment PG40: 1244A, Bamberger, Ibid, p. xci).

The concept and practice of *hesychia* developed by Evagrius and by other monks who lived lives of rigorous ascetic self-discipline became one of the primary approaches to mystical practice recognized by religious authorities in the Eastern Orthodox branch of Christianity.

Visions of Yang in Early Daoism

An old, pre-Daoist text called *Chu-ci*, "The Elegies of Chu", written by an anonymous Chinese seer living in the third century BCE, contains a poem entitled *Yuanyou*, "The Far-Off Journey". It describes a shamanic flight in which the poet sees a vision of "the shining brightness of the Glittering Gem" and sees "Yang in its gentle flashes, not quite bright, … / Plunging and soaring, we go up and down, / Wandering on floating waves of unsteady mist… / Traversing fresh blue clouds, I am floating freely (Kohn, 1993, pp. 254-255)." Centuries later, another Daoist master wrote about seeing visions of a purple cloud that developed a bright inner disk of light: "A purple breath… enters into my *hsüan-tan* palace. It fills the palace and penetrates to the center of the purple breath. Then I see it as a fiery pearl within the darkness (Maspero, quoted in Robinet, 1993, p. 130)." Another Daoist teacher describes this same vision as "a purple pneuma [*chi*], as large as the pupil of your eye, but wrapped in several tens of layers and flashing brilliantly… This is called the flying root of solar efflorescence (Bokenkamp, 1997, p. 315)."

Round Shapes with Bindus in Tibetan Texts

Karma Lingpa, a Tibetan lama who wrote *The Natural Liberation of Seeing: Experiential Instructions on the Transitional Process of Reality-Itself,* a treatise on Highest Yoga Tantra, describes the first light visions that meditators see as "lamps of pristine absolute space". He states that each of these "lamps" looks like "the eye of a peacock feather". What comes next, according to Lingpa, is the vision of "the lamp of the empty *bindus*" that looks like the "concentric circles of ripples when you throw a stone into the pond" or the "round plates of a shield". He advises meditators to concentrate their attention on the very center of that vision, where they'll see a tiny dot of light that is brighter than the round plates: "Inside that form like the round plates of a shield, there appears a *bindu* about the size of a mustard seed or a pea. Inside the *bindu* are the so-called '*vajra*-strands of awareness' which look like knots tied in a strand: 'like a horse's tail, like a string of pearls, like an iron chain, like a lattice of flowers moving with the breeze' (Lingpa, in Chagmé, 2000, p. 164)." Lingpa's reference to "vajra-strands" alerts meditators that this formation of tiny lights has the potential to move them forward along the path that leads to the ultimate spiritual experience—the explosion of the "Lightning Bolts" that give Tibetan *Vajrayana* Buddhism its name.

Lingpa's description of the vajra-strands of awareness resembles a passage in a Hindu text, the *Chandogya Upanishad,* where it's said that "in the city of *Brahman* there is an abode, a small lotus flower; within it is a small space. What is within, that should be sought, for that, assuredly, is what one should desire to understand (8: 1.1, in Radhakrishnan, 1992, p. 491)."

The Rainbow Serpent of the Australian Aborigines

The Rainbow Serpent is an important mythological creature for the Aboriginal tribes of Australia. They take care to respect this spirit and to be vigilant for signs of its presence because the spirit is said to possess awesome powers that it can use for both good and ill. Caution is especially important when members of the tribes travel through unfamiliar regions or when they see a rainbow appear after a storm. The ancestors of the Australian Aborigines created the myth of the Rainbow Serpent to explain why some of the colored lights that appear in a rainbow are also seen by the tribes' spiritual leaders when they perform a ritual that enables them to enter into an Otherworld called "The DreamTime".

Anthropologist David McKnight explains how the myth Rainbow Serpent came into being in his book, *People, Countries, and the Rainbow Serpent: Systems of Classification among the Lardil of Mornington Island* (1999). His informants, members of the Nardil tribe, told McKnight that during the lives of their ancestors, the annual rainy season was a time of great suffering. People were often forced to take refuge in primitive shelters and to stay there for several days, enduring wet, cold, and hunger. One ancestor decided to try something different: he built himself a hut where he could wait out the terrible storms in relative comfort. He finished building a hut just before the first storm of the season broke. When rain began pouring down, he refused to let anyone else take refuge inside his hut—not even his sister who begged him to let her come in because her infant was sick and needed shelter. The man refused. When the baby died, the mother wanted to get revenge. She watched her brother's hut, studying his habits so she could judge when it was likely that he would remain inside for a while. When she felt the time was right, she crept up to the wall of the hut and set it ablaze. When her brother came running out, he was writhing in agony as flames spread over his body. He ran to a nearby waterhole and threw himself into the depths to extinguish the flames. He never resurfaced; once he disappeared in the waterhole, he was transformed into the spirit of the Rainbow Serpent.

The myth envisions that the Rainbow Serpent can manifest to humans in either of two guises: when he appears as a rainbow arching across the sky after a storm he's called the "Day-Crawler"; when he resides in the spiritual world of the DreamTime, waiting for the next storm to erupt, he's called the "Eye-Thing". One day McKnight was working in the field with some Aborigine companions when a storm erupted. When it was all over, a rainbow appeared high overhead. He saw one of the men point up to a rainbow stretched high overhead and overheard him say to the other worker: "Poor old man. Look at him all burnt, crawling up in the sky (p. 195)." That exchange between McKnight's Aborigine companions implies that the red, orange, and yellow colors in a rainbow are thought to represent the fire burning the back of the ancestral spirit. If that's indeed the case, then the other colors that appear in a rainbow—the green, blue, and purple colors—must represent the body of the ancestor when he dives back into the waterhole to extinguish the agonizing flames. McKnight's informants told him that there were men in their tribe who knew how to create the image of a "sacred waterhole" that they used to transport themselves into the DreamTime. In the Nardil tribe, these men are called *nhuyin*, or "doctors", but the name varies by tribe; some ethnographic studies of Aboriginal culture report that these practitioners are called "Wise Men" while other studies refer to "Men of High Degree" (Elkin, 1977).

Once the Wise Men enter the DreamTime, they see visions of the Rainbow Serpent manifesting in his guise as the Eye-Thing. While McKnight's informants didn't know what their tribal Wise

Men actually saw, it's reasonable to infer, based on the ancient myth, that the Wise Men must see lights with the colors that would be left if a rainbow were stripped of the fire-like colors of yellow, orange, and red. That suggests that when the Wise Men enter the DreamTime and see the Rainbow Serpent manifesting as the "Eye-Thing", they see visions of lights with green, dark blue, and purple colors.

The hypothesis that the Wise Men see visions of green light is supported by what's known about the details of the ritual that they use when they want to enter into the DreamTime. The Wise Men separate themselves from the rest of the tribe, paint their bodies with red ochre, and add puffs of white bird down for decoration. Then they construct a symbolic waterhole called an *Ilbantera* by placing more feathery white puffs in circles to form a set of concentric rings. In photographs of *Ilbanteras* taken by anthropologists, the number of concentric rings varies between four and six—a number consistent with the number of the green light-ring visions that get generated during meditation-induced trance states and also with the number of synchronous spindle bursts discharged during stage 2 NREM sleep.

Once the symbol of the sacred waterhole is finished, the Wise Men seat themselves around its edges and focus their attention on the concentric rings of the *Ilbantera:* "He is sitting down by himself with his thoughts in order 'to see'," an Aborigine informant told Adolphus Elkin, an anthropologist who spent working with Aboriginal tribes, "He is gathering his thoughts so that he can feel and hear. Perhaps he then lies down, getting into a special posture, so that he may 'see' when sleeping (Elkin, *Aboriginal Men of High Degree: Initiation and Sorcery in the World's Oldest Tradition*, 1970, p. 56)." The concentric rings of the *Ilbantera* provide a resonant symbol that anticipates the series of green light-rings that the Wise Men expect to see, based on what they've been told or based on their own past experience, once they've entered into the DreamTime. They believe it's the flow of green light-rings that transports them into the DreamTime where they see the Rainbow Serpent manifesting as the "Eye-Thing". There's an interesting photograph of several Wise Men sitting around an *Ilbantera* and staring intently at rings of bird feathers in Robert Lawlor's book, *Voices of the First Day: Awakening in the Aboriginal Dreamtime* (1991, p. 108). The Wise Men sometimes describe their visions of the Eye-Thing as "little rainbows". They believe that those among them who enter the DreamTime and see the lights of the "Eye-Thing" acquire special powers (McKnight, p. 194).

Quetzalcoatl, "The Plumed Serpent" of Mesoamerica

A classical Mayan civilization flourished in the Yucatan Peninsula and Guatemalan Highlands between 250 and 900 CE. The walls of many ancient temples and many of their freestanding stone stellae contain carvings of Mayan hieroglyphic symbols that scholars have only recently deciphered. Their research reveals that one of the most important mythical beings in the Mayan pantheon was *K'awil*, god of the life-force and of transitional states. An interesting portrait of K'awil at work is pictured on the walls of an ancient Mayan temple at Palenque. In the book, *Mayan Cosmos: Three Thousand Years on the Shaman's Path* (2001) by David Friedel and colleagues, there's a line drawing that reproduces the main elements of the carving at Palenque that portrays K'awil as a symbol of transitional states (Figure 4: 9, p. 194). It shows a dead king named Pakal falling backward off a high pedestal. There are three details that demand attention: first, one of the king's feet has been replaced by the head of a snake; second, there's an axe implanted in Pakal's forehead; and, third, there's a cloud of smoke drifting out of that wound. This carving that the researchers call "Pakal-becoming-K'awil" reveals important insights about ancient Mayan myths. We need to analyze the symbolic significance of each of those details, and, equally important, we need to ask why all three details are portrayed in that same carving.

David Friedel and his co-authors write that the ancient Mayans believed the spirits of dead kings get transported up to a dark spot in the night sky called the "Black Transformer" where the king's spirit becomes a star. But to reach that destination, the king's spirit has to ascend through the dark gullet of a "Vision Serpent" called *K'ukumatz*. When the carvers at Palenque replaced one of Pakal's feet with the head of the Vision Serpent, this was a sign that the dead king's spirit was ascending through gullet of *K'ukumatz*.

There's a carving that depicts a Vision Serpent on the walls of a Mayan temple at Yaxchilanwall: it shows the spirit of an ancestral warrior after he's descended through the gullet of the Vision Serpent to return to earth. His spirit is shown emerging out of the mouth of a strange creature—"a frightening, double-headed beastie with a half-flayed body decorated with feather fans (Friedel et. al., p. 208)". The feather fans are a prominent feature on this carving, so much so that it's important to ask what the feather fans would have signaled to Mayan audiences. Feathers clearly evoke associations with birds and hence with flying, but it's not the Vision Serpent itself that flies; rather, it's the spirits of the dead kings and famous ancestral warriors that fly through the Vision Serpent's dark gullet. To decipher the symbolic role of the feathers depicted on the body surface of the Vision Serpent, we need to know more about the second and third symbols given prominent placement in the carving of Pakal-as-K'awil at Palenque: we need to know why there's a flint axe implanted in the dead king's forehead and why there's smoke coming out of that wound.

The Mayans believed that the flint stones they gathered in the forest and used to make axe blades were created by lightning bolts that struck the earth and melted the dirt into stone. Given this association of flints and lightning, it seems clear that the carving at Palenque of King Pakal with a flint axe implanted in his forehead is a symbol that points to lightning and the smoke coming out of the wound is a symbol that points to a fire burning inside Pakal's head.

In Mayan mythology, *Jurakán*, the god of storms and lightning, could initiate three different types of lightning (*caculhá*). He could hurl down bolts of lightning, called "one-legged lightning". He could also ignite flashes of heat lightning inside clouds, called "dwarf lightning". The Mayan people would have been familiar with those types of lightning because they often saw those flashes in their natural environment. But the Mayan priests also claimed that *Jurakán* could send a very different kind of lightning called *Räxa-Caculhá* (Friedel et al., pp. 199-200). An eminent anthropologist named Mary Preuss, author of the *Gods of the Popol Vuh* (1988), has proposed that the term, *Räxa-caculhá*, can be given any of three different meanings—it can be translated as "green lightning" or as "blue lightning" or as "precious lightning" (p. 76). Pruess proposes that *Räxa-Caculhá* most likely refers to some lightning-like phenomenon that appears to the dead king's soul as it begins to fly up gullet of the Vision Serpent on its way to become a star. That hypothesis can be supported by what we've learned from our neurologically grounded, reverse-engineering analysis of meditation-induced light visions. If we combine all three alternative meanings proposed by Mary Preuss to create a single, composite phrase—if we translate *Räxa-Caculhá* as "precious green-and-blue lightning"—then the meaning of *Räxa-Caculhá* is that there is a type of lightning that occurs, not in the world of natural events, but in the supernatural world of spirit beings. This means that *Jurakán*, the god of storms and lightning, has the power to ignite visions of lightning flashes that occur only within human consciousness, visions that are "precious" because they have spiritual significance—and the color of those "precious" flashes of the *Räxa-Caculhá* lightning are green and blue.

This hypothesis provides an explanation for why King Pakal has a flint axe implanted in his forehead with smoke coming out of the wound while at the same time he's falling backward with one foot having been transformed into a serpent's head: the combination of these three symbols in the statue of Pakal-as-K'awil signifies that the dead king's spirit is seeing *Jurakán's* "precious green and blue lightning" as it "feathers out" in the dark gullet of the Vision Serpent. To create a statue that incorporates all of these symbolic references, those "feathers" of precious lightning have to be carved on the outer surface of the statue even though the symbolic function of those feathers decorating the Vision Serpent's body is to remind viewers about what's happening within.

Visions of light with green and blue colors are often mentioned in Mayan myths. Pruess also reports that the *Popol Vuh*, an early account of Mayan myths compiled by a priest who accompanied the conquering Spaniards, states that the conquered people believed that, in the beginning, long before the world as we humans know it came into existence, there was nothing but water, darkness, and silence. Hidden beneath the water were green and blue lights that had been placed beneath the water to protect spirit-entities who had not yet emerged to become the Mayan gods. One of the gods that would later emerge out of that cover of green and blue lights, according to the *Popol Vuh*, was the Vision Serpent named *K'ucumatz* who became the god of transformations (Goetz and Morley, *Popol Vuh*, 1950, pp. 81-83).

How did the Mayan priests come up with all these ideas? One possibility is that they had a ritual practice of inducing empty-mind trance states, like many religious practitioners all around the world, and that while they were in that trance state they saw visions of green light-rings and dark blue clouds. To make sense of the otherworldly lights they sometimes saw during their visionary experiences, the priests might well have concluded that they were experiencing the same kind of spiritual transformations that K'awil, the god of transformations, conferred on dying kings. They might have thought that their prayers conveyed their spirits into the dark gullet of the Vision Serpent and that, once there, the lights they saw—the "feathers" of "precious green and blue lighting"—were the same visions of feathery light that the spirits of dead kings rising up the gullet of the Vision Serpent would see.

More support for this hypothesis about the "feathers" of the Vision Serpent in Mayan myths surfaces when we consider what happened when the Mayan armies were defeated by the Aztecs of central Mexico. The Aztec priests adopted the Mayan myth of *K'ucumatz,* the Vision Serpent, but they gave the spirit a new name: they called it *Quetzalcoatl,* "The Quetzal-Feathered Serpent". This reference to the feathers of quetzal birds makes quite clear what colors the Aztec priests associated with the "feathers" of the Vision Serpent: in the jungles of Mesoamerica, the feathers of quetzal birds shine with iridescent green and blue hues that precisely match the colors of the early-stage light visions. For the Aztec priests to feel confident about adopting Quetzalcoatl as a god, they must have been able to see for themselves, when they were immersed in prayer, that visions of green and blue lights appeared to ruffle out like waving "feathers" in the dark in front of their closed eyes.

In the Aztec kingdom, quetzal birds were a protected species. Each year the king would send hunters out to capture quetzals and pluck the feathers for ceremonial use, but the hunters were given strict orders to release the birds back into the wild so they could be captured again in future hunts. In the Aztec kingdom, killing a quetzal was a capital offence.

Visions of the Hidden Sun in Amazonia

Anthropologist Gerardo Reichel-Dolmatoff spent many years living with the Tukano Indian tribes who inhabit remote regions of the Amazon jungle in Columbia. He describes the most important religious ritual of those tribes as *yajé* rituals (Reichel-Dolmatoff, 1975). The tribal shamans welcomed all members of the tribe who wanted to participate in these rituals which involved ingesting the hallucinogenic drug, *ayahuasca*. The shamans primed the participants by telling them stories about the kinds of experiences they would likely have once the drug took effect. While many of the strange, kaleidoscopic visual symptoms experienced during these rituals fall outside of our primary interest in meditation-induced light visions, Reichel-Dolmatoff's reports reveal that before and after the drug produced its hallucinatory effects, the participants often saw visions like those that appear in early in a meditation-induced sequence. For example, after the participants drank the beverage and while they were waiting for the hallucinogenic drugs to take effect, they would sit quietly in a group, sometimes singing or swaying, always maintaining a solemn, introspective demeanor. Some tribal members told the anthropologist that, during the waiting period, they saw ring-shaped visions. In his book, Reichel-Dolmatoff includes a photograph of a Tukano shaman using a stick to trace a set of concentric rings in the sand to illustrate the ring-like images he often saw at the outset of a *yajé* ritual. The background of that same photo shows part of the façade of the longhouse that's used for ritual events where the out wall is decorated with paintings of concentric rings similar to rings the shaman drew in the sand.

The Tukanos regard these visions of inner light as "closed forms" that involve "states... that appear and disappear" and that point beyond themselves to a world of spiritual experiences

(Reichel-Dolmatoff, 2005, pp. 170-171). Tribal myths connect the seeing of these closed-form light visions with other kinds of ethereal lights that can occasionally be glimpsed in the natural world. For example, when people hike through the dark forest, they often see shafts of sunlight streaming down from the forest canopy that contain tiny sparks of light reflecting off the motes of dust that are floating in that shaft of sunlight. Other kinds of hidden lights that manifest in special circumstances include rainbows, shooting stars, and lightning flashes.

The Tukanos regard all of these sightings as glimpses of a radiant life-energy they call "*bogá*". They believe that everything that appears in the natural world is animated by the "*bogari*" energies, even when the animating lights remain invisible. When the Tukanos see these hidden lights suddenly flash out, they say that these lights emanate from the "Father Sun", a spirit that is otherwise invisible (Reichel-Dolmatoff, 1996, pp. 32-38). It's not surprising, then, to learn that the Tukanos believe that the visions of light that appear in the mind's eye while they're waiting for the *yajé* to take effect represent another form of *bogari* energy emanating from the hidden sun: "A significant category of *bogari* energies is perceived during narcotic trance states," Reichel-Dolmatoff writes, "but they can also be observed during fleeting states of dissociation, day-dreaming, hypnagogic states, isolation, sensory deprivation, or other situations of stress."

When Reichel-Dolmatoff decided to join in one of the tribal *yajé* rituals as a participant observer, he planned to make a contemporaneous tape recording to describe what he was seeing and feeling. It turned out that he couldn't do that; it proved to be much too difficult. The visions he saw were too elusive, too fast-moving, and too hard to describe. He was only able to record a few observations that came to him during the early stages of the preliminary waiting period while his inner experiences were evolving more slowly. He describes seeing green light-rings with dark blue centers that reminded him of the green rings with dark blue centers that appear near the tip of a peacock feather. Then a new type of vision appeared—a vision of dark blue light that reminded him of the decorations woven into Persian tapestries. Here are the notes he took during these visions:

> I'm seeing something… well, like… it's dark, but I see something like the tail of a peacock… but at the same time it's like… everything in movement… like fireworks, no? Much like a… the background of, let's say… of certain Persian miniatures. There's something Oriental about all this. Oh, tapestries, Tibetan tapestries… (Reichel-Dolmatoff, 1975, p. 164).

Once the hallucinogenic *yajé* drugs reach effective levels in the bloodstreams of the participants, the meditation-like visions get eclipsed by a rush of new, drug-driven visions that manifest as chaotic combinations of light sensations and dreamlike images that evolved rapidly in ever-changing, kaleidoscopic patterns. While the drug was active, the participants said they saw visions of people, places, and things that were familiar to them. They also saw the kinds of strange images from the world of spirits that the shamans had primed them to expect. These visionary experiences were charged with emotional intensity and a sense of having experienced something that was deeply meaningful. That shouldn't surprise us because we know the constant flux of hallucinations coated with strong emotional reactions means that a barrage of strong excitation has streamed down into the hippocampi, the terminals of the visual pathways, and that, from there, the waves will be relayed out to the emotional association centers of the limbic brain. The end result will be similar to what happens in déjà vu, the phenomenon we discussed earlier where stimulation of the emotional association centers in the brain will coat whatever happens to be in front of that person's eyes as a scene that feels familiar, deeply moving, and personally meaningful, even if the person never actually encountered any of the constituent parts of that scene before.

After the climax of the drug-driven hallucinations, a third and final stage in the ritual takes place while the participants are waiting quietly for a sense of calm and normality to be restored. During this last stage of quiet contemplation and recovery, there is a return to seeing the same kinds of visions as those that appeared earlier during the waiting phase of the ritual. Many participants told Reichel-Dolmatoff that they saw visions of amorphous blobs of green light that looked like swirls of smoke: "Now there is said to prevail a yellowish-green light like young coca leaves," Reichel-Dolmatoff writes, "the light of paradise (1975, pp. 172-3)".

CHAPTER 9

Visions of Meditation-Induced Seizures

When I Saw the Dark, Moving Tunnel

In chapter one, I described how I was lying in bed, waiting to fall asleep while I watched a familiar set of light visions flow in and out of my visual field: I saw the green light-rings, then the dark blue clouds with porous textures and amorphous borders that developed bright inner nodes that looked like eyes. Then something happened that I'd never seen before. The dark blue cloud and its bright inner node suddenly condensed into a tiny, star-like cluster formed by thin white filaments flashing in and out of existence. The image looked exactly like a "twinkling star" in the night sky, and it seemed to exert a magnetic effect, pulling all my attention into its orbit. The intensity of that "star" gave me an ominous feeling, and I now realize, in retrospect, that the star was an early warning sign that there was an epileptic-like focus gathering strength in those areas of the visual cortices containing the neurons that represent central vision. After watching for only a few seconds, my head gave an involuntary jerk backward as the "star" abruptly vanished. In that same instant, a stream of black rings flooded the visual field.

The black rings followed the same trajectory as the green light-rings that had appeared earlier—they flowed in from the peripheral rim of the visual field, as if they'd just come from behind my head and then shrank steadily in diameter. These black rings were flooding into the visual field at a rate of two or three rings per second (2.0 to 3.0 Hz), ten times faster than the green light-rings which enter at five-second intervals (0.2 Hz). Seeing so many rings flowing so fast with each ring shrinking in diameter in such close conjunction with the other rings that had come before created the illusion of a dark tunnel rapidly receding toward some unseen point in the dark void. The individual black rings were barely visible against the dark charcoal gray of the visual field, but the sensation of "optic flow" was so powerful that I felt I was being sucked into the vortex of that dark, moving tunnel. Sometimes the sensation of optic flow seemed to shift direction, making it seem I was pulled backward through the dark, moving tunnel instead of being propelled forward. It was the kind of visual impression you get when you're riding on a subway train that's speeding through a dark tunnel when you're standing beside the back window of the train's last car and looking out.

I mentioned before that this vision of the tunnel reminded me of what I'd read in the accounts of some near-death experiences where survivors reported that they saw a dark tunnel that picked them up, carried them away, then dropped them off in the middle of a bright, all-enveloping light. As they floated in that light, they were infused with feelings of joy and bliss. Some of the survivors said they weren't really sure they wanted to leave that beautiful light and return to their physical bodies. As I stared into the dark, moving tunnel pulling me in, I wondered if this might be the same kind of dark tunnel described by those near-death survivors. But then why would it be appearing to me?

Visions of Tunnels Seen by Near-Death Survivors

In *Light & Death: One Doctor's Fascinating Account of Near-Death Experiences* (1998), Dr. Michael Sabom tells the story of Lori, a woman who began having grand mal seizures in her mid-fifties. In someone her age, this symptom raised the specter of brain cancer, and, indeed, that's what her physicians found when testing her: there was a large tumor in her right temporal lobe. She was scheduled for a surgical procedure that would full seven hours. During surgery, Lori suddenly went into cardiac arrest, and that's when she felt herself being moved through a dark space:

> I went down this dark corridor. It was like "time to go" down this corridor. It was like the wind and I were the same… At the end of the corridor was this bright light. Brighter than any sunlight. Brighter than any star. Brighter than anything you can think of. It permeated everything. Everything was that light (1998, p. 29).

While Lori does not use the word, "tunnel", her description suggests a sensation of optic flow and a feeling she was being blown through a "dark corridor" by a wind coming from behind and pushing through that dark space. (Her reference to a "wind" anticipates what we'll encounter later in this chapter when we discuss visionary experiences described in early Daoist texts where meditators say they felt as if they'd been caught up in a *piao*—in a "whirlwind". Tantric Hindu texts also include references to a sensation of "churning… that must be performed with whirling force until there appear the dazzling sparks".)

Dr. Sabom also tells the story of Pam Reynolds, a thirty-five-year-old woman being operated on for a giant aneurysm in one of the arteries that enters through the base of the skull and carries blood to the brain. The size and location of her aneurysm was such that the surgeons had to use a new and radical technique called hypothermic cardiac arrest that required them to put Pam temporarily in a death-like state. Her body temperature would have to be lowered to sixty degrees, which would cause her heart and her breathing to stop and her brainwaves to flatten out in the EEG monitor. Then, in the final step, she would be placed on a device that turned her body upside down to allow most of the blood to drain out of her head. In a difficult operation like this, the patient's physiological processes had to be monitored very closely. That's why Sabom makes a point of emphasizing that in this case "the documentation far exceeds any records from before and provides us with our most complete scientific glimpse yet into the near-death experience (p. 15)." During the early stages of the operation, after Pam's body was inverted to drain out her blood, she began to have a near-death experience:

There was a sensation like being pulled, but not against your will. I was going on my own accord because I wanted to go. I have different metaphors to try to explain this. It was like the Wizard of Oz—being taken up in a tornado vortex, only you're not spinning around like you've got vertigo. You're very focused and you have a place to go. The feeling was like going up in an elevator real fast. And there was a sensation, but it wasn't a bodily, physical sensation. It was like a tunnel, but it wasn't a tunnel. / At some point very early in the tunnel vortex I became aware of my grandmother calling me, but I didn't hear her call me with my ears... The feeling was that she wanted me to come to her, so I continued with no fear down the shaft.

It's a dark shaft I went through, and at the very end there was this very little tiny pinpoint of light that kept getting bigger and bigger and bigger. / The light was incredibly bright, like sitting in the middle of a lightbulb. It was so bright that I put my hands in front of my face, fully expecting to see them, and I could not... / I noticed that I began to discern different figures in the light—and they were all covered with light, they *were* light, and had light permeating all around them—they began to form shapes I could recognize and understand. I could see that one of them was my grandmother (Sabom, 1998, p. 18).

Pam uses several different metaphors to describe sensations of movement consistent with optic flow: "being taken up in a tornado vortex", "like going up in an elevator real fast", and "a sensation... like a tunnel but it wasn't a tunnel". All of these metaphors point to sensations of rapid movement through a dark, empty space similar to what Lori, the patient described above, also reported.

In one of Dr. Sabom's earlier books, he provides another, similar account of someone's tunnel-like experience:

There was total blackness around me. I want to say that it felt like I was moving very, very fast in time and space. I was traveling through a tunnel. It didn't look like a tunnel, but when you're in a tunnel, all you see is blackness around you. If you move very fast you can feel the sides moving in on you whether there are sides there or not because of the darkness (Sabom, *Recollection of Death: A Medical Investigation*, 1981, p. 41).

There's also another researcher whose work is essential reading for anyone interested in this subject. Psychologist Susan

Blackmore, a scientific researcher who specializes in the study of extrasensory perception and other anomalous phenomena, became interested in near-death experiences after she had a near-death experience herself. In her article, "The Physiology of the Tunnel", published in *The Journal of Near-Death Studies* in 1981, Blackmore and her co-author, Tom Troscianko, report that during her near-death experience she saw visions of dark "bands" moving through the visual field in a fast-moving stream that made it feel as if she were moving through a tunnel. She also writes that the tunnels she often experienced were "of varying textures," and she specifies that they could be tunnels formed by "bright lights" in addition to those formed by "bands of darker and lighter gray (p. 17)". I'm confident that Blackmore is describing the same kind of black-ring phenomenon that I've seen because her reference to seeing "bands of darker and lighter gray" is a good description of how there's a thin space between each of the black rings that takes on the charcoal-gray color of the visual field. And obviously that gray-colored gap will also have a ring shape because it's sandwiched in between two black rings. Blackmore also writes that she's seen "tunnels made of… bright lights". While this description is ambiguous, I think it's likely that she's referring to the vision of a bright spray of tiny sparks radiating out through the periphery of the visual field, a vision that erupts immediately after the dark tunnel disappears.

Seizure Onset and the Visions of Dark Tunnels

When I started searching through the medical literature for studies about the brain mechanisms that would have to become active in order to generate the stream of black rings, I was already in possession of two important clues. First, I knew that the black rings had the same shapes and followed the same shrinking trajectories as the green light-rings I'd seen. The resemblance was striking, and I assumed there would have to be some kind of connection. But what would cause sleep rhythm oscillators in the brain stem to suddenly start firing spindle bursts ten times faster than they'd been firing before? And why didn't those rings take on the same green color instead of black? The second clue pertained to the postural contortions and the muscle tremors in my fingers, face, and toes. These symptoms had to be produced by some kind of paroxysmal episode. Both clues pointed in the same direction—I would need to find out more about how the brain mechanisms that govern a normal transition to sleep could be disturbed in a way that would trigger the eruption of a seizure.

It didn't take long to find relevant research articles. They revealed that there is a type of seizure that often erupts in epileptic patients when they're about to fall asleep or when the brain initiates one of its regular transitions between rapid-eye-movement (REM) sleep and slow wave NREM sleep. That shift takes place several times during a typical night. The reason why epileptic patients are especially vulnerable to having seizures when the slow waves of NREM sleep begin to take over is that when the synchronous spindles waves that inaugurate slow wave sleep arrive in those areas of an epileptic patient's brain where the neuron circuits are damaged, some of those neurons are likely to be chronically hyper-excitable. Those hyperexcitable neurons will respond to the synchronous spindle waves from the brainstem by firing their own synchronous discharges. As these two kinds of synchronous waves reverberate back and forth between the hyperexcitable neurons in the cortical regions and the brain stem, this creates a positive feedback loop that increases the amplitudes and frequencies of the brainwaves. The build-up can happen very rapidly and cross a threshold that causes sleep rhythm oscillators in the brain stem to suddenly destabilize. When that happens, the destabilized sleep rhythm oscillators will shift to firing bursts at the "hypersynchronous" rate of two-to-three bursts per second (2.0 to 3.0 Hz), a firing rate ten times as faster than normal timing of spindle bursts which are fired with clocklike regularity at a rate of one burst every three to ten seconds (0.3 to 0.1 Hz). This shift marks the onset of a hypersynchronous seizure. When that kind of seizure gets detected by a scalp EEG, the tracing pins register two or three "spike-wave complexes" being fired every second. A team of researchers led by Mircea Steriade, a leading expert in this field of study, found that activation of this mechanism of sleep rhythm destabilization can occur "with surprising ease" (Steriade et. al., 1998, p. 1476).

The reason why the ring visions generated by onset of a hypersynchronous seizures are so black is because the spindle waves that are flowing so rapidly up the sides of the RTN that they impose almost continuous waves of inhibition on the axons of the LGN vision-relay neurons situated directly beneath those inhibiting waves. There is not enough time between the ascending spindle wave inhibitions for the vision-relay neurons to recover and fire their normal rebound spikes. Each wave of inhibition has the effect of cutting off all light-related signals, which is why the meditator sees the spike-and-wave complexes manifesting in the visual field as black rings devoid of all light. Between each black ring there is a momentary glimpse of the normal charcoal gray color of the visual field which takes on a ring shape because it's sandwiched in between two black rings.

Why would this kind of hypersynchronous seizure that's usually experienced by epileptic patients erupt in someone like me who doesn't have any kind of epileptic disorder. What disrupted my normal routine of falling asleep to produce this dramatic outcome? There are two likely suspects: I'd acquired a substantial sleep deficit before I got in bed, and I'd been feeling mildly depressed. Studies have demonstrated that both of these conditions can cause a person's cortical neurons to become more hyper-excitable than normal. It is reasonable to assume that when I got in bed at such a late hour while feeling mildly depressed and having already acquired a substantial sleep deficit that the convergence of these three factors caused some cluster of neurons in my visual cortices to become hyperexcitable. That would facilitate a build-up of excitation as the synchronous spindle waves of stage 2 NREM sleep were flowing up from the brainstem to the cortical regions where they stimulated the hyperexcitable neurons in my visual cortices to respond by firing their own synchronous bursts. This means that what happened to me was similar to what happens in patients with epilepsy except that in those cases it's the epileptic brain lesions that cause their cortical neurons to be hyperexcitable.

This analysis suggests that what happened to me when I was meditating after having accumulated a substantial sleep deficit can also happen to other meditators who, like me, are not epileptic. It's important for us to keep this in mind when we study what was happening in the lives of the founders of the world's major religions and in the lives of many other famous mystics that led to them seeing visions of fiery light during their prayer or meditation vigils. For most of those mystic seers, there is no credible evidence to support the inference that they saw the vision of fiery light because they suffered from some kind of epileptic disorder that triggered the seizure that generated their vision.

Researchers who use scalp EEGs to study what happens in the brains of expert meditators when they signal that they're inducing their "peak experiences" often overlook or ignore the possibility that the "peak experience" is being generated by the onset of hypersynchronous seizures. There's an interesting anecdote that was sent to me in a personal communication from Dr. György Buzsáki, a prominent neuroscientist. It was a response to my having sent Dr. Buzsáki a copy of my book, *Meditation & Light Visions: A Neurological Analysis*, to thank him for the pioneering research he'd published over the years that proved to be so useful when I was doing the research for my book. Dr. Buzsáki sent a response acknowledging that he'd skimmed *Meditation & Light Visions*, that he found it to be quite interesting, and that it brought to mind an incident that had occurred earlier in his life. He was attending a medical conference where representatives of the Maharishi Institute had set up an information booth. When Dr. Buzsáki stopped by the booth, he was shown some EEG recordings of the brainwaves of expert meditators taken while they signaled that they were transcending normal consciousness. He recognized that many of the EEG tracings he was being shown were filled with spike-wave complexes that indicated these meditators had induced hypersynchronous seizures:

> It is interesting that in the first-ever international meeting that I attended (the International EEG meeting in Amsterdam, 1977), there was a poster from the Maharishi Institute showing scalp EEGs of highly trained meditators. I could not help but point out to the presenter that it is a spike and wave (absence) pattern. In retrospect, it makes sense because these individuals train their brains to isolate the outer world from the inner world, i.e., generating an absence from reality. (Personal communication, 2010)

In an article, "The Transits of Consciousness", written by Dr. Edgar Wilson and published posthumously in *The Journal of Subtle Energies and Energy Medicine* (1994; 4(2): 171-185), the author reports that when he conducted a study of the brainwave patterns of an experienced "therapeutic touch healer" as he induced the state of consciousness he used to induce healing, the scalp EEG recorded alpha waves, then shifted to slower waves in the theta- and delta-band frequencies, then slowed even more, reaching "really low frequencies, like low delta, then suddenly the EEG registered a surge of activity in which high-amplitude waves in all frequency bands—in the theta, delta, and gamma bands—soared up to very high levels, producing readings of twenty to thirty-nine microvolts (µV)." Wilson didn't know what to make of this anomaly, but then he was even more surprised to find out that the same sudden surges of high-amplitude waves could also be observed in EEG studies of novice meditators.

Wilson was invited to perform before-and-after EEG tests on volunteers who were attending a well-known and highly reputed training course that touts the use of biofeedback techniques to teach attendees how to deepen their meditation practices. The attendees listened to audiotapes that were primed with binaural beats set at delta band frequencies. When Wilson conducted the post-training tests using scalp EEGs, he found that "a sudden shift from slow waves to temporal lobe activation occurred in 80% of these subjects, with temporal activation reaching 64 Hz in one female subject." That woman reported that what she experienced during the post-training EEG test had the same "ecstatic" feelings and the same "out-of-the-body" qualities that she'd felt during the meditation training session. The high-amplitude surges in the scalp EEGs of many of Wilson's subjects were clustered around the central vertex of the mediator's head or localized over the temporal lobes. Seven years after the publication of Wilson's article, these two distinctive EEG patterns—the "table-top" distribution and the "earmuff" distribution—were identified as the product of hypersynchronous seizures in the temporolimbic regions of the brain in that article published by Pacia and Ebersole that we discussed in detail in Chapter 3.

What I find particularly interesting about Dr. Wilson's work is that he had to struggle with balancing two contradictory ideas. His medical training taught him that the high-amplitude gamma surges he'd observed were most likely caused by temporal lobe seizures: "When people are really going up into ecstatic or transcendent experiences, I've seen them go up to 120 to 150 µV activity in the temporal lobe. The first time I saw this evidence of temporal activation, I thought the person probably had a temporal lobe seizure, and I continued to think that for some time because of the intensity of that response (Wilson, Ibid., p. 181)." But later he reconsidered this interpretation on the grounds that it would be inappropriate for him, as a scientist and an observer who is limited in what he can know about the inner, "felt qualities" of a person's experience, to conclude that the deeply moving spiritual experience described by his subjects was "nothing more" than a temporal lobe seizure. He decided that it would be more appropriate to call these meditation-induced ecstasies "transits of consciousness", leaving open questions about causality because he anticipated that someday these meditation-induced ecstasies might be regarded as the gradual emergence of a new and spiritually elevated form of human consciousness. But Wilson never explicitly rejected his initial finding that the high-amplitude surges could also be triggered by partial seizures spreading through the limbic regions.

Edgar Wilson's reports about brainwave patterns in therapeutic touch healers and novice meditators recall the EEG studies we reviewed in Chapter 3 where researchers recorded brainwave patterns in Tibetan monks who were specially selected for their meditation skills. When the monks signaled that they'd induced their typical "peak experience", their scalp EEGs recorded sudden surges of high-amplitude brainwaves consistent with the "table-top" and "earmuff" patterns that signal the onset of hypersynchronous seizures. (Readers interested in a more comprehensive and detailed analysis of this phenomenon of expert meditators inducing partial seizures are invited to consult some of my earlier publications—my book, *Meditation & Light Visions: A Neurological Analysis,* or an article published in *Medical Hypotheses* entitled "Does Meditation Predispose to Epilepsy? EEG Studies of Expert Meditators Self-Inducing Simple Partial Seizures" (*Medical Hypotheses* 2006; 66(3): 674-676)).

The Hypersynchronous Vision of a Spray of Sparks

We've discussed why meditators who induce hypersynchronous seizures see visions of black rings that create the illusion of being pulled into a dark, moving tunnel, but that same hypersynchronous seizure can also generate a very different kind of vision—a vision that manifests as a spray of radiating sparks. Studies show that, when hypersynchronous seizures are underway, there can be an alternation between the firing of hypersynchronous spike-and-wave complexes, the kind of excitation that generates the visions of black rings, and "cortical fast-runs", the kind of excitation that generates the spray of tiny sparks. That kind of shift is what happened to me: I was staring into the dark, moving tunnel of black rings, feeling as if I were being sucked into its vortex, when suddenly everything changed: instead of seeing a tunnel that seemed to be streaming inward, I saw thousands of tiny sparks begin radiating out through the peripheral regions of my visual field as if they were aimed at my forehead.

The spray is shaped like a cone of water spraying out of a jet nozzle. The spray of tiny sparks flows only in the peripheral regions of the visual field; the center of the visual field remains empty and dark. I suspect that Blackmore saw the same vision when she described "tunnels made of... bright lights". The vision of the radiating spray creates a sensation of the optic flow that makes the seers feel as if they are moving in the opposite direction from the feeling of inward movement generated by the tunnel of black rings that was active only moments before. I felt as if I were being "pushed back", not "pulled forward." When the spray of radiating sparks began streaming out toward my forehead, I felt an obscure compulsion to arch my back, pull my head back against the pillow, and let my mouth fall slack. At the same time the muscles in my face and fingers began to twitch. These were clearly paroxysmal symptoms, although it turned out that they were relatively mild compared to what was to come.

When a hypersynchronous seizure is generating the vision of a spray of sparks, this is a sign that neurons in the visual cortices are firing synchronous "fast-runs" at the rapid rate of ten to fifteen discharges per second. Because cortical neurons are connected in large, locally connected networks, these "cortical fast-runs" send waves rippling outward in all directions, forming a pattern epileptologists describe as an "expanding epileptic penumbra". The waves of excitation generated by the cortical fast-runs are transmitted down through the neuron circuits that connect the visual cortices with the LGNs where they stimulate vision-relay neurons in the LGNs to fire in a pattern that mirrors the expanding epileptic penumbra.

The waves of excitation generated by the cortical fast-runs are processed first in the upper regions of the LGNs where vision-relay neurons represent central vision. Then those waves keep moving down the sides of the LGNs where the vision-relay neurons represent ever-more peripheral regions in the visual field. But there is an important difference between what happens in the visual cortices and what happens in the LGNs. Studies reveal that fewer than half of the LGN vision-relay neurons fire discharges in response to the incoming waves of excitation. They also report that none of the vision-relay neurons located in the uppermost regions of the LGNs—the neurons that represent central vision—respond to the receipt of waves generated by the cortical fast-runs. That means meditators who induce this type of hypersynchronous seizure will see tiny flecks of light suddenly flash out and then go dark again, and those sparks will seem to be flowing in an outward direction through the periphery of the visual field as if they were heading toward the outer rim of vision. That perception that the individual sparks are moving is only an illusion; what's really happening is that the waves of excitation are moving, and as those waves flow down from the tops to the bottoms of the LGNs, they trigger individual vision-relay neurons to fire as they pass by, but then as each wave keeps moving down the sides of the LGNs, it triggers individual vision-relay neurons located lower down. Each descending wave generates its first spark-like flashes in the middle regions of the visual field and then continues to generate sparks in ever-more peripheral regions of the visual field. But since none of the vision-relay neurons associated with central vision respond to the waves generated by cortical fast-runs taking place in the visual cortices, the central region of the visual field remains dark.

The Vision of a Gradual Brightening and Bluing

As I watched the spray of tiny, bright sparks radiate out through the peripheral regions of my visual field, I realized that the visual field was beginning to brighten. At first this brightening was very subtle, but then it continued until the entire visual field looked like a bright blue sky.

While the visual field was slowly brightening, the tiny sparks that had been radiating out through the visual field faded away and the paroxysmal symptoms that accompanied the spray of sparks—the postural contortions and muscle tremors—also disappeared. I felt a deep calm as I stared out into that bright blue sky. And I remembered the stories told by survivors of near-death experiences who described being pulled through a dark corridor and then dropped off in the middle of a bright, all-encompassing light that filled them with joy and bliss. Now I was floating in a bright, all-encompassing blue light, but where was the joy and bliss? They hadn't arrived. At least not yet.

Now, in retrospect, after studying the medical literature, I have a better idea about what happened back then. When the brightening began to appear, the hypersynchronous seizure had already been underway for a while—it had already generated the vision of the dark tunnel and the vision of radiating sparks—and all that while the ongoing seizure would have been sending a barrage of hypersynchronous excitation down into the hippocampi, the terminal structures in the visual system. That gradual build-up would register in the visual field of those meditators who know what to do to remain conscious as a gradual brightening of the visual field. In order for meditators to see a shift in which the bright blue visual field suddenly erupts with bright, flashing lights, many of the neurons in both hippocampi would have to shift from firing hypersynchronous discharges to firing in paroxysmal bursts.

Visions of Tunnels, Sparks, and Brightening Skies in the Myths of World Religions

The Whirlwind of Unitive Fusion in Early Daoism

There are very few reports in the mystical literatures of world religions in which meditators see visions of the kind of dark, moving tunnels that I've described. There are, however, interesting accounts in some early Daoist texts of meditators about being caught up in a strange sensation of movement that appears just before a spray of tiny sparks. In the Daoist *Ta-tung ching*, "The Book of Great Profundity", meditators are urged to use the technique of *Shou-i* ("Guarding the Light of the One") or *Cun-jian* ("Retentive Visualization") to attract the attention of celestial deities and get them to send down visions of celestial light. They are taught that the first light sent down from the heavens will be wheels of green light: "The splendor of yang starts to shine and spread its light… Its breath [*chi*] turns and circles like the wheels of a chariot (Robinet, 1993, p. 110)." Next, the meditators will see "a purple breath, as large as the pupil of your eye, but wrapped in several tens of layers and flashing brilliantly (Bokenkamp, 1997, p. 315)." While watching these visions of the purple cloud, meditators may see that "the sun… penetrates to the center of the purple breath… a fiery pearl within the darkness (Robinet, p. 130)." It's then, after seeing meditation-induced visions of green light-rings and dark blue clouds with bright inner cores, that something very different is said to happen.

The Daoist texts warn that meditators will suddenly find themselves caught up in sensations that make them feel like they're "whirling" or "twisting". This mystical "whirlwind" is called *piao*, a word that can be translated as a "violent or wild or fiery wind" or as a "fast chariot". Meditators are taught that once the *piao* begins, they will feel their bodies "twirled around like a falling leaf" or buffeted "like a cloth fluttering in a strong wind (Robinet, pp. 113-114)". What is being described here as the buffeting of a "violent or wild wind" is most likely a reference to the visual effect produced by the vision of a dark, moving tunnel and the sensation of optic flow generated by the onset of a hypersynchronous seizure.

Then, according to these Daoist texts, the effects produced by the *piao*—by the whirlwind—suddenly change: the sensations of whirling and twisting will disappear and the meditators will then see the vision of "the ten thousand things". This is clearly a reference to the spray of tiny sparks radiating out through the periphery of the visual field. What happens next is that the spray of sparks fades out as the visual field becomes brighter and bluer. This is a change that's also described in the Daoist texts: "... suddenly the respiration disperses the form of the ten thousand things and, at the height of the movement, there is a tranquility again—obscurely, all around, the Miracle of the Emperor One" which "brightens everything like a 'like a white sun'" (Robinet, 1993, pp. 109-110, 116-117). That's why the *piao* whirlwind can also be described as a "chariot"—because it brings about the "fusion" in which meditators experience the Miracle of the Emperor One.

The Tantric guru traditions of India also advise meditators that they may experience a sensation of movement while staring into the dark space of the visual field. This sensation is called "the churning" or "the mystical whirling", and it's a promising signal that the meditators are about to see the next vision—a spray of tiny sparks: "the churning... must be performed with whirling force until the dazzling sparks appear (*Shivasutravimarchini* II: 3, in Silburn, 1988, pp. 42, 59, 74)."

The Tibetan Vision of "Flaring Fireflies"

The *Svetasvatara Upanishad* states that "fireflies" are among "the preliminary forms which produce the manifestation of Brahman in yoga (II: 11)". In Patañjali's *Yogasutras*, written several centuries after the *Upanishads*, the author advises meditators to keep paying close attention to the "fireflies" because that vision is a signal that the *atman*, the radiant spiritual "self" that's split off from the primordial radiance of Brahman and implanted in every human, is about to appear: "Once the flux ends, the *atman* comes (4.24)." In the *Taittiriya Upanishad*, it's said that the *atman* will manifest as a bright protrusion "that hangs down between the palates like a nipple (1: 6.1)". In the *Katha Upanishad*, it's said to look "like a flame without smoke" and to be about the "size of a thumb (2: 1, 13)". All of the Hindu texts agree on this: when the vision of the *atman* appears, the "Abounding Brahma-Light" is not far behind.

In the Tantric Buddhist tradition of India, there is a similar account in which meditators are told to expect that they will see a vision called "The Flaring" that "will appear as a yellow radiance (Naropa, *The Epitome of the Six Yogas*, 'The Yoga of Psychic Heat' 1: 98-9, p. 123)". And in another chapter of this same text—in "The Yoga of the Bardo State"—Naropa uses a similar metaphor to describe the vision that looks like fireflies: "The internal sign looks like the apparition of fireflies. This is the time of the Ignition (5: 15-16)."

The Tibetan Vision of a Dawn Before the Dawn

The Hindu *Rig Veda* has nothing to say about visions of dark tunnels and the spray of sparks, but it does describe a vision of brightening and bluing that takes over the visual field. This vision is sent to the priests participating in the Soma ritual by *Usas*, the goddess of dawn. Usas sends the vision of a "conscious dawn", a dawn that appears before the arrival of the natural dawn. One hymn states that "Many are the days that dawned before the rising of the sun," and adds that "our ancestors discovered this hidden light and created the Dawn (RV 7.76.2)." Those ancestors "glorified the conscious dawns... and the purple dawn appears (RV 4.1.11-17)."

The Tibetan Buddhist tradition also teaches that the vision of apparitional fireflies will give way to a vision of "something resembling the light of dawn, and something resembling a cloudless sky" (Naropa, *Six Yogas*, 'The Yoga of Psychic Heat' 1.98, p. 195).

The Neural Mechanisms that Generate the Bulb-Shaped Vision

Why did I see the image of a small, white, translucent bulb-shape begin glowing in the upper right quadrant of the bright, sky-blue background? Earlier I explained what caused the gradual brightening and bluing of the visual field—that was produced by the steady barrage of hypersynchronous excitation streaming into the hippocampi. But in order to generate the intense white dome-shaped glow that seemed to push out from the bright blue background, there must have been some additional stimulation bearing in on some small region with one of the hippocampi. The shape of the bulbous white glow provided an important clue about what had to be happening to produce that vision. In Chapter 3 we discussed how each hippocampus has an anterior "nose" region that consists of a tube with a rounded tip that stretches forward from the main body of the hippocampus, then bends back and flattens out against the main body. The anatomy looks a lot like a human thumb that's been flattened against the palm of the hand. The anterior nose of the hippocampus is covered by a thin sheet of neurons gets selectively stimulated when meditators fixate their attention intently on that part of the visual field located just beyond the tip of their noses. That attention-driven stimulation of the bulbous nose region of the hippocampus adds to the excitation imposed on all hippocampal neurons by the barrage of hypersynchronous pulsations. The greater intensity of the stimulation taking place in the anterior nose region of a hippocampus has the potential to produce an image brighter than the general brightening of the entire visual field. What meditators see is, in effect, a translucent white "ghost image" of the tip of the anterior nose of one of the hippocampi located deep inside their brain.

But why did this differential brightening occur in only one of the two hippocampi? Researchers studying epileptic seizures report that it's typical for the initial hypersynchronous activity to build with greater intensity in one hippocampus, which is why the sudden outbreak of paroxysmal discharges usually occurs first in one of the two hippocampi. Given that I saw the white bulbous glow appear on the right side of my visual field and that it's the left hippocampus that processes signals coming from the right side of the visual field, it's reasonable to infer that the build-up of excitation became most intense in the anterior nose region of the hippocampus located on the left side of my brain. One reason why it the left hippocampus might have been more vulnerable than the right is that I'm left-handed, a handedness that is sometimes associated with having a hippocampus that's a bit smaller on the left side and thus more vulnerable. It might also be relevant that, as I mentioned earlier, I've been diagnosed with complex post-traumatic stress disorder, and studies have shown that patients with PTSD can sometimes have residual damage in their hippocampi. It's possible that might have affected the condition of my left hippocampus.

As I watched the translucent white surfaces of the bulbous figure brighten, it's posterior regions seemed to get longer. That change created the illusion that the bulbous figure had just moved forward. If my attention wavered, even momentarily, the white light would dim and, with that, some of the bulb's posterior extension evaporated. These changes in the perceived size of the bulbous image created the illusion that it could "protrude", then "pull back", then "protrude" again. This back-and-forth movement continued for a relatively long time, but then there was a sudden and dramatic change: the white bulb seemed to flash more brightly than ever before, and, in that same instant, it disappeared. The bright blue background also disappeared in that same instant, restoring the normal charcoal gray of the visual field. In the same space formerly occupied by the white bulb I saw three thin white rays extending out from a single base. The tips of the rays splayed apart, forming a trident figure, and in this first appearance the rays extended only halfway to the outer rim of the visual field.

This dramatic change in which all the visual phenomena that were being generated by the hypersynchronous seizure suddenly disappeared and were replaced by a different kind of discharge is consistent with what's known about how a hypersynchronous excitation builds in intensity until it triggers the outbreak of a more powerful "paroxysmal" seizure. That's the best fit explanation for the vision sequence I just described. Given that there were only three rays jutting out in the first appearance, it's reasonable to infer that three neurons in the anterior nose region of the left hippocampus were the first neurons to begin firing paroxysmal discharges. It's also reasonable to infer that the excitation generated by those first paroxysmal discharges would begin to flow along the axons of those neurons, recruiting other neurons located in that same region of the same hippocampus to fire their own paroxysmal bursts. That would explain why, one second later, the three rays doubled in number and also extended all the way to the outer rim of the visual field. Then one second later there was a third transformation: the tips of all six rays slowly spread apart in what looked like flower petals "wilting" as they were struck by the sun.

Nothing else changed in the visual field as I counted the passing seconds, but I knew something else had to be happening somewhere in the brain. What seems most likely is that the paroxysmal excitation continued to flow through all the intra-hippocampal circuits and then spread out into the limbic and temporal lobe regions located downstream. When that paroxysmal excitation reached those temporo-limbic structures, that would initiate the outbreak of a bilateral partial seizure with visions of bright, fiery flashes filling both sides of the visual field.

Visions of Bulbous Protrusions and White Rays in World Religions

Hindu Visions of the Bulb-Shaped Atman

The *Taitttirrihya Upanishad* describes a "space that is within the heart: Therein is the Person [*Atman*] consisting of mind, immortal and resplendent. That which hangs down between the palates like a nipple (1: 6.1)." Some other descriptions refer to "the person the size of a thumb… like a flame without smoke (*Katha Up.*, 2: 1, 13)", or that this vision has a round top which makes it "seem to be the size of a goad (*Svetasvaratara Up.*, 5: 9)". It's also said that this thumb-shaped image of the self "looks like white wool (*Brhadaranyaka Up.*, 2: 3, 6)." In the Tantric Hindu yoga texts that were written long after the Upanishads, there are verses that claim "The Egg-of-Brahma looks like a uvula, a womb, an ivory tusk, a linga [penis], or like the stomach of a fish (*Tantraloka* 5)." That same text also describes the vision of three rays jutting up out of the Egg-of-Brahman: "From the navel there arises a trident whose points… reach a cosmic *dvadasanta* (15)", where *dvadasanta* refers to the "opening to Brahman" that occurs when the visions of light seen by meditators pierce the sacred sheath that binds the light of the "inner self" to the human body. Another passage in that same text states that "The Supreme energy blossoms… like a five-hooded cobra as she rises (29: 248)."

When the Hindu guru, Patañjali, wrote his famous *Yogasutras*, the last chapter was about the visions that lead to *Kaivalpa* ("Liberation"). The author assures meditators that when they see "Those countless speckles striking… they have a purpose (4.24)." That purpose is to bring on the bulbous image and, when that happens, meditators are warned to pay close attention to "That bending image (*nimnam*)" because "behind it comes *Kaivalpa* (4.25)." They are advised to look for the "cut" in the bending image: "That cut—from it more forms will arise (4.26)."

The Tibetan Vision of "The Pure Illusory Body"

Naropa's anthology of texts describing the meditation practices of Highest Yoga Tantra, *The Epitome of the Six Yogas*, advises meditators that they've reached a pivotal moment when they see "The internal sign looks like fireflies. This is the time of the Ignition ("Yoga of the Bardo State" 5: 15-16)". The next vision is "Something resembling the light of dawn, and something resembling a cloudless sky ("Yoga of the Psychic Heat" 1: 98)." It's after the bright sky appears that the meditators see "The Pure Illusory Body", a bulbous figure poking out of the bright blue background: "The Pure Illusory Body looks like a fish leaping out of a pond, like the moon's reflection in water" ("The Yoga of the Clear Light" 4: 34). This vision of a white bulbous figure is described in another chapter as "the invisible psychic protuberance... which is filled with transmuted seminal fluid" ("The Yoga of the Psychic Heat 1: 144-5). Meditators then see the white rays jut out and undergo the transformations that lead to the explosion of the fiery light: "The transmuted white seminal fluid issues forth in an intense flow upward to the crown of the head which it permeates completely ("Yoga of the Psychic Heat 1: 143-6)."

Daoist Visions of a "Turtle's Head"

After meditators are caught up in the *piao* "whirlwind" that I described earlier in this section, and after they've see "obscurely, all around, the Miracle of the Emperor One" that brightens everything "like a white sun", then they see blue light filling the visual field. In the Daoist texts, that's described as "The Great Ocean of Energies, which covers the whole" and "wherein a large turtle swims" (Karl Schipper, 1993, *The Taoist Body*, pp. 106-7). Someone who sees a turtle swimming in the ocean will only really see the turtle's bulbous head poking up above the surface of the water, so this is an apt metaphor to describe the vision of a bulbous protrusion. Schipper also notes that the bulb-shaped image emerging out of the Great Ocean of Energies is described differently in some other Daoist texts: there the bulbous protrusion is not described as a turtle but rather as "*Kun'lun*, the sacred, inverted mountain with its narrow base widening toward the top, giving it the outline of a mushroom (Schipper., pp. 106-7)." In both of these descriptions, the essence of the image is that it displays a bulbous shape.

CHAPTER 10

The Anomalous Visions of the Hebrew Patriarchs

The God Who Manifests as Fire

The Hebrew patriarchs—Abraham, Moses, Elijah, and Ezekiel—are all said to have seen visions of God manifesting as a vision of Fire. Abraham awoke from sleep and saw a flaming torch leaping back and forth between animal bones he'd piled up in a sacrificial altar (Genesis 15: 17). Moses was herding sheep near Mt. Sinai when he saw a bush burst into flames without burning any leaves (Exodus 3: 2). God ordered Elijah to step out of the remote cave where he was hiding and showed His power by mounting whirlwinds, initiating earthquakes, and spreading fire across the sky (1 Kings 19: 11-13). None of these stories provide any evidence that would suggest the patriarchs were doing something to cause those visions to appear; rather, the visions of fire are depicted as miraculous events initiated by God as occasions for issuing commands or reassurances to the seer.

There is a dramatic contrast between the visionary experiences presented in those three stories and the visionary experiences of a fourth patriarch, the prophet Ezekiel, a Judean priest who spent most of his life living as an exile in Babylonia. In chapter one of the Book of Ezekiel, the prophet writes that he was meditating on the banks of a river in Babylon when he saw an elaborate sequence of visions erupt. He begins by describing visions of flames and flashes of lightning, but he also reports seeing visions of colored light—visions that looked like "something like a wheel within a wheel" and others that looked like a "crystal dome" that had a "sapphire" color" (Ezekiel 1: 26). These descriptions show that Ezekiel must have known how to use meditation to induce visions of light. On this occasion, his meditation progressed to the point that it triggered the eruption of a partial seizure that generated visions of bright, fiery flashes. After seeing this culmination of his elaborate vision sequence, Ezekiel fell on his face (1: 28).

How can we account for the stark differences between the visionary experiences attributed to Abraham, Moses, and Elijah that are depicted as having erupted spontaneously with the experiences described by Ezekiel himself which match the descriptions of visions that appear in meditation-induced sequences? To see how we might go about explaining these differences, we need to take a closer look at the lives and visions of the patriarchs. We also need to consider where and how those stories came into being because that history might have shaped what got preserved in those accounts. I'll begin at the beginning—with Abraham, the first Hebrew patriarch.

The Visions of Abraham

Abraham, the shaman/sheikh of a nomadic tribe that had emigrated out of the kingdom of Ur, is said to have established a special relationship with a powerful God who promised to give Abraham and his heirs control over the land of Canaan and its riches (Genesis 17: 1-19). In an anguished prayer to that God, Abraham asked if he and his wife, Sarah, could be blessed with a male heir (15: 2). God commanded him to travel alone into a wilderness area to perform a ritual sacrifice (Genesis 15: 9-17). When he arrived at the destination, Abraham killed the animals he'd brought with him and cut the bodies in halves. He stacked the body pieces in a pile to create a sacrificial altar. But then, "As the sun was going down, a deep sleep fell upon Abraham," and later when he woke up, a "deep and terrifying darkness descended upon him." Quivering in the intense darkness, he heard the voice of God promising him that he would indeed have offspring and that they would inherit the land of Canaan. That would happen even though, at the time, Abraham was 100 years old and his wife, Sarah, was 90 years old. To seal the covenant between them, God sent Abraham a vision in which "a smoking fire pot and a flaming torch passed between the pieces" of the sacrificed animals (Genesis 15: 17). That is the only vision of fire attributed to Abraham.

The Book of Genesis does not suggest that Abraham was meditating, nor does it say that he was performing a ritual of extreme stimulus overload, so neither of the two prerequisites for seeing visions of light that were identified earlier in our neurologically-grounded, reverse-engineering analysis of clear light visions were present when Abraham saw the visions of a "fire pot" and "a flaming torch". The assertion that he was sleeping and woke up to find himself immersed in a "deep and terrifying darkness" just before he saw the visions suggests that this experience might have been generated by a sleep-related epileptic seizure of the sort we discussed in Chapter 9—a seizure that can be triggered when hyperexcitable cortical neurons at the site of an epileptic focus in the person's brain destabilize sleep rhythm oscillators in the brainstem. The inference of epileptic seizure is supported by another passage in Genesis where Abraham is said to "fall facedown" while receiving communications from God.

This happened back when God first established his covenant with Abraham, designating the 99-year-old man as "the father of many nations (Genesis 17: 2)". So there is some ambiguous evidence suggesting that Abraham might have suffered from recurring seizures that erupted spontaneously, the preliminary criteria for diagnosings an epileptic disorder. There is no evidence that he induced those visions while he was meditating.

Some clues about the messages that the authors of the book of Genesis want to convey in their stories about Abraham can be found in passages that describe what happened when he was 137 years old. After Abraham's wife, Sarah, passed on, God decided to test him to determine if he was still God's faithful servant. He gave Abraham a command: "Take your son, your only son, Isaac, whom you love, and go to the land of Moriah, and offer him there as a burnt offering on one of the mountains that I shall show you (Genesis 22: 2)." Abraham did not argue with God, and Isaac did not argue with Abraham; the two of them gathered supplies and traveled to the appointed destination. When they arrived, Isaac was surprised to learn that Abraham was planning to make a sacrifice because they hadn't brought any animals with them. But then Isaac got an even bigger surprise when Abraham made his next move: "He bound his son Isaac, and laid him on the altar, on top of the wood." This claim that a 137-year-old man would and could forcibly bind a man who was 37 years old, then pick him up and place him on top of a sacrificial altar, challenges the credibility of the story, but then as it continues it gets even more incredible. It's said that "Abraham reached out his hand and took the knife to kill his son." But then, just before he plunged the blade into Isaac, Abraham heard the voice of an angel ordering him not to kill his son. The angel told Abraham he was being tested him to see if he was still God-fearing enough to act on the command to sacrifice his only son (Gen. 22: 10-11). As Abraham helped Isaac come down from the improvised altar, a miracle occurred: a ram appeared, entangled in a nearby bush. They used that ram for a substitute sacrifice. From a modern, rational perspective, Abraham's behavior is what we'd expect from a severely deranged psychotic, not from a pious religious figure, and, indeed, that's the hypothesis proposed by Doctors Evan Murphy, Miles Cunningham, and Bruce Price in their article, "The role of psychotic disorders in religious history considered," published in 2012 in *The Journal of Neuropsychiatry and Clinical Neuroscience* 24: 410-426.

When the priests and scribes who wrote the book of Genesis reached the end of Abraham's story, they included an anecdote that suggests why they went to the trouble of making up such an incredible tale. They write that Abraham gave the site where he had demonstrated his willingness to sacrifice Isaac a symbolic name: "Abraham called that place 'The Lord will Provide.' And, to this day it is said, 'On the mountain of the Lord it will be provided' (Genesis 22: 14)." That's a revealing anecdote, because it shows that the moral of the story was to emphasize the theological principle that those who fear God and who want to receive His favor must be willing to do whatever God commands them to do, even if they they know that act would be regarded as immoral by others in their community. In practical effect, this means that humans must be willing to do whatever it is they *think* God is commanding them to do because the individual involved has no independent way to verify that the command did indeed come from the supernatural realm rather than being something coughed up by mental illness or delusion. Another theological principle underscored in this story is that God has the power to intervene and change the course of human events, even to the extent of enabling a 100-year-old man and a 90-year-old woman to conceive a child. Both of those theological doctrines that first surfaced in the story of Abraham were adopted by the Christian and Islamic religions when they split off from Judaism.

The Visions of Moses

Moses was herding sheep in the vicinity of Mt. Sinai when he saw "a flame of fire coming out of a bush; and he looked, and the bush was blazing, yet it was not consumed (Exodus 3: 2)." The *Torah* doesn't give any details about the circumstances—if he was alone, if it was day or night, if he was doing something other than watching the sheep when it happened, or if he happened to be meditating at the time. It seems strange that Moses was not frightened when he saw this "strange sight". He moved closer to get a better look, and that's when he heard a voice that identified itself as the voice of the God of Abraham, the God of Isaac, and the God of Jacob. The voice of God ordered Moses to return to the land of Egypt, where he'd been born and raised, to carry out the God's goal of liberating the Hebrew tribes from the control of the Egyptian pharaoh (Exodus 3: 1-22). Moses was eighty years old when he saw this vision.

Forty years earlier he'd been forced to give up his life of privilege in the Egyptian court and to flee the country when he'd killed a man. When Moses was on the run, he encountered a tribe of Midian nomads that welcomed him to live with them. The tribe was led by a shaman/sheikh named Jethro. The two men formed a close bond. Moses married one of Jethro's daughters, and when the couple produced a child, Moses realized that he was "a foreigner in a foreign land (Exodus 2: 22)". The relationship between Moses and Jethro provides some clues about how and why Moses did some of the things he is said to have done. It also provides some clues about Moses's visionary experiences that we'll take up later as the story unfolds.

After seeing the vision of the burning bush, Moses followed God's command and returned to Egypt where he performed magic feats that convinced the pharaoh it would be prudent to let the Hebrew tribes leave the country. Moses led the tribes on a three-week journey that took them to the foot of Mt. Sinai, the same site where he'd seen the vision of the burning bush. The Hebrew tribes set up camp and waited for God to send a sign of what He wanted them to do next. On the third day of their encampment, Mt. Sinai was enshrouded by a thick cloud flashing with lightning and rumbling thunder (Exodus 19: 16-25). This was the omen the tribes had been waiting for, but now, faced with such an intimidating display, the tribal elders told Moses that the people were frightened, that they wanted him to go up the mountain alone to consult with God on their behalf and to bring down the messages he received: "Speak thou with us, and we will hear, but let not God speak with us, lest we die (Exodus 20: 20)."

Moses hiked up the slopes and entered into the dark clouds. There he encountered the same God who'd sent him the vision of the burning bush, the God who wanted to be known as *Yahweh asher Yahweh*. Moses conferred with Yahweh and then hiked back down to the Hebrew camp to convey God's instructions to the assembled tribes. This initial ascent of Mt. Sinai was the first of eight trips that Moses took to meet Yahweh at the summit. On one of those trips, God gave Moses two stone tablets inscribed with the Ten Commandments. Yahweh warned Moses that these were the commandments that the Hebrew people would have to obey, and He promised that if the tribes agreed to obey these commands, and if they also worshipped Him exclusive of all other gods, then He would designate them as His "Chosen People". To celebrate the new covenant, Moses built an altar, ordered young tribesmen to sacrifice some bulls, then took the blood of the sacrifice and splashed it over the altar. When he read the new covenant that Yahweh gave him to the assembled tribes, they responded with "All that the Lord has spoken we will do, and we will be obedient." Moses then cast the rest of the sacrificial blood out over the assembled crowd, saying "This is the blood of the covenant that the Lord has made with you in accordance with all these words (Exodus 24: 4-8)."

The tribes organized a feast to celebrate the new covenant. The Biblical account states that, during the Feast of the Covenant, Moses and seventy tribal elders had a mystical experience that involved them seeing visions of dark blue lights: "Then Moses and Aaron, Nadab, and Abihu, and seventy of the elders of Israel went up, and they saw the God of Israel. Under his feet there was something like a pavement of sapphire stone, very like the heavens for clearness (Exodus 24: 9-10)." While this passage might seem to suggest that Moses and the elders saw God, this would not be correct because we know from other passages in Exodus that God had appeared to Moses in a blast of fire and had warned him to let it be known that no human could see Him directly and survive such an encounter: "Go down and warn the people not to break through to the Lord to look; otherwise many of them will perish (Exodus 19: 21)". Moses also had to heed this warning himself:

> Moses said, "Show me your glory, I pray." And he [God] said, "I will make all my goodness pass before you, and will proclaim before you the name, 'The Lord', … [But] you cannot see my face, for no one shall see me and live." And the Lord continued, "See, there is a place by me where you shall stand on the rock, and while my glory passes by I will put you in a cleft of the rock, and I will cover you with my hand until I have passed by, and you shall see my back, but my face shall not be seen (Exodus 33: 17-20).

If we assume that Moses and the elders saw a vision of dark blue light during the Feast of the Covenant, clearly it would not have been a vision of God Himself. What was it that they did see? The authors of *The New Oxford Annotated Bible* interpret the meaning of Exodus 24: 10 to be that "The leaders did not see God directly; they saw only the lower part of the throne room—the sapphire pavement (firmament) above which the Lord was enthroned (p. 101)."

What's most interesting about this vision attributed to Moses, given that we're focused in this investigation on the content of actual visions seen by real people, is that the story suggests that Moses might have known how to use meditation to induce visions of light when he saw the vision of the burning bush. During the forty years Moses lived in the Midian tribe, he would have had ample opportunities to learn shamanic arts from his father-in-law, Jethro, a Midian shaman as well as a sheikh. We know from the Biblical account of Moses' return to Egypt that he had to perform many acts of magic to convince the pharaoh he had to release the Hebrew tribes (Exodus 7: 1-25). And the years that Moses spent living with the Midian tribes was the only opportunity he would have had to learn shamanic magic. But if Moses had been trained in the shamanic arts before he returned to Egypt, he would most likely have acquired those skills before he went out herding Jethro's sheep at the foot of Mt. Sinai where he saw the vision of the burning bush. If one of the shamanic arts that Jethro taught Moses was how to use meditative trance states to self-induce visions of light, including visions that looked "something like sapphire stones, like the very heaven for clearness", that suggests the possibility that Moses might have meditating just before he saw the vision of the burning bush. There is some credible evidence that suggests that might indeed have been the case.

Modern scholars suspect that Mt. Sinai was a Midian holy site long before it became identified with the Hebrew tribes (Kirsch, *Moses: A Life*, 1998, p. 135). One clue that points to this relationship is that when the Hebrew tribes camped at Mt. Sinai after escaping from Egypt, Jethro, the Midian shaman/

sheikh, visited the camp and officiated at some of the religious ceremonies. Scholars have even suggested that the name God used to identify Himself—the name *Yahweh asher Yahweh*—came from one of the gods the Midian tribes had been worshipping at the Mt. Sinai site long before the coming of the Hebrew tribes. These observations about the relationship of Moses and Jethro raise interesting questions about might have happened when Moses saw his vision of a burning bush. Perhaps it was not a coincidence that Moses led his sheep to the foot of Mt. Sinai: he might have chosen the site, not just because it offered good pasture, but also because he had an ulterior motive. Moses might have been planning to seek spiritual guidance from the god of Mt. Sinai about what he should be doing with his life now that he was eighty years old. It's not hard to conjure up a realistic scenario that could explain what happened. Suppose it was night, the sheep were asleep, and Moses took the opportunity to put himself in the kind of deep trance state he'd learned from Jethro. If he did induce an empty-mind trance in the dark of night, it's likely he would have seen a vision that was "something like a pavement of sapphire stone, very like the heavens for clearness", the same kind of vision that he saw much later when he and the elders of the Hebrew tribes were celebrating their new covenant with Yahweh (Exodus 24: 9-10). And if Moses kept pushing his meditative trance ever deeper, he might have pushed to the point of destabilizing the sleep rhythms oscillators that generate the visions of dark blue light, and, if so, that would trigger an eruption of the fiery light. This is a clearly a speculative hypothesis, but it offers an explanation that does not require any supernatural intervention to explain how and why Moses might have seen the vision of a fiery light engulfing a bush without burning its leaves.

There is also an alternative hypothesis. Given that the vision of the burning bush is said to have erupted spontaneously and given that the fire didn't burn the leaves of the bush it seemed to be engulfing, it's possible that what Moses experienced during this episode was the eruption of an epileptic seizure. In the Biblical account, it's said that Moses saw visions of fire that erupted spontaneously on more than one occasion—that's how Yahweh always chose to appear when Moses met with Him inside the dark cloud covering Mt. Sinai—and that suggests that the two clinical criteria used to make clinical diagnoses of epilepsy, namely, that there are "recurring" seizures that are "not being provoked", are both present in this case. But that's the only evidence in the Biblical record that points to Moses having some kind of epileptic disorder.

The Visions of Elijah

The prophet Elijah lived during the ninth century, BCE, long after the death of Moses. In the Hebrew scriptures, Elijah confronted King Ahab "because you have abandoned the commandments of the Lord and followed the Baals (1 Kings 8: 16-18)". He told the king that God was angry that Ahab built a temple to Baal to humor his wife, Queen Jezebel, and he warned that no rain would fall in the kingdom until the king repented and destroyed the temple. To provide a convincing demonstration of the power of Yahweh, Elijah issued a challenge to Ahab and Jezebel: he dared them to gather the priests of Baal for a public contest of miracle-making. During the contest, Elijah, with God's help, performed a series of miracles. He then challenged the priests of Baal to get their god to do something equally impressive. The priests of Baal were unable to do that. Elijah then called out to God, asking Him to hurl down a fire to destroy the buildings that surrounding the square, and that's what God did. As the assembled crowd watched this stand-off, they realized that what

Elijah had been telling them was true—that "The Lord indeed is God." Elijah commanded the crowd kill all the priests of Baal gathered in the square, and they did what he commanded. Queen Jezebel became enraged and convinced the king to send soldiers to capture Elijah and kill him. But Elijah had fled the capital to take refuge in a tiny cave situated high up on the slopes of Mt. Sinai.

One day, as Elijah was languishing alone in the cave, ruminating about what to do with his life, a disembodied voice rang out: "What are you doing here, Elijah? (1 Kings 19: 13)." The prophet recognized that this had to be the voice of a divine messenger, if not the voice of God himself. He began complaining about how badly things had turned out for him—about how he'd been rejected by the people he was trying to teach, even though he'd done everything God wanted him to do, and about how he was in despair because it seemed as if God had abandoned him. The voice ignored all of Elijah's complaints and commanded the prophet to step outside the cave to watch God pass by. As Elijah stepped out of the cave, a whirlwind began blowing so hard that it dislodged rocks from the slopes and broke them into pieces. Then the earth began to quake. When the strong winds and the earthquake suddenly ceased, a fire spread across the sky. Then the fire disappeared, and Elijah found himself enveloped by a "sheer silence" that made him feel afraid. He tried to hide himself by wrapping his face in his cloak. It was then that the voice spoke out once again: "Elijah, what are you doing here?" Elijah began repeating the same litany of complaints, but the voice ignored him and commanded him to make preparations to leave the cave and return to Damascus. The voice said God would be with him, that God would take revenge on his enemies, and that Elijah would succeed at convincing the Israelites to change their ways and to live lives of righteousness (1 Kings 19: 11-13).

The Stories of the Patriarchs: How They Came to Be

We've seen how the three patriarchs who are celebrated as the founders of the ancient Hebrew religion were all inspired by seeing their God appear to them in a vision of fire. The question we now have to ask is whether these stories about the visionary experiences of the patriarchs are credible enough to be included in an investigation of visionary experiences that have actually been seen by real people. During our review of the stories about Abraham, Moses, and Elijah we found that it was difficult, if not impossible, to fit their visionary experiences into any of the three scenarios that we identified earlier in our neurologically grounded, reverse-engineering analysis of light vision characteristics and the behaviors that cause them to occur. That suggests we need to tack in a different direction if we want to uncover clues that can help us answer the question of whether or not it's appropriate to include the visions attributed to Abraham, Moses, and Elijah as examples of veridical experiences. We can begin that inquiry by studying the circumstances in which these stories were originally composed.

The Judean Exiles and the Babylonian Captivity

In 720 BCE, the king of Assyria destroyed Samaria, the capital of the northern kingdom of Israel and forced some of the wealthy and powerful citizens to move to the Assyrian capital of Babylon and live there in exile. The southern Israeli kingdom of Judea escaped the destruction meted out to their northern neighbors by agreeing to become a vassal state of Assyria. In the wake of the

Assyria attack, many Israelis from Samaria fled south into Judea, significantly increasing the size and wealth of the Judean population. Judea soon rose to become one of the dominant powers in the region. But then Judea faced a new challenge: during the intervening years, the Assyrians had been decisively defeated by the armies of a king named Nabopolassar who adopted Babylon as the new capital for his Neo-Babylonian Empire. When King Nebopolassar died, his son, Nebuchadnezzer II, ascended to the throne and began plotting to expand his empire. The Hebrew kingdom of Judea became a pawn in the ensuing struggle between the Neo-Babylonians and the Egyptians to determine who would dominate the lands located between them. Nebuchadnezzer II eventually defeated Egypt. He then forced Judea to become a client kingdom. He put a loyal puppet ruler in charge, but many Judeans who secretly resented Neo-Babylonian influence began conspiring with Egyptians who wanted to organize a revolt against Babylonia.

When the news of this conspiracy reached Nebuchadnezzer II in 587 BCE, he attacked Jerusalem, the capital of Judea. The Babylonian army breached the walls of the city and went on a rampage: they killed many of the inhabitants, sacked and burned the Holy Temple, and destroyed most of the city. Nebuchadnezzer then imposed a new exile mandate: he forced the Judean king and many of the upper class to move to Babylon where it would be easier to keep a watch over them. The forced exile of the Judean elites that began in 587 BCE may have involved several waves of deportations. The Babylonian Captivity of the Judean elites lasted for forty-eight years—half a century—and it only ended in 539 BCE when Babylon was conquered by Cyrus the Great, founder of the First Persian Empire.

King Cyrus gave the Judean exiles permission to return to their native land. Some exiles chose to remain in Babylon, perhaps because they wanted to continue living in a rich, cosmopolitan environment where their lives would be settled, prosperous, and predictable, but many exiles did choose to return to what was now a desolate, poverty-stricken land. When they arrived back in Judea, the returnees quickly seized political and religious power and set up a new theocracy ruled by a king named Josiah and the high priests. One of the top priorities of the new rulers of Judea when they returned to power was to legitimize their right to rule. They launched the construction of a new Temple and assembled a group of priests and scribes to write a history of the Hebrew people that would prove that there was a straight line of ascent from legendary times when Judea and Israel were both part of a single United Monarchy ruled by divinely anointed kings like David and Solomon, all the way up to the reign of the newly installed ruler, King Josiah. The priests and scribes set about their assigned task, collecting all the old traditions they could find along with the recollections of the oldest Judeans, then working hard to integrate all that information. They used those resources to write five books that came to be known as the *Torah*. Those five books trace a genealogy that is said to have begun in ancient times with leadership of the early patriarchs like Abraham and Moses. It follows the migration of the Hebrew tribes into Canaan and celebrates the formation of the Kingdom of Israel, a United Monarchy ruled over by divinely anointed kings like Solomon and David. Then, as the priests and scribes had been instructed by their rulers, they traced a direct line of ascent from Solomon and David all the way up to King Josiah who'd assigned them to carry out this project. But some of those traditional stories have recently been contested.

Modern Scholarship and the Myth of the United Monarchy

In June, 2020, Ruth Margalit, a reporter working for *The New Yorker*, published a fascinating article, "In Search of King David's Lost Empire", in which she reported what she'd learned from interviews with three prominent Israeli scholars about their discoveries, based on their archeological research, regarding the traditional biblical stories. When Margalit interviewed Israel Finkelstein, Nadav Na'aman, and Ze'ev Herzog, she asked them if the rumors were true that many traditional stories in the *Torah* that purported to trace Jewish history and religion back to a United Monarchy and the lives of David and Solomon could not substantiated by evidence. The researchers told her that this was indeed what they'd discovered. Here are some of the most striking quotes reported by Margalit:

> There is no archeological record of Abraham, or Isaac, or Jacob. There is no Noah's Ark, nothing from Moses. Joshua did not bring down the walls of Jericho: they collapsed centuries earlier, perhaps in an earthquake (Na'aman, quoted in Margalit, Ibid., p. 42).

> There was a world war [in archeology departments] over whether Abraham was historical. Then there was a big debate about the conquest of Canaan. Today, there isn't. We know these things didn't happen (Finkelstein, Ibid., p. 44).

> Following 70 years of intensive excavations in the Land of Israel, archeologists have found out: The patriarchs' acts are legendary, the Israelites did not sojourn in Egypt or make an exodus, they did not conquer the land. Neither

is there any mention of the empire of David and Solomon, nor of the source of belief in the God of Israel. These facts have been known for years, but… no one wants to hear it (Herzog, Ibid., p. 46).

Finkelstein pointed out that the need to reconstruct a communal Jewish identity began long before the Babylonian Captivity. When the Assyrians destroyed the Northern Kingdom of Israel in 720 BCE, many Israelis escaped by moving south into Judea. There were so many immigrants that the population of Judea increased twelvefold. To integrate these newcomers, it became critically important to find a way to construct a communal Jewish identity that could gain the allegiance of all factions in the society. That same imperative surfaced again at the end of the Babylonian Captivity when the Judean exiles returned to Judea and confronted the task of reconstructing what had been lost. Finkelstein believes that the returnees had to conjure up a "dream of a past golden age—real or imagined—when their ancestors were settled securely in well-defined territories and enjoyed the divine promise of eternal peace and security (Finkelstein, in Margalit, p. 46)." The newly installed king, Josiah, succeeded in accomplishing this task, Finkelstein explains, by commissioning a team of priests and scribes to write a history that reconstructed a past golden age: "The core of the Bible was composed during his time as an attempt to lend his rule divine legitimacy by rewriting the stories of his ancestors—Moses, Joshua, and David." What implications do these observations published by contemporary archeologists have for our investigation of visionary experiences as they're described in the Hebrew *Torah*?

Visions of Fire and the Zoroastrian Influence

As the priests and their scribes strived to carry out their commission, they confronted a formidable challenge: they encountered confusions, contradictions, and gaps in the traditional stories that made it inevitable that they would have to do some improvising. The challenges would have been especially acute when they attempted to write the books of Genesis and Exodus in which they had to reconstruct what happened in the most ancient times. They wanted to tell stories about the lives of the two early patriarchs, Abraham and Moses, but how could they go about filling in all the missing pieces to come up with a coherent, convincing story about men who were said to have lived so long ago?

In the pages that follow, we'll weigh evidence supporting the hypothesis that the priests and scribes working for King Josiah were influenced, consciously or unconsciously, by ideas that they'd absorbed from the Zoroastrian culture that had surrounded them during the decades that they lived in exile. The Babylonians were immensely more powerful and more prosperous than the Judeans. How could the priests and scribes succeed in defending and propagating their traditional religious ideas when faced with the example of a culture with very different religious ideas that had been able to decisively defeat the Judeans. They would have wondered why their God let that happen. Why would He look on but not intervene while the Babylonian soldiers were destroying His Temple in Jerusalem and forcing His Chosen People into captivity?

Coping with this kind of conflict in which traditional values are threatened by the values of a new and more powerful culture would have been especially acute for the children of the Judean exiles. Born and raised Babylon, they would have grown up surrounded by a culture in which the models of behavior were different from the old traditions their parents wanted to instill. Those new ideas and new values being implemented all around them would be likely to appeal to some of those young Judean exiles because they could see that the new ideas and new values of the foreign culture were more effective at producing the kinds of outcomes that those young Judeans hoped to achieve in their lives. This kind of cultural crisis is the subject of Weston La Barre's book, *The Ghost Dance: The Origins of Religion* (1970). La Barre, an anthropologist with psychoanalytic training, describes the kind of dilemma faced by the young Judeans who were being buffeted by an ongoing cultural crisis. In that situation, La Barre suggests, young people in the traditional culture have to ask themselves, "Shall the models for my behavior be the old ambivalently loved persons of my tribe?—or the new ambivalently hated persons of a more powerful alien tribe? (p. 338)."

La Barre's work suggests that, in a situation like that faced by the Judean exiles in Babylon, it would not only be understandable but even likely that some of the values of the Babylonian culture would begin to subtly migrate into the subconscious minds of the exiles. When King Josiah commissioned the Judean priests and scribes to write a new, comprehensive genealogy of the Hebrew people, it would not be surprising if those writers were to incorporate some of the Zoroastrian ideas they'd learned during the Babylonian Captivity. And, indeed, it does appear that some ideas from the Zoroastrian religion of Babylon were incorporated into the books of the Genesis and Exodus. This is especially true for the stories of Abraham and Moses. Here are some ideas that scholars trace to Zoroastrian origins:

1. There is only one God, and that supreme God lives in a world of Light.
2. God is continually striving to win a cosmic struggle between the forces of Light and Good and the forces of Dark and Evil.

3. Each human being has to choose which side to support: the forces of Light and Good, or the forces of Darkness and Evil, and each human soul, after death, has to face a Day of Judgment. For the Zoroastrian, this moment came when it was time to cross a bridge called *Cintuuant* and to find out if the soul's fate was to fall into the hellish reservoir of molten metal below or to make it across and into a paradise of light.

4. God created Fire in his own likeness and gave Fire to humans as a symbol of His presence, so if He manifests to humans, He manifests as Fire.

The idea that the Hebrew God, Yahweh, always manifests in a vision of fire appears again and again in the Hebrew Scriptures. All of the patriarchs—Abraham, Moses, and Elijah—are said to have seen God appearing spontaneously in a vision of fire to deliver some message or command. But none of those traditional stories mention what the patriarchs were doing to induce their visions of fire; instead, the visions are described as having been initiated by God as the preliminary to issuing a divine command or reassurance. The Judean priests and scribes needed a convincing way to demonstrate to their readers that the patriarchs had been chosen by God to become the founders of the Hebrew religion and the progenitors of a new, divinely inspired kingdom. It would appear, then, that they portrayed the Hebrew God manifesting in a manner similar to the Zoroastrian god, *Ahura Mazda,* who manifested his presence in a vision of fire.

The credibility of this hypothesis can be tested by comparing the visions of the Patriarchs that described as having broken out spontaneously with the experiences of the prophet Ezekiel. Ezekiel, who lived much of his life as a Judean exile living in Babylonia, would have been a near contemporary of the Judean priests and scribes who wrote the early books of the Hebrew

Bible. Many scholars believe that Ezekiel wrote most of the book that appears in the Bible under his name, so to come up with a credible story about Ezekiel and his visions, the priests and scribes who composed the first books of the Hebrew *Torah* did not have to resort to creative fiction. Ezekiel reported that he saw visions of fiery lights, like the early patriarchs, but his visions, unlike theirs, describe a wide range of experiences that are consistent with what we now know about the kinds of light visions that appear during a meditation-induced sequence.

The Visions of Ezekiel: A Case for Comparison

Ezekiel was a priest living in Jerusalem when Nebuchadnezzar II and the Neo-Babylonian armies first conquered the city of Jerusalem in 597 BCE. Nebuchadnezzar forced Jehoiachin, the king of Judea, and members of the Judean elite, including Ezekiel, to move to Babylonia. He installed a puppet king to rule over Judea. After Ezekiel was deported to Babylon, he began issuing prophecies: he warned his compatriots that God was displeased with them because they'd strayed from the path of righteousness—because they tolerated foreign ways, desecrated some of the time-honored rituals that had been celebrated in the Temple, and allowed injustice to flourish in the land. It was the impieties of the Hebrew people that led to the tragedy they'd just experienced at the hands of the Assyrians, Ezekiel claimed, and he warned the people of Israel and Judea that if they did not repent and change their ways, they should expect that an even worse fate would befall them in the future. No one at the time anticipated just how prescient Ezekiel's prophecies would turn out to be.

In 586 BCE, Nebuchadnezzer learned that the puppet king he'd installed in Judea was plotting with Egyptians to escape from Babylonian control. He quickly mobilized an army and attacked Jerusalem a second time. During this invasion, the Neo-Babylonian armies raged through the city, killing many inhabitants, sacking and pillaging, and destroying the Holy Temple. They then forced more Judeans to move to Babylon to join the earlier wave of exiles. After the destruction of Jerusalem, Ezekiel's prophecies that the Hebrew kingdoms would face an imminent catastrophe if they were not able to align their lives with righteousness now seemed prescient and divinely-inspired.

It was in 592 BCE, five years after Ezekiel was forced into exile and two years before Nebuchadnezzer's second attack, that the prophet was overwhelmed by the intrusion of an intense visionary experience while he was praying on the banks of the Chebar River in Babylon. The visions were so powerful that they caused him to lose consciousness and fall to the ground. When he woke up, he was "stunned" and couldn't speak for seven days (Ezekiel 1: 3-12).

There's a stark contrast between Ezekiel's descriptions of what he saw, when he saw it, and what he was doing both before and after the visions appeared, compared with the cursory descriptions of the visions attributed to Abraham, Moses, and Elijah, that are said to have erupted spontaneously when God wanted to attract attention and issue a command. Ezekiel also saw a vision of fire, like the Patriarchs, but his vision didn't erupt spontaneously:

As I looked, a stormy wind came out of the north: a great cloud with brightness around it and fire flashing forth continually, and in the middle of the fire, something like gleaming amber. In the middle of it was something like four living creatures. / In the middle of the living creatures, there was something that look like burning coals of fire, like torches moving to and fro among the living creatures; the fire was bright, and lightning issued forth from the fire. The living creatures darted to and fro, like a flash of lightning (1: 13; 10: 4).

If this were the only vision seen by Ezekiel—and if, in his case, the fiery light suddenly flared forth without any warning, as it always did with the Patriarchs—then there would be no significant difference between his visions and those attributed to Abraham, Moses, and Elijah. But Ezekiel also describes seeing many other kinds of light visions, including this vision that we discussed earlier that clearly refers to his having seen visions of green light rings, the kind of vision that appears first in a meditation-induced sequence:

> I saw a wheel on the earth beside the living creatures, one for each of the four of them. As for the appearance of the wheels and their construction: their appearance was like the gleaming of beryl; and the four had the same form, their construction being something like a wheel within a wheel. When they moved, they moved in any of the four directions without veering as they moved. Their rims were tall and awesome, for the rims of all four were full of eyes all around. When the living creatures moved, the wheels moved beside them… for the spirit of the living creatures was in the wheels (Ezekiel 1: 15). / … When they moved, I heard the sound of their wings like the sound of mighty waters, like the thunder of the Almighty, a sound of tumult like the sound of an army (Ezekiel 1: 24).

This description of green light-rings provides clear evidence that Ezekiel knew how to use empty-mind meditation to induce visions of clear light—and that suggests he must have inducing a deep meditative trance as he was sitting on the banks of the Chedar River. We know, given our neurology grounded, reverse-engineering analysis of meditation-induced light visions that this vision of green light rings would have been the *first* vision Ezekiel saw, assuming that he is reporting what happened during the course of a single vision; however, in his account, the wheel visions don't appear until he's halfway through his account. That detail suggests the Biblical account of his vision on the banks of the Chedar River is not a report of what happened during a single vision but rather an amalgamation of images Ezekiel saw during many different visionary experiences.

In addition to seeing the visions of green light-rings, Ezekiel also saw visions of light sensations that had rounded shapes "something like a dome", translucent surfaces that were "shining like crystal", and "sapphire" colors. This is obviously a very ambiguous description, hence one that's difficult to decipher. Ezekiel seems to be confused about what it is that he's really seeing and how to describe what he's seeing in words his contemporaries can understand. That's why he keeps using the phrase, "something like". Here's his description of a vision that clearly refers to him seeing "something" that looks like "sapphire":

Over the heads of the living creatures there was something like a dome, shining like crystal, spread out about their heads… And above the dome over their heads there was something like a throne, in appearance like sapphire, and seated above the likeness of a throne was something which seemed like a human form… and there was a splendor all around. Like the bow in a cloud on a rainy day, such was the appearance of the splendor all around. This was the appearance of the glory of the Lord… When I saw it, I fell on my face (1: 22-28).

Ezekiel's descriptions of what he saw during this elaborate visionary experience contain many details that enable us to identify parallels between what he's describing and what we know now about the kinds of light visions that appear in a predictable meditation-induced sequence. If he saw visions of green light-rings (the kinds of vision generated when a deep meditative trance activates stage 2 sleep rhythms), and if he also saw visions of a dark blue "sapphire" light shining like "crystal"(the kind of vision generated when a deep meditative trance activates stage 3 sleep rhythms), then we have good evidence that it was his meditative prowess that eventually led to the eruption of a temporolimbic seizure and the visions of lightning, burning coals, and torches moving to and fro.

When we compare Ezekiel's visions with the descriptions of visions of fire allegedly seen by Abraham, Moses, and Elijah, the differences are stark and revealing. Ezekiel is the only one whose visions can be matched with what we now know about what causes visions of fiery light to erupt.

PART III.

Visions as a Legacy of Child Trauma

CHAPTER 11

Trauma and Visions: Buddha, Muhammed, and Jesus

The Life Trajectories of Three Founders

As I studied the traditional sources to trace the lives of mystic seers who said they saw visions of fiery light, I was surprised by how often I would come across striking similarities in their life trajectories. There would often be evidence that the future mystic experienced serious trauma as an infant or young child. Then their stories would skip the intervening years of adolescence and young adulthood and pick up again at midlife when they were faced with a major life crisis. Sometimes it was an external misfortune—like a serious, life-changing injury—or it could be some internal disturbance like a sudden, inexplicable welling-up of feelings of despair or depression. How the founders responded to the challenge of that major life stressor turned out to be the most important factor for explaining why they ended up seeing visions of fiery light. The future mystics chose to respond to their life crises by relying on the dissociative coping strategies that they were forced to learn to survive a traumatic childhood.

If caregivers are unable to provide the kind of reliable and effective nurturing that helps ameliorate pain and distress, leaving their children in a state of high arousal, the body's autonomic nervous system will intervene to restore homeostasis by forcing a parasympathetic collapse. We discussed those autonomic mechanisms earlier in relation to rituals of extreme stimulus overload, but a similar process has been observed in young children. When this happens, young children enter a psychological state called "conservation-withdrawal," a precursor of adult dissociation. We'll study this phenomenon of infant conservation/withdrawal and its relationship to adult dissociation in more detail in Chapter 13.

What's important to keep in mind now, as we begin our review of the lives of these three founders of world religions, is that adults who have legacies of child trauma often learn to rely on dissociation as a primary coping strategy when they are confronted by major life challenges. The elements of their dissociative coping strategies include choosing to isolate themselves from other people, adopting extreme ascetic regimens designed to suppress the unruly urges of their minds and bodies, and immersing themselves in intense meditation sessions to pray for spiritual guidance from some supernatural source they consider to be more trustworthy than fellow humans. Those meditation vigils often extend late into the night, night after night. When the seekers accumulate sleep deficits, this causes their cortical neurons to become abnormally excitable, a condition that makes it easier to trigger meditation-induced seizures. The hyperexcitability of cortical neurons can also be affected by depression, a condition which is often present in seekers who choose to retreat on solitary spiritual quests. These considerations will all become relevant in our discussion of three founders whose lives and visions we're about to examine. All three were feeling depressed or uncertain about their futures when they decided to go on a solitary spiritual quest; all of them adopted rigorous ascetic regimens; and all of them employed dissociative strategies like spending long hours in late-night prayer or meditation vigils that led to the accumulation of substantial sleep deficits.

If seekers see a vision of fiery light erupt during their prayer or meditation vigils, the emotional ecstasy that accompanies a limbic seizure helps erase the feelings of emptiness and loss of meaning that initially led them to isolate themselves on a spiritual retreat to seek guidance from a supernatural entity. In the wake of that kind of vision, the seers typically experience the emergence of the distinctive cluster of symptoms associated with the temporal lobe behavior syndrome—hyper-emotionality, hyper-religiosity, hypergraphia, and hyposexuality. Given the convergence of all these powerful experiences, it is eminently understandable that these mystic seers would become convinced that their visions could only have come from God or some other supernatural entity and that the visions were a reward for their dedication and purity of purpose.

Now it's time to take a closer look at some individual cases to see if you agree that the life trajectories of mystic seers often share a common pattern. I'll begin by focusing on the lives of three founders of new religions that ended up spreading worldwide—on the lives of Gautama the Buddha, the Prophet Muhammed, and Jesus of Nazareth. As you read these life stories, look for evidence you consider relevant for determining if each man's life trajectory fits into a common pattern that includes:

1. Traumatic childhood experiences;
2. A major life stressor that intrudes at midlife;
3. Self-isolation to seek guidance from a source more trustworthy than humans;
4. Meditation or prayer vigils that extend late at night, night after night;

5. Seeing a vision of fiery light erupt; and,
6. Experiencing the emergence of a temporal lobe behavior syndrome.

Let me say at the outset that, for me, these men are personal heroes. In what follows, I am not trying to undermine their ideas or their contributions to the welfare of their fellow humans. The focus in this investigation is to discover as much as we can, based on the paltry information available in traditional sources, about what was happening in the lives of those seers that led them to see visions, about what they saw during those visions, and about how seeing the visions transformed their lives. Please keep that qualification in mind as you read on.

Gautama the Buddha

When Gautama was born, his mother died. The next time Gautama's name surfaces in the traditional sources, he's twenty-nine years old and said to be living a sheltered life in a wealthy family. His father was determined to spare his son from learning about the desperate lives that led many less fortunate people to early deaths, but whatever illusions Gautama had about the human condition were shattered one day when his carriage rolled past an old man in a skeletal condition hobbling along the road. Gautama was shocked to realize that human life could ever become so desperate and so close to death. He was flooded by an upwelling of despair that came from somewhere inside him. When that deep depression did not lift, he decided to take desperate measures: he abandoned his wife and child, gave up the privileged life of his wealthy family, and became a solitary "renunciate". This path is prescribed in the Hindu *Upanishads* for those who become desperate to find *moksha*, "release", from the karmic burdens that beset them.

Gautama retreated into the forest, lived by himself, and practiced a regimen of extreme austerities. After seven years of uncompromising asceticism, Gautama realized that this strategy was not working. Not only had he not achieved release; the ascetic practices almost ruined his health. Burdened by an even greater sense of despair than what first led him into the forest, he hiked to the edge of a small village, sat beneath a shade tree, and vowed to remain in place, meditating continuously, until he either died or achieved his goal.

In the *Majjhima-Nikaya*, an important text in the Buddhist Pali Canon that is said to preserve the earliest written accounts of the Buddha's life and teachings, Gautama is reported to have told his followers that during that first night of continuous meditation he saw many "limited light-manifestations" that lasted throughout the night (128.3.161). Then, just before dawn, his visions suddenly changed: the "Divine Eye opened [*Caksus uppada*]", flooding his consciousness with "boundless light-manifestations" and "boundless material shapes" that kept going "for a whole night and a whole day". In the *Samyuda Nikaya*, another early text preserved in the Pali Canon, Gautama gives a similar description of that culminating vision that reveals how it affected him intellectually and emotionally:

> *Caksus uppada! Caksus uppada!* Coming to be! Coming to be! At the thought, there arose in me, brethren, "Eye," there arose in me knowledge, insight, penetrating wisdom; a radiant light arose (*Samyuda Nikaya* 12, 1, 10, Gonda, 1963, p. 306).

Gautama testified that seeing this vision extinguished all of his karmic entanglements "like the blowing out of a candle flame", leaving him in a state of ecstasy he called *nirvana*. This

"Enlightenment" transformed Gautama from just another spiritual seeker into "Buddha, the Awakened One".

Given his familiarity with the Hindu *Upanishads*, Gautama would have known that he'd just seen the vision of the "Abounding Brahma-Light", considered to be the ultimate vision in the Hindu mystical tradition. But he was surprised to see the "Abounding Brahma-Light" manifest without having been preceded by the penultimate vision that the sacred texts described as the *atman*, a spiritual "self" or "person" said to reside in the human body until the moment of Realization. The *atman* is described in the Upanishads as a substantial figure that has a bulbous shape like a "female uvula" or like a "human thumb". Gautama did not see any evidence of an *atman* that would match what he expected to see; he saw only the serial flashes of the "boundless light-manifestations" that were wholly devoid of any substantial imagery. The Buddha would build on this insight gleaned from that initial visionary experience when he formulated a new doctrine called *an-atman*, or "no-self"—that a human self has only apparitional reality.

Buddha, The Awakened One, shared his story with some of the hermits who'd been living near him in the forest practicing the same kinds of ascetic regimens that he'd been using. When he told them about seeing the "Divine Eye open" and about the joy and insight that vision brought him, the hermits became the Buddha's first followers. Soon rumors about this new teacher spread to the local villages and beyond. People started flocking in large numbers to hear the Buddha teach about what he'd learned and about what they could do themselves to make progress toward attaining Enlightenment. Eventually the Buddha and his followers organized communities called *sanghas* where those who wanted to take up the lifestyle of a celibate monk could dedicate themselves to the practice of meditation with the goal of Enlightenment. Some monks became the missionaries and traveled to India, Tibet, China, and Japan where they established new monasteries for monks and new temples for Buddhist worshippers.

Before we leave the story of Gautama the Buddha, I want to analyze what it was that he most likely saw when he watched the "limited light-manifestations" that continued throughout the night leading up to his Enlightenment. The books of the Pali Canon that purport to preserve the Buddha's early sayings do not provide any details about those preliminary light visions, but we can infer, based on our neurologically grounded, reverse-engineering analysis of light vision characteristics, that what the Buddha saw were visions of green light-rings followed by visions of dark blue clouds. That inference is supported by evidence that is circumstantial but also credible: in Buddhist works of religious art that incorporate colors, there are many examples where the artists chose to depict the Buddha using the same green and dark blue colors that appear in the visions of light induced by meditation. The paintings that decorate the walls of the many Buddhist caves that line the ancient Silk Road provide an excellent example of this phenomenon: the artists make dramatic use of the distinctive green and dark blue colors that appear during meditation to signal who it is that they want to portray in a painting, what that person is reputed to have seen, and how the person now lives in an divine otherworld surrounded by green and dark blue light. Sometimes the central figure is The Buddha himself wearing a robe decorated with green and dark blue and floating in a sky painted with those same colors. Sometimes there's also a blue halo inserted behind the Buddha's head or his curly hair is blue. There are also many statues of the Buddha, carved in stone or molded with plaster, and on most of those statues it is still possible to make out traces of dark blue paint that once decorated the Buddha's curls. Many of the cave paintings also include images of followers of the Buddha who attained Enlightenment themselves by following the example of their leader. These followers, known as Bodhisattvas, wear robes with the same green and dark blue colors, and, like The Buddha himself, they're often depicted floating in a mist of green and dark blue colors.

Evidence that the Buddha saw green light-rings and dark blue clouds is also found in the Tibetan Buddhist meditation texts that were written long after the texts that compose the Pali Canon. In Naropa's *Epitome of the Six Yogas*, the visions of light that appear first during a meditation session are said to be visions of "fiery effulgences" shaped like "four wheels". Other Tibetan texts describe meditators seeing visions of "the five halo-like signs" or visions of the "lamp of pristine absolute space… [that looks] like the eye of peacock feather".

In the Theravadan sect of Buddhism, the teachings about meditation and visions of inner light are very different from the Tibetan Vajrayana tradition in which meditation-induced light visions are considered to be a vehicle of spiritual ascent. The Theravadan tradition focuses on the Buddha's teaching that all earthly phenomena are mere apparitions, that the primordial radiance of the universe is empty of all substance and is always undergoing change. Theravadan meditators are advised to regard all earthly phenomena as being "impermanent, painful, and not-self", and that diagnosis also applies to meditation-induced visions of clear light. But in this Buddhist tradition there is also a recognition that meditation-induced visions of light can serve some useful purposes but only in the special circumstance where novice meditators are trying to learn how to concentrate their attention. This exception for novice meditators was proclaimed by an early Buddhist teacher named Buddhaghosa who wrote the book, *Visshuddhimagga*, "*The Path of Purification* (Nanamoli, 1991)", that became one of the foundational documents for the Theravadan religious tradition. For novice meditators who are still trying to learn how to focus their attention inwardly and how to fixate on the dark, empty visual field, Buddhaghosa suggests that they watch closely to see if visions of light begin to flow spontaneously. He tells the novice meditators that they can expect to see "formations of light" that get "perpetually renewed" but that are also "short-lived like dew-drops at sunrise... like a bubble on water... without a core, like a conjuring trick... like a mirage (Nanamoli, pp. 655-656)." Once the novice meditators begin to see those "formations of light", they're said to have achieved a "beginner's insight". But then, in order to continuing making progress toward attaining the Buddhist goal of Ultimate Insight, meditators are instructed to not let their attention get distracted by visions of inner light that might intrude into consciousness. They are told to treat those visions of light like all of the apparitional thoughts, images, and sensations that are inherently "impermanent, painful, and not-self". Buddhaghosa warns meditators to heed this advice because otherwise they might find it to be too easy for them to become attached to the feelings of emotional serenity that often accompany the appearance of meditation-induced light visions. Or even worse, some meditators might be seduced into thinking that, by virtue of their having seen visions of inner light, they've already achieved the goal of Ultimate Insight.

While there are clearly some very dramatic differences in the types of meditation practices used by Theravadan Buddhists and Tibetan Buddhists, the ultimate goal of Enlightenment is envisioned as being virtually the same by both traditions: the ultimate goal is to recognize that all phenomena perceived by humans, including mental experiences, are ultimately illusory. So while it's true that Buddhists in the Tibetan Vajrayana tradition emphasize meditation-induced visions as the most effective vehicle for attaining Enlightenment while the Theravadan Buddhists proscribe the use of those very same visions, it turns out, in the end, that both of these traditions describe Ultimate Reality as a formless, ever-changing radiance. That state of mind that the Theravadans call "Insight" is indistinguishable from the state of mind that Tibetan Vajrayana Buddhists achieve when they see the visions of fiery lightning and become "Wielders of the Thunderbolt" who've learned that "When illusory forms contact the Formless… / … one gains understanding of the Pervading and the Real, / And mastery of the Very Bright and of the Enduring, and of the Siddhi of Transformation (Naropa, *The Epitome of the Six Yogas*, "The Yoga of Clear Light," 4: 35-36)."

*　　*　　*

The life of the Buddha provides a good example of a life trajectory that follows the path I described at the outset of this chapter. Is there evidence of a legacy of child trauma? Yes. His mother died in childbirth. Is there evidence of a midlife crisis? Yes. At the age of twenty-nine, he felt crushed by feelings of despair about the meaning of life. The sudden onset of a deep depression suggests that, in addition to the traumatic effects associated with the death of his mother during childbirth, he most likely suffered other traumas during his early childhood. Did Gautama choose to cope with his feelings of depression and hopelessness by relying on a dissociative coping strategy? Yes. He totally abandoned his former life, choosing to become a hermit, and for the next seven years he inflicted his body and mind with extreme austerities that eventually broke his health. Did he engage in prolonged meditation vigils that caused him to lose sleep? Yes, probably many such vigils although the traditional sources focus on the night when he saw visions of "limited light-manifestations" that led to him seeing the "opening of the Divine Eye". It's also relevant that on that night, Gautama was experiencing feelings of despair and suffering from ill health. Did he see a vision of fiery light? Yes. He saw a vision of "boundless light-manifestations". In the wake of this visionary experience, did the Buddha develop symptoms that would be consistent with the emergence of a temporal lobe behavior syndrome? Yes. His mood shifted from depression to elation. He felt a sense of enhanced personal destiny that motivated him to begin preaching about what he'd learned from his visionary experiences. He succeeded in organizing ever-larger communities of disciples who followed his teachings and who helped him found a new Buddhist religion to preserve their leader's spiritual insights for future generations.

The Prophet Muhammed

Muhammed's father died shortly before his birth. His mother was too ill to nurse him, so the newborn was entrusted to the care of a Bedouin wet nurse named Halima. She became his surrogate mother. His biological mother, whom he seldom saw, died when he was six years old. Another serious trauma struck Muhammed when he was only eight years old. According to Ibn Ishaq, one of the first and most important biographers of Muhammed's life, the young boy and his Bedouin companion were guarding a herd of sheep in fields near their encampment when Muhammed suddenly collapsed and lost consciousness. The other boy ran to summon Halima. By the time they returned, Muhammed had recovered consciousness and he told them this about what he'd experienced during the collapse:

> While I was with a brother of mine behind our tents shepherding our lambs, two men in white raiment came up to me with a godly basin full of snow. They then seized me and opened up my belly, extracted my heart and split

it; then they extracted a black drop from it and threw it away; then they washed my heart and belly with that snow until they had thoroughly cleaned them (Ishaq, 1955, pp. 72-73, quoted in Peters, 1994, *Muhammed and the Origins of Islam*, pp. 103-104).

When the elders of the Bedouin tribe heard about this incident, they were worried that it might be an early warning sign of impending epilepsy and that the tribe would be blamed if the boy were to start experiencing seizures while he was living with them. They ordered him to be returned to his surviving relatives in Mecca. That meant Muhammed had to leave behind the only mother and the only home he'd ever known. He was taken in by his paternal grandfather. The two of them soon became very attached, but then, only a year later—when Muhammed was nine years old—his grandfather died. Muhammed had to move again, this time joining the family of an uncle, a prosperous businessman in Mecca who sponsored merchant caravans. As a young man, Muhammed began traveling with some of his uncle's caravans, working first as an apprentice, but then, as he gained experience, taking on more and more responsibility. Eventually he came to be recognized by fellow Meccans as a reputable merchant in his own right. When Muhammed was twenty-five years old, he was approached by a wealthy widow and businesswoman named Khadija who presented him with an offer of marriage. He accepted, and that was the start of a happy and prosperous marriage.

When Muhammed was forty years old, he began to feel a pervasive sense of discontent. He felt he was losing the sense of purpose that had shaped his life. He became so concerned that he decided to put his work aside in order to go on a solitary retreat where he would be able to pray for spiritual guidance without any interruptions. He packed supplies and traveled to a small cave located high up on the side of a mountain not far from Mecca.

That was the first of what would turn out to be a series of retreats. During these retreats to the mountain cave, Muhammed spent a lot of time immersed in prayer. Much later, after he'd become an important religious leader, his followers often asked him for details about how he prayed. He told them that if they'd seen him while he was praying, they would think that he'd fallen asleep—but that was definitely not the case, he told them: "My eyes are closed, but my heart is awake." This comment suggests that Muhammed knew how to empty his mind of distracting content and to focus his attention on the dark, empty visual field as he waited for some signal to arrive from the supernatural world.

It was during one of these solitary retreats while he was immersed in prayer that Muhammed began to see visions. Much later in his life he confided in A'isha, his youngest wife that "The beginning of the revelation was the True Vision that came like the break of day (*falaq as-subh*) every time he saw it, there being no obscurity." A'isha passed this insight on to a man named Bukhari who was writing a book that collected all the "sayings (*hadith*)" that were being attributed to Muhammed (*Bukhari's Hadith*, I: 3; Notes 171-173). The Arabic phrase that Muhammed used when he was talking with A'isha—the phrase, *falaq as-subh*—has a special meaning for Arabs who live in the desert. According to Maxime Rodinson, a French historian and sociologist who wrote an influential biography of Muhammed, for desert-dwellers this phrase connotes "the abrupt rendering asunder of the darkness of those lands where there is no twilight or dusk by the rising of the sun (Rodinson M, *Muhammed*, 1961, p. 70)." In other words, A'isha's report describing Muhammed's first vision—his "True Vision"—points to a bright flash of light that looked to him like the sun suddenly bursting above a dark horizon. That's the kind of vision that fits within our definition of a fiery light.

A'isha also told Bukhari that after Muhammed saw his first vision, "then the love of seclusion was bestowed on him (Notes

171-173)". He began taking more solitary retreats, and during his prayer vigils in that isolated cave he saw two more visions. His descriptions of those visions are very ambiguous, making them difficult to decipher. Here's his description of those two visions that he included in the *Holy Quran* in Surah 53:

> He was taught by one mighty in power, one possessed of wisdom, and he appeared while in the highest part of the horizon. Then he approached and came closer, and was at a distance of two bow lengths or closer. And he inspired his servant with what he inspired him. His heart did not falsify what he saw. Will you then dispute with him over what he saw? Indeed, he saw him descending a second time, near the lote tree that marks the boundary. Near it is the garden of the dwelling, and behold, the lote tree was shrouded in the deepest shrouding. His sight never swerved, nor did it exceed its limits. Indeed, he saw the signs of his Lord, the Greatest (Surah 53: 1-18, in Peters, 1994, p. 142).

What is Muhammed trying to communicate when he says he says he saw the "one mighty in power, one possessed of wisdom" on a distant horizon and that he saw that figure approach to within several feet of his face? It's not clear what he's describing here in the first of these two visions that constitute Surah 53, but it's important to notice what he does *not* say: he does not say he saw an angel with a human-like body. There is no mention of the angelic messenger named Gabriel. That name that did not surface until long after the verses in Surah 53 were committed to writing; it wasn't until after Muhammed had been recognized as the Prophet of Allah and after he and his followers were forced to move from Mecca to Medina to escape persecution that the name, Gabriel, began to be generally used for the divine messenger described in Surah 53.

In the second vision that Muhammed describes in Surah 53, he mentions a detail that might offer an important clue about the nature of his visionary experience. He says he saw the "one mighty in power, one possessed of wisdom" appear once again, and in this second appearance the spirit "descended" to a location that was "Near the lote tree that marks the Boundary / Near it is the Garden of the Abode (53: 13-18)." This phrase led me to search online for photographs of mature, healthy lote trees in Arabia. What I discovered turned out to be quite striking: mature lote trees have symmetrical, disk-shaped bowers with leaves that have the same green colors as the green light-rings that appear first in a meditation-induced sequence. That suggests that when Muhammed said he saw a vision that looked like a "lote tree", he might well have been referring to something that looked like a disk of green light. It's important to note that Muhammed said he couldn't be sure of what it was he was seeing because the image was "shrouded in the deepest shrouding". Given these parallels, Muhammed's description of seeing green, disk-shaped images receding away from him and then abruptly disappearing when they reached the same location in the visual field would be consistent with his having meditation-induced visions of green light-rings in which the centers of the light-rings fill in with green light to become green disks just before they vanish.

Given what I learned about Muhammed's method of prayer from his own testimony, it is reasonable to infer that Muhammed knew how to use meditation to induce deep trance states. And given his description in Surah 53 of seeing a vision that looked like the green bower of a "lote tree" but was so "enshrouded" that he couldn't make out the details, it is reasonable to infer that Muhammed saw meditation-induced visions of green light-rings and watched as those rings filled with green light to become disks just before they all disappeared in a similar manner. These observations are important because they raise the question of whether Muhammed was using meditation to induce visions of light before the original eruption of the "True Vision" of fiery light. Or did that "True Vision" erupt spontaneously, without having been preceded by any other visions, in which case that might raise the specter of his having experienced an epileptic seizure? That second alternative would resonate with the traditional accounts of Muhammed having lost consciousness and collapsed when he was still very young, an episode that suggests he might have had some hidden epileptic vulnerability. And A'isha told Bukhari that the "True Vision" looked the same "every time he was it ". But there is no evidence that he had seizures during his adult life other than those occasions when the "True Vision" appeared, and that vision might have occurred, not as a spontaneous eruption, but as a vision induced by his immersion in meditative prayer vigils where it looked like he was asleep. There is not enough information for us to solve this issue. But there is yet another vision that we need to bring into the equation.

Muhammed continued to go on his spiritual retreats long after he saw the visions described in Surah 53, and on one of these vigils he was startled and frightened by hearing a disembodied voice suddenly speak out: "You are the Messenger of God," the voice said. "I had been standing," he would later tell his followers when he told them about this experience, "but I fell to my knees and crawled away with my shoulders trembling (*Bukhari's Hadith*, Note 173)." Hearing this disembodied voice struck him as a very different experience from seeing visions: it made him feel afraid that he might be losing his mind or that he was about to be possessed by desert spirits that the Arab tribes called *jinns*. When this happened, he quickly got back up on his feet, packed his bags, and left the cave. A'isha told Bukhari what happened next: "Allah's Apostle returned with the Inspiration and with his heart beating severely. He went to Khadija and said, 'Cover me! Cover me!' She covered him till his fear was over, and, after that, he told her everything that had happened and said, 'I fear that something may happen to me' (*Bukhari's Hadith*, Vol. 1, Book 1, No. 3)." Khadija comforted Muhammed and suggested that the two of them should visit to one of her uncles, a man named Waraqa who had a reputation for being knowledgeable about mystical phenomena.

Waraqa reassured Muhammed that he was not being possessed by *jinns* and that, moreover, he should regard what just happened to him as an omen. Waraqa told Muhammed that it appeared as if he were about to receive the kind of visions that had been given to the Hebrew patriarch, Moses, when Moses was most in need of God's guidance. There is a story in the Hebrew Torah that also appears in the Muslim *Quran* about divine messenger who came to Moses's aid. Waraqa advised Muhammed to return to the cave and to pray for instructions from "the same one who keeps the secrets Allah sent to Moses (*Hadith* 1:1:1)".

Muhammed followed Waraqa's advice: he kept going back to the cave and praying for answers, but nothing more happened for a relatively long time. He became discouraged and depressed, but he didn't give up. Then one day he heard the voice speak out again. This time the voice identified itself as the voice of Allah, the Supreme God, the God of Abraham and Moses, the God worshipped by both the Hebrews and the Christians. Allah told Muhammed that He was now prepared to send humans his third and final set of commandments, and He announced He'd chosen Muhammed to be His Chosen Prophet. Allah ordered Muhammed to begin receiving messages that would be implanted in his mind and to then recite them out loud in order to make sure he would remember them.

The two Arabic words that Muhammed used to describe how he received these messages from Allah are *wahy* and *ahwa*. In the *Quran*, Muhammed states, "It was not for a human being that Allah should speak to him except by *wahy*, or from behind a veil (Surah 51)." According to Richard Bell, a prominent trans-lator of the *Quran*, the literal meaning of *wahy* as it's used in the Quranic verses is "suggested", "prompted", or "put into the heart of". The meaning of *awha* is "signed", which signifies that the ideas implanted in Muhammed's mind had Allah's signature. According to Bell, it was only later, after Muhammed's initial articulation of the *wahy* and *ahwa* that these two Arabic words began to be interpreted by commentators as "revelations":

> Even when the agent of *wahy* is Allah, and the recipient a messenger or prophet, what is communicated are not the words of a revelation, but... a practical line of conduct, something to do, not to say... To Muhammed, it is "sug-gested" that he should follow the religion of Abraham (Surah 56: 124)... These practical "suggestions" are indeed often formulated in direct speech, as if it were a form of words that had come into a person's mind... These formulations, however, are always quite short, the sort of phrase, one may remark, which might flash into a person's mind after consideration of a question, as the decision and summing up of the matter (Bell, 1934, pp. 146-148).

When Muhammed told friends and acquaintances in Mecca about what happened to him and about the messages he'd received from Allah, many who heard him speak chose to become followers. But others were hostile and rejected Muhammed's claim to have been chosen as the Prophet of Allah. That conflict eventually forced Muhammed and his followers to leave Mecca and move to Medina, a city where they would be free to practice the new religion that had come to be called "Islam", the religion of "submission to the will of God".

The new religion was uncompromising in its insistence on the Otherness and Inscrutability of Allah, but it also welcomed all who chose to submit themselves to God and to God's community. This eagerness to proselytize distinguished the Muslim community from the Jews of that era who held religious views that were similarly monotheistic but who made a point of keeping themselves separate from all others and to continue regarding themselves as "God's Chosen People". Both religious cultures agreed that there was only One God, and they both agreed that the One God was Wholly Unknowable to human beings. But they both also recognized that there was one exception to that rule—that God could choose to intervene in human affairs and to prescribe rules for how human beings should live, and that by virtue of His having done that, the otherwise unknowable God did reveal something about Himself.

*　　*　　*

This review of the life of the Prophet Muhammed traces a trajectory of life events that, like the life trajectory of the Buddha, unfolds according to the pattern we discussed at the outset of this chapter. Is there evidence of child trauma? Yes. He was taken away from his biological mother soon after he was born and placed with a surrogate caregiver. Then when he was still only eight years old, Muhammed was torn away from his beloved surrogate mother, Halima, the only woman who'd ever nurtured him, and torn away from the Bedouin community where he'd grown up. He was sent to live with relatives in Mecca who would have been virtual strangers. It would have been clear to the young boy that he'd been rejected by the Bedouins because of his fainting attack, and that recognition would almost certainly have made him feel like an outcast. Moreover, during that fainting episode, he'd had a vision of being assaulted by two men who cut his chest open, a vision likely to instill fears that could not be easily put aside. Then soon after he developed a new love relationship with his paternal grandfather, the old man died. Muhammed was forced to move in with some other relatives. All in all, Muhammed experienced a much more traumatic childhood than any of the other visionaries we'll discuss in this book, and those traumatic events clearly affected his life. Did Muhammed have a midlife crisis? Yes. At the age of forty, he began to feel that his life had lost its meaning and he needed to search for spiritual guidance. Did he resort to dissociative strategies to cope with this midlife crisis? Yes. He began taking solitary retreats and engaging in long, meditative trances that he described as being sleep-like in their outward appearance. Did he see a vision of fiery light? Yes. He saw the "True Vision" erupt with a blast of light that looked like a bright sun rising about the dark desert horizon. After he saw the True Vision, did he experience any symptoms pointing to a temporal lobe behavior syndrome? Yes. He became obsessed with continuing his practice of religious retreats and persisted despite long periods in which nothing happened. Then he began receiving "suggestions" (*wahy*) that were implanted in his mind by a God named Allah. He felt emboldened by an enhanced sense of personal destiny. He came to believe that he had chosen to become the Prophet of Allah and that his mission was to pass along the teachings he'd received. Muhammed was a charismatic prophet who was able to recruit many loyal followers and lead them in founding the new religion of Islam. He and his army of followers would eventually end up conquering much of the Middle East and North Africa and converting the inhabitants to become members of the new religion of Islam.

Jesus of Nazareth

The young man who'd worked as a carpenter for years in his native village of Nazareth decided in midlife that he had to get away from that village and from everything he'd had to endure for so long. He'd heard rumors about a preacher named John the Baptist who'd set up camp on the banks of the Jordan River at a spot that was close to the main road Jewish pilgrims used when they traveled to and from the holy city of Jerusalem. John was summoning all who would listen to heed the message of the ancient Hebrew prophets—that all Jews must repent their sins and strive mightily to purify their souls if they want to escape punishment when God decides to install His kingdom on earth and to subject all Jews to His Day of Judgment. John claimed that he could purge his listeners of their sins by performing a ritual baptism. He briefly immersed those who chose to become penitents in the waters of the Jordan River, lifted them up, and urged them to begin living their lives in accordance with God's commandments. By becoming baptized, he told them, their souls had been born again. By baptizing penitents in the natural waters of the Jordan River, John was making a dramatic demonstration that God's priority was spiritual purity, not the conventional demonstrations of piety that involved taking regular ritual baths in prescribed facilities.

Jesus hiked west from Nazareth and arrived at John's camp where he was welcomed to join the disciples who helped John carry out his mission. Like all of the disciples, Jesus adopted the same wild look modeled by their leader, dressing themselves in loincloths and in rough, camel-hair tunics to signal their commitment to simplicity and authenticity.

When John baptized Jesus, the new disciple had a powerful spiritual experience. The Gospels claim that Jesus saw a vision coming from Heaven: "Straightway coming up out of the water, he saw the heavens rent asunder, and the Spirit as a dove descending upon him, and a voice came out of the heavens, thou art my beloved son, in thee I am well pleased (Mark 1: 9-11)." This story has all the elements of a creative fiction inserted by the authors of the Gospels to underscore Jesus' special relationship with God, but even if it's the case that the vision of the heavenly dove never actually happened, it's clear that Jesus' baptism by John was a deeply moving emotional experience.

Jesus felt compelled to make this dramatic change when he was in his early 30s. Like many of the other spiritual seekers we've studied in this investigation, he was finding it harder to tolerative the effects of traumatic events that had begun when he was still a child. The writers of the *New Testament* include details in their stories about the life of Jesus that suggest he'd been stigmatized as an outcast from the time of his birth. It's no wonder, then, that he felt compelled as an adult to escape all that by leaving his native village and joining an intentional community that did live by God's command to "love your neighbor as yourself".

To trace how Jesus' early life shaped his visionary experiences and his career as a charismatic rabbi, it's important to begin by examining how certain evidence about Jesus' birth created problems for the authors of the first books of the *New Testament*. They faced the challenge of coming up with some way to counter the persistent rumors that Jesus was born an illegitimate child, that his mother, Mary, had been impregnated out of wedlock.

One reason why this rumor about Jesus' birth received such wide circulation was that Gospel writers who were translating the original Aramaic texts into the Greek language used the word, *parthenos,* to describe the condition of Jesus' mother when she gave birth. In Greek, *parthenos* does mean "virgin", but this was a bad choice because the word was used in the original Aramaic texts was "*almah,*" a word that meant "a young woman of child-bearing age". That Aramaic word did not connote that the woman was also a virgin:

> The famous text in Greek, "a maiden (*parthenos*) shall conceive," became "a virgin shall conceive" when Matthew

was translated into Latin during the second century, and the change of a word fed the development of the legend of Jesus' miraculous birth. Both *almah* in Isaiah's Hebrew and *parthenos* in Matthew's Greek (and come to that, even the Latin virgo) refer to a "maiden" rather than a biological "virgin" (Bruce Chilton, *Rabbi Jesus*, 2000, p. 8).

This interpretation of the Aramaic word as "a young woman of child-bearing age" rather than "virgin" is confirmed by the renowned Jewish scholar, Geza Vermes:

In both the Greek and Hebrew parlance of the Jews, the term 'virgin' was used elastically. It was certainly not confined to denoting men and women without experience of sexual intercourse… A similar imprecision is manifest in the Greek version of Genesis, where the Greek word for virgin (*parthenos*) renders three different Hebrew words: *bethulah* = virgin, *na'arah* = girl, and *'almah* = young woman (Vermes, *Jesus the Jew: A Historian's Reading of the Gospels*, 1973).

This mistranslation turned out to have far-reaching effects. The writers of the Gospels could not cite specific facts about what really happened to counter the rumors because Jesus' birth had occurred so long ago that relevant information was no longer available. And they couldn't ignore the fact that the Greek versions of the Gospels that were receiving wide circulation did specify that Mary was a virgin when Jesus was born. The Gospel writers decided to make a virtue of necessity and to argue, yes, it was true that Mary was a virgin when she gave birth, but they added that it was God who instigated the conception. Arranging for Mary to give birth to God's "only begotten son" was said to be part of God's plan to bring His kingdom to earth. This miraculous birth was said to be only the first of many miracles that would bring God's plan to fruition. There were critics who ridiculed this explanation as biologically impossible, but the story of the virgin birth survived and eventually attracted more credibility than the Gospel writes could ever have hoped to achieve. The belief that Jesus was the incarnated Son of God became a foundational belief that would give rise to a new Christian religion.

If we move beyond this controversy about a virgin birth as a mistranslation, we can look instead at author Bruce Chilton's credible account of how and why a controversy over Jesus' birth might have been initiated in the village of Nazareth. In his book, *Rabbi Jesus: An Intimate Biography* (2000). Chilton suggests that the controversy most likely arose because of the insular customs that were common in the small villages of rural Galilee. Mary lived in Nazareth, but she was betrothed to a man named Joseph who lived and worked in another town—in Bethlehem—so the inhabitants of Nazareth would have known nothing about him and would not have seen him courting Mary. On one occasion when Mary was in Bethlehem visiting Joseph, the man she'd been pledged to marry, she became pregnant. Because the couple's courtship—and their initiation of sexual activity—took place in Bethlehem, out of sight of the Nazarenes, those who wanted to gossip could point out that nobody who lived in their village had been able to observe what Mary had really been up. Maybe Jesus' biological father was not Joseph but rather someone else, someone living in Bethlehem whom they didn't know. Someone even suggested that she might have been impregnated by a Roman soldier. Today this kind of gossip strikes us as being petty, gratuitously mean, implausible, and eminently forgettable, but this kind of insular gossip would not have been unusual in the small, rural, tight-knit communities of that time and place. And that kind of gossip could have serious consequences: it led to Jesus being stigmatized by some villagers and perhaps also by the local religious authorities. Chilton points out that the Book of Deuteronomy states that if there is any question about the legitimacy of someone's birth, that person should be classified as a *mamzer*. Here's Chilton's explanation of what would mean:

> Jesus was not illegitimate in the modern sense of the word (i.e., a child born out of wedlock). The term *mamzer* refers specifically to a child born of a prohibited sexual union… The fundamental issue was not sex before marriage (which was broadly tolerated) but sex with the wrong person. An unmarried woman impregnated by a man outside of her own community was in an invidious position, suspected of illicit intercourse… [And] given that Joseph had lived in Bethlehem and she in Nazareth when she became pregnant, it was virtually impossible for her to prove he was the father (Chilton, 2000, p. 13).

The Book of Deuteronomy also specifies that "No mamzer shall enter the congregation of the Lord (Deut. 23: 3)." If Jesus was stigmatized as a mamzer, he would not have been allowed to accompany his father to the synagogue. But even if that were not the case, even if Jesus grew up as a normal child, we know that when Jesus returned to his hometown after having become a respected religious teacher elsewhere in Galilee, some villagers were upset and said it was presumptuous for him to proclaim that he'd discovered a new spiritual path:

> He came to his hometown and began to teach the people in their synagogue, so that they were astounded and said, "Where did this man get his wisdom and these deeds of power? Is not this the carpenter's son? Is not his mother called Mary? And are not his brothers James and Joseph and Simon and Judas? And are not all his sisters with us?

Where then did this man get all this?" And they took offense at him. But Jesus said to them, "Prophets are not without honor except in their own country and in their own house." And he did not do many deeds of power there, because of their unbelief (Matthew 13: 54-58, *The New Oxford Annotated Bible*).

This scene suggests that the villagers still regarded Jesus as someone who couldn't escape his sullied past, that it was outrageously presumptuous for him to put himself forward as a spiritual leader in a town where the locals could remember that he'd once been stigmatized as a mamzer. If Chilton is right about Jesus having grown up an outsider in his own village, that insight might help explain why Jesus, once he became a spiritual leader, would often make a point of emphasizing the teachings of Leviticus in the third book of the Hebrew *Torah:* "You shall love your neighbor as yourself (19: 18)," and "You shall love the alien as yourself, for you were aliens in the land of Egypt (9: 34)." Jesus often repeated those ancient teachings in his own sermons: "You shall love your neighbor as yourself. There is no other commandment greater than this (Mark 12: 31)."

To dramatize what it meant to observe this commandment, Jesus told several parables in which he described the good deeds of individual Samaritans who were members of a minority population despised by most Orthodox Jews. In 'The Parable of the Good Samaritan', Jesus tells the story of a man who'd collapsed by the side of a road in a desperate condition. As he lay there, two prominent Jews passed by, ignoring the plight of the desperate man. When a Samaritan passed by, he saw the fallen man and took action to rescue him (Luke 10: 25). Another story describes an incident in which Jesus approached a well to get a drink of water. He noticed that a Samaritan woman had just drawn up a full bucket, so Jesus asked her if she'd give him a drink. When she graciously complied, he drank from the cup she'd handed to him. These behaviors would have scandalized the Orthodox Jews of his time: he'd used a utensil that had been touched by a Samaritan which would be considered "unclean" given the strict dietary regulations that most Jews observed (John 4: 26).

To illustrate how Jesus might have been well aware, even at a young age, that he would never find a true home in Nazareth, Chilton cites an incident that took place when Jesus was twelve and had traveled to Jerusalem with his family to celebrate the festival of Passover. In the Biblical story, it's said that Jesus managed to slip away from his family and to elude them for three whole days while he wandered through the Temple and its surrounding precincts, listening to many different religious teachers (Luke 2: 41). When Jesus' distraught parents finally tracked him down, his mother asked him, "Child, why have you treated us like this? Your father and I have been searching for you in great anxiety." Jesus replied, "Why were you searching for me? Did you not know that I must be in my Father's house?" This event may be merely apocryphal, but if something like that it did happen, it would imply that Jesus, even at the young age of twelve, already knew that he would have to look beyond life in Nazareth to find his true vocation. Chilton states that "Jesus was forced by the circumstances of his birth to look outside the provincial establishment for an understanding of who he was and what it meant to be an Israelite (Ibid., pp. 16, 21)."

Once Jesus left his native village and began living in the community of disciples who were helping John the Baptist, he began to wonder, given the emotional transformation that took place when he'd been baptized, if he was being called to become a spiritual teacher in his own right. He decided to test that idea by leaving John's community of disciples long enough to go on a solitary retreat in the wilderness where he could seek God's guidance about what to do with the rest of his life.

During that retreat, Jesus spent many hours in prayer and he also had to struggle on occasion against importuning thoughts that "tempted" him to make use of his talents in ways that would further his own personal self-interest:

> Then Jesus was led by the Spirit into the wilderness to be tempted by the devil. He fasted forty days and forty nights, and afterwards he was famished. The tempter came to him and said, "If you are the Son of God, command these stones to become loaves of bread." But he answered, "It is written, 'One does not live by bread alone, but by every word that comes out of the mouth of God'" (Matthew 4: 1-4).

Jesus would later report that during that solitary retreat he saw a vision of a bright, fiery light that looked like lightning. Seeing that vision convinced him that God was now ready to begin installing His kingdom on earth—and that He wanted Jesus to help him implement that plan. This was a message that would oblige Jesus to go beyond the teachings of his mentor, John the Baptist, who was still calling on Jews to ready themselves for something that would not happen until sometime in the distant future. Jesus didn't reveal that he'd seen this vision until much later in his ministry. He brought up the vision during a meeting with his twelve disciples and seventy other followers, all of whom had been spending their time traveling alone or in pairs to convey the good news about the coming of God's kingdom. During that reunion, some of the disciples expressed surprise that they'd been able to perform exorcisms by themselves, even though Jesus was not present. They asked their master why they were able to perform those miracles, and that's when Jesus told them about his vision: "I watched Satan fall from heaven like a flash of lightning," he said (Luke 10: 18, *The New Oxford Annotated Bible*). Jesus' description of his vision resonated with some apocalyptic ideas that had been circulating in Galilee. An example of an apocalyptic text that was popular at the time, *The Assumption of Moses*, is described by two Biblical scholars, Gerd Theissen and Annette Merz:

> At that time, the defeat of Satan was an expectation for the future. The *Assumption of Moses* 10.1 says: "And then His kingdom shall appear throughout his creation, and then Satan will be no more, and sorrow shall depart with him." This writing was in circulation shortly before the appearance of Jesus in Palestine. Jesus now asserts that what is expected has already taken place in heaven. Evil has been conquered. He states this as a visionary seer… It is quite conceivable that a visionary experience of Jesus led him to be able to replace John the Baptist's fear of judgment in his preaching with the certainty of salvation (Theissen and Merz, *The Historical Jesus: A Comprehensive Guide*, 1998, pp. 211-212).

Based on these apocalyptic imaginings, Jesus' vision of Satan falling out of heaven was a signal not only that God was now ready to install His kingdom on earth, but also that Jesus saw that vision because he'd been chosen by God to lead a movement to implement that goal. Theissen and Merz suggest that Jesus most likely saw this vision during his first retreat into the wilderness after being baptized by John:

> The vision of a fall of Satan may have only been handed down in the Lukan special material, but there is a legendary echo of it in the tradition in the temptation story. Perhaps a reference to a vision of Jesus at his call has been preserved in Luke 10: 18. Primitive Christianity later associated the overcoming of Satan with the cross and

resurrection... But already in his earthly activity Jesus presupposes a fall of Satan. It becomes a certainty to him as a result of his exorcisms: if the demons flee, that is a sign that the power of evil has been fundamentally broken. The saying about exorcism (Matt. 12: 28; Luke 11: 20) has rightly been cited as the main evidence for a present eschatology. If the demons are being driven out, the rule of God has already arrived (Ibid., p. 258).

When Jesus began to preach the new message, this may have caused some conflict with John the Baptist—or John and Jesus might have been collaborators working toward the same end. No one knows what transpired between them. But even if it were the case that Jesus' teachings ruptured the relationship, the dispute would have died soon after Jesus began his ministry because John the Baptist was captured by the soldiers of King Herod Antipas, put in prison, and executed. What's important about the relationship between Jesus and John is that many of John's teachings lived on in the teachings of Jesus:

He took over from John the images, themes and problems of his preaching, probably to a greater degree than we can recognize today, so that there could be some unknown sayings of John the Baptist among the sayings of Jesus which have been handed down. But soon Jesus showed his own profile everywhere, most clearly in the priority of grace over judgment in his preaching (Theissen and Merz, Ibid., p. 235).

Jesus' confidence that he and his disciples were implementing God's plan and his confidence that God was now prepared to back them up, no matter how dangerous their mission might become, explains why Jesus and the disciples deliberately chose to provoke the Jewish Temple authorities and the Roman governor during one of the most sensitive times of the year—during the Passover celebration when crowds of worshippers always gathered in Jerusalem. To make sure that the challenge to existing authorities was abundantly clear, Jesus chose to enter the city at the head of a ceremonial procession, draping himself in symbols that the Jewish people would recognize as heralding the coming of the Jewish Messiah who would end Roman domination, restore the rule of the Davidic kings, and lay the foundations for God's plan to install the Kingdom of God on earth. fruition. Jesus chose to ride into Jerusalem on a donkey rather than walking, as he would have normally done, and the symbolism of the donkey clearly resonated with the crowd of onlookers. They recognized that what they were seeing now was something that their prophet Zechariah had predicted long ago about the coming of the Messiah:

> Rejoice greatly, O daughter of Zion! Shout aloud, O daughter of Jerusalem! Behold, your king is coming to you; righteous and having salvation is he, humble and mounted on a donkey, on a colt, the foal of a donkey. I will cut off the chariot from Ephraim and the war horse from Jerusalem; and the battle bow shall be cut off, and he shall speak peace to the nations; his rule shall be from sea to sea, and from the river to the ends of the earth (Zechariah 9: 9-10).

The crowd that had assembled along the road began to chant: "Hosanna! Blessed is he who comes in the name of the Lord!" Others in the crowd then responded, "Blessed is the coming kingdom of our father David! Hosanna in the highest!" Some of the onlookers spread their cloaks out on the road while others strewed palm branches. Jesus proceeded all the way to the Temple. There are two different accounts of what happened during Jesus' first visit to the Temple: Mark states that Jesus entered the Temple, looked around, and left (Mark 11: 11). But Matthew claims that Jesus became angry and violent when he saw what was happening all around him: "When Jesus entered the temple and drove out all who were selling and buying in the temple, and he overturned the tables of the money changers and the seats of those who sold doves… He said to them, 'My house shall be called a house of prayer, but you are making it a den of robbers' (Matthew 21: 12)."

After visiting the Temple, Jesus led his disciples to a small village located just outside Jerusalem near the Mount of Olives to celebrate the Passover meal. When the meal was over, Jesus led his disciples (except for Judas Iscariot, who'd excused himself) to the Garden of Gethsemane located nearby on the western slope of the Mount of Olives. When they arrived, Jesus stepped away from the others to pray. It was then that the Roman soldiers, led by the traitor, Judas, entered the garden and took Jesus into custody (Matthew 26: 36-47).

I've emphasized the triumphal mood of Jesus' entry into Jerusalem because the evidence suggests that Jesus must have believed that God had given His blessing for this provocative challenge to the existing order. Jesus must have believed that God was prepared to intervene to make sure that the plan did succeed. This is a very different interpretation from the traditional story where it's said that Jesus, because of his divine birth, knew in advance about everything that was going to happen to him—that he warned his disciples that one among them would betray him to the Temple authorities and their Roman allies, that he would be arrested and put on trial, and that he would be sentenced to suffer a painful death, and that then, after being buried, he would rise from the dead to rejoin his Father in Heaven (Matthew 16: 21). The Gospels portray the story of

Jesus' crucifixion and resurrection as a dramatic demonstration of God's promise to humans that their suffering on earth does not go unnoticed and that death is not the end of life for those who let themselves believe in that divine promise (Mark 10: 33-34).

*　　*　　*

The life of Jesus, as I've reconstructed it here, fits the trajectory that I described at the outset of this chapter. Was there child trauma? Yes. An unfair stigma acquired through no fault of his own and through no fault of his parents which nevertheless resulted in his being identified as a mamzer. Midlife crisis? Yes. In his late twenties, Jesus felt compelled to abandon his mother, his profession as a handyman and carpenter, and the village where he'd lived all his life in order to become the disciple of a radical religious prophet. Did he resort to dissociative strategies to cope with his midlife crisis? Yes. His life as a disciple of John the Baptist would have introduced him to ascetic practices and strict self-discipline. Then he decided to go on a solitary retreat into the wilderness to pray to God for spiritual guidance without having to countenance any interruptions. While on that retreat, did he engage in long meditation vigils? It's reasonable to infer that that's how he spent most of his time, day and night, clearing his mind of distractions so he'd be open to whatever messages might come to him. Did he adopt a regimen of extreme austerities while on his spiritual retreat? Yes. The traditional story states that most of the time he relied on God to provide the few edible items and pools of water that he consumed. Did he see a vision of fiery light? Yes. He saw a vision of bright flashes that he described as "Satan falling in a hail of lightning". Is there evidence, in the wake of that vision, of the emergence of a temporal lobe behavior syndrome? Yes. After his wilderness retreat, Jesus felt inspired to begin his new career as a religious leader who could rightly claim that he'd been divinely appointed to speak on God's behalf. Jesus radiated a powerful charisma that enabled him to convince twelve men to leave their families and their professional livelihood in order to become his fulltime disciples. There is no evidence that Jesus ever got embroiled in sexual relationships. His sense of confidence in his personal destiny was strong enough that he was able to convince himself that God would come to his aid if he deliberately placed himself in danger and precipitated a crisis by provoking Roman authorities during a Passover celebration.

*　　*　　*

What stands out in these three examples of founders who were inspired by visions of fiery light is that in all three cases, there is credible evidence that they each experienced some kind of trauma when they were infants or young children. As adults they each became depressed and disillusioned about their lives and felt compelled to withdraw from society to seek spiritual guidance from a supernatural being they trusted more than fellow humans. On those solitary quests, they engaged in long meditation and prayer vigils that often extended late into the night, increasing the likelihood that they accumulated substantial sleep deficits. That combination of depressed mood and sleep loss would cause cortical neurons to become hyper-excitable and thereby set in motion certain changes in the brain that would facilitate a destabilization of sleep rhythm oscillators and the onset of a hypersynchronous seizure.

These three men are the only founders for whom there is enough credible evidence about their childhoods to reveal the connection between traumatic childhoods and adult decisions that led to them seeing visions of fiery light. But there are many other religious mystics who had similar experiences, men and women who did not start new religions but who did see visions of fiery light and who used their visionary experiences to revitalize their existing religious traditions. In the next chapter, we'll focus on the lives and visions of some men and women who were exposed to trauma as young children but who then succeeded, once they became adults, in finding ways to transcend their legacies of child trauma to become inspirational religious leaders.

CHAPTER 12

Trauma and Visions: Other Famous Seers

Hildegard von Bingen (1098-1179)

Hildegard was the tenth child born to a noble family living in Böckelheim, Germany. At the time of her birth, her parents promised they would give her as a "tithe" to the church, a practice known as "oblation". Hildegard began to see visions when she was only three years old: "I saw an immense light that shook my soul," she would later recall. She soon learned that she shouldn't tell anyone about her visions: "I tried to find out from my nurse whether she saw anything at all other than the usual external objects. And she answered, 'Nothing.'… Then I was seized with a great fear and did not dare reveal this to anyone" (Acta Inquisitions VIII, in *Jutta and Hildegard: Biographial Sources,* tr. by Anna Silvas, 1999, p. 267).

When Hildegard was eight years old, her parents made good on their pledge and sent their daughter to live in a small community of nuns attached to the church of the Benedictine monastery at Disibodenberg. There she was assigned to the care of a nun named Jutta von Spanheim who was only six years older than Hildegard. Jutta had a reputation of being someone who regularly subjected herself to a regimen of extreme austerities including self-flagellation, fasting, and prolonged prayer vigils.

Hildegard was devastated by being torn away from her biological mother at such a young age. She would later recall "weeping bitterly for the loss of my mother and also for all my sorrows and all my wounds. And so many tears did I shed (*Scivias* I, V)." But there was no going back, so Hildegard had to adjust to her new life. Jutta taught her young charge the rudiments of reading and writing and modeled the lifestyle that would be appropriate for an ascetic nun.

Six years after Hildegard had begun living with Jutta, her mentor decided to become an anchoress and to commit herself to enter into "Enclosure", the strictest form of isolation. She convinced Hildegard, who'd just taken holy orders herself at the age of fourteen, to join her in making this move. Being in Enclosure meant they would have to live together in a small cell cut off from the rest of the world with no visitors. Meals would be passed to them through a small window or left outside the door. They were expected to spend most of their time in prayer and contemplation and to engage in the practice of the most extreme austerities. Enclosure was like entering a tomb—it meant death to worldly concerns—which is why the two women were administered the last rites during a symbolic burial service performed just before they entered Enclosure. This momentous change would be a difficult undertaking for anyone, but obviously it would be particularly onerous for an adolescent girl who was only fourteen years old. Hildegard endured it all, and it no doubt strengthened her skills of prayer and self-discipline, but it could not have been easy or pleasant. One of Hildegard's biographers, Fiona Maddocks, author of *Hildegard of Bingen: The Woman of Her Age*, asks "What effects did these excessive acts of piety have on the young Hildegard? The fact that Hildegard recalls the later years of her childhood and youth—the period she was enclosed with Jutta—as more difficult and fraught than her infancy cannot be ignored (Maddocks, 2001, p. 42)." When Jutta's reputation for uncompromising piety and virtue began to attract visitors seeking spiritual guidance, a compromise was reached in which she would be allowed to give instruction even though she was, technically speaking, still in Enclosure. She was also allowed to prepare young women who came to her to take holy orders. Then Jutta decided to leave Enclosure when she was offered the opportunity to become the Abbess in charge of the nunnery at Disibodenberg. That's when Hildegard was finally released from her imprisonment.

When Hildegard was a teenager, she confided to Jutta that she was worried because she was still seeing visions. Jutta passed this information on to a monk named Volmar who'd been assigned to oversee the spiritual welfare of the nuns stationed at Disibodenberg. When Volmar heard Hildegard's stories about her visions, he was very impressed. He urged her to put aside her self-doubts and to allow the visions to keep coming because he thought the visions were coming from God. Volmar offered to help her keep a written record of what she saw. With his help as her amanuensis, she wrote two books, *Scivias* and *The Book of Divine Works*.

Once Hildegard became comfortable with sharing what she saw during her visionary experiences, she described the vision of "an extremely strong, sparkling, fiery light coming from the open heavens" that began to appear when she was twenty-four years old (Maddocks, Ibid., p. 55). These visions continued to appear and became more and more powerful. She wrote that when she was forty-two years old "a fiery light of exceeding brilliance came and permeated my whole brain (Ibid., pp. 55, 60)." And in a letter she sent late in life to a monk named Guibert of Gembloux who was her friend and confidant, she describes two extraordinary visions of fiery light she said she often saw—the visions of "the cloud that carries the sun" and the "living light":

> The light I see is not confined to one place, but it is far, far brighter than a cloud which carries the sun; nor can I gauge its height or length or breadth, and it is known to me by the name, "the reflection of the living light"… and the words in this vision are not like those which sound from the mouth of man, but like a trembling flame, or like a cloud stirred by the clear air. / I also have no means of knowing the form of this light, in the same way that I cannot look directly at the ball of the sun. In the same light I sometimes (but infrequently) see another light— but when and how I see it, I cannot tell. And while I am looking on it, all sorrow and all perplexity are drained from me… / But at no hour is my soul without the light I spoke of, which is called "the reflection of the living light." I see as though I were in a shining cloud, looking at a firmament without stars (Hildegard, "Letter to Guibert of Gembloux," quoted in Fiona Bowie and Oliver Davies, *Hildegard of Bingen: Mystical Writings*, pp. 145-146).

Hildegard became an avid painter who often placed halos with blue or gray colors behind the subjects she featured in the foreground. Many examples of paintings with prominent ring-shaped images can be found in Matthew Fox's anthology of Hildegard's paintings, *The Illuminations of Hildegard of Bingen* (1985). For example, in her painting, "The Almighty", a series of concentric rings appear beneath the throne of Jesus. In "Creator Mundi", she depicts herself in the lower left corner of the canvas looking up at Jesus who is surrounded by many concentric blue rings. I've never seen paintings in which Hildegard uses green ring images instead of the usual blue, but all of her blue ring images have the same shapes as visions of green light-rings. We know Hildegard was someone who prayed often and for long intervals, and we know that she often inserted ring-shaped images in her paintings, so it would be reasonable to infer that she often used meditation to induce visions of green light-rings. But then why did she choose to use blue colors when she painted in the ring-shaped halos? I suspect that she was concerned, and rightfully so, that as a Roman Catholic nun living in a Roman Catholic country in an historical era dominated by the Roman Catholic Church, it would be risky for her to reveal that she saw visions of a green light, much less to publicize that fact in her paintings. That admission might have led religious authorities to take some action against her if they concluded that her visions were coming from Satan, not from God.

But Hildegard was not wholly deterred from acknowledging the role of green lights in her visionary experiences. She found another way to go about expressing her belief in the profound significance of the color green as a mystical symbol of rebirth when she proposed that there is a divine energy that infuses all creation, a divine energy she called *Veriditas*, "Green Truth". She coined this word to merge the meanings of the Latin word, "*Viridis*", which means "green" with the Latin word, "*Veritas*", that means "Truth." For Hildegard, the Truth of *Veriditas* is that there is a green life-force that gets resurrected every spring when plants start to blossom. And that spirit of *Veriditas* also infuses the lives of human beings, providing them with the energy they need to find spiritual renewal. Hildegard would have felt that green energy begin to pulse in her body and mind when she induced a meditative trance and entered into a dark world where green light-rings would begin to appear spontaneously. The link between her having seen visions of green light and her concept of a universal green energy becomes explicit in a painting entitled "Vision Four" in her *Book of Divine Works*. In that work, Hildegard painted some blue, ring-shaped halos in a position where they provide an aperture that enables the viewer to see how all humans are connected with the green of *Veriditas*.

Hildegard also painted visions of eye-like images, often superimposing several of them on ring-shaped halos. In her description of the painting, 'God Enthroned Shows Himself to Hildegard', she writes: "I saw a great mountain the color of iron, and enthroned on it One of such great glory that it blinded my sight," and then she adds, "Before him, at the foot of the mountain, stood an image full of eyes on all sides, in which, because of those eyes, I could discern no human form (*Scivias*, Part 1, Vision 1)." This comment reveals that she saw visions of dark blue clouds that condensed into visions of "Third Eyes". Hildegard sometimes includes dark blue colors in her paintings that mirror the patterns displayed by visions of dark blue lights. For example, in *The Illuminations of Hildegard of Bingen*, Matthew Fox includes a painting entitled "The Man in Sapphire Blue" that depicts a vision that Hildegard described as "a bright light, and in this light the figure of a man the color of sapphire... which was all blazing with a gentle, glowing fire... and the bright light and the glowing fire poured over the whole human figure, so that the three were one in the light in one power of potential (*Scivias*, 1990, p. 159)." Hildegard makes a point of specifying that "the three were one in the light", making it clear in the text that what she actually saw was a vision of sapphire-colored light that glowed like a cloud on fire, not an angelic figure. Her characterization of this painting is yet another instance of Hildegard using a politically savvy strategy to assure the theological correctness of her vision: even if she did not actually see a human-like figure in her vision of the dark blue light, she says she intuited that there must have been something divine hidden in that light—that it was a vision embodying the Christian principle of the Trinity, the Three in One, where God is Father, Son, and Holy Ghost.

In our discussion of the life trajectories of Gautama, Muhammed, and Jesus, I suggested that their legacies of child trauma led them to feel an upwelling of dissatisfaction in midlife and that they responded by relying on dissociative coping strategies—by going on solitary spiritual quests and disciplining their bodies and minds by self-inflicting extreme austerities. In the case of Hildegard of Bingen, her adoption of dissociative coping strategies was not a matter of choice; from the age of eight she was obliged to obey the nun, Jutta, who was her mentor and demanding taskmaster. Having grown to maturity within the confines of such a strict religious environment, Hildegard did not need a midlife crisis to push her to choose a dissociative coping strategy—she'd already lived most of her life in a highly structured environment where dissociative coping strategies were a daily routine.

Hildegard saw many visions of a bright white light, so it is not surprising that she experienced the symptoms of a temporal lobe behavior syndrome—deepened emotions and a compulsion to communicate in books and in paintings that depicted what she'd seen in her visions. She also became an important religious leader: when Jutta died, Hildegard took over as Abbess of that small group of nuns living at Disibodenberg. That was only her first initiative as a religious leader: she went on to establish several new convents and to become an advocate for reforms designed to improve the lives of nuns. By the time of her death, Hildegard was already regarded as a saint in her native Rhineland region, even though it was not until 2012 that she was officially canonized by the Roman Catholic Church.

Adi Shankara (788-820 CE)

Shankara was born in India in the state of Kerala to parents who were both very old. His father died soon after his birth, leaving his mother to raise her son in an extended family where rumors were circulating that Shankara had to be an illegitimate child. In the traditional story, it's said that the boy left home at the age of eight hoping to find a guru who would accept him as student. If this story is accurate, it suggests that he felt that his life in that extended family had become intolerable.

As Shankara matured, he traveled to many different Hindu monasteries to study with the resident gurus and to participate in religious discussions. He became a formidable debater and determined that he wanted to revitalize the ancient Vedic traditions. Those traditional concepts and practices were being challenged by Indian Buddhists and by the Muslim invaders who'd recently conquered the northeast region of India. Shankara is credited with having almost single-handedly creating a new and more systematic exposition of the ancient Vedic belief that there is an Ultimate Reality that consists of a primordial, ever-changing radiance, the "bright-like-lightning" of the *Rig Veda* and the "Abounding Brahma-Light" of the *Upanishads*. His systematization of traditional Vedic beliefs came to be known as the religious philosophy of *Advaita* ("Non-Dual") *Vedanta*.

The teachings of Advaita Vedanta underpin an important yoga meditation practice known as *jñana* yoga, or "wisdom" yoga. In this practice, meditators cultivate seeing the visions of inner light that endow the seers with the "wisdom" that comes with "spiritual knowledge". In this philosophy, all natural phenomena are said to consist of ever-changing "apparitions" that have only an illusory reality. Shankara advises seekers who want to attain spiritual insight to become meditators and to learn how to use meditation skills to penetrate beneath the apparitions of phenomenal reality to see visions of the primordial light of the Cosmic Self. In modern versions of Advaita Vedanta, it's said that meditators can reach that goal by cultivating the rise of a spiritual energy that is latent in every human body until it gets activated by the practice of a proper discipline of meditation. That hidden resource came to be called "*kundalini*" energy. When the kundalini begins to rise, it activates a series of subtle energy centers called "cakras" that are said to be aligned in a vertical hierarchy. As each cakra gets activated in turn by the rising kundalini energy, meditators see a light that emanates the distinct shape and color associated with that particular cakra. It's said that when the rising kundalini energy activates the penultimate cakra associated with the top of the skull, meditators will see a tiny, thumb-shaped bulb of light known as the *atman* or *purusha*, the light of the spiritual "inner self". If they keep their attention fixated on the vision of that *atman*, they will enable the energy infusing that bright, bulb-shaped light to suddenly pierce through the invisible sheath that binds the "inner self" to the physical body. When that happens, the light of the "inner self" can merge with the primordial radiance of the Brahma-Light from which it originated. Meditators see the flashes of fiery light and feel themselves caught up in an ecstatic rapture. This event is described as a "realization" of the individual meditator's "inner self" and also as a "Realization" that restores the unity of the original "Cosmic Self." It's said that meditators who attain this ultimate visionary experience live the rest of their lives in a state of inner bliss and spiritual freedom.

Shankara's revitalization of the ancient Vedanta tradition was informed by his own visionary experiences: "It is precisely because of ignorance (*a-jñana*) that the self seems to be in bondage. But once that is resolved, the *atma* shines forth and reveals itself absolute and free as the sun does when it is no longer covered by clouds" (*Shankara Atmabodha: Self-Knowledge*, trans., Raphael, transl., 2003, p. 28). In another passage in that same work, Shankara writes that when "the previous darkness is dissolved by the solar illumination, the atma, like the sun, spontaneously unveils (p. 52)". Most interesting of all Shankara's descriptions of visionary experiences, given our focus in this investigation on visions of fiery light, is his confident assertion that "lightning is the end of the road beginning with light" (Thibaut, *Vedanta-Sutras with the Commentary by Shankarakarya, Part II.* p. 386).

Eleazar of Worms (c. 1176-1238)

Eleazar's father was a famous scholar in the German city of Mainz. His father died when the young boy was only five years old, and his mother died three years later. Very little is known about his early years. The biographies written about him don't provide many details until he became a young man who worked as a teacher during the day and then studied most nights with a relative named Judah ben Samuel "the Pious". His mentor taught him the secrets of the Jewish mystical practice known as *Kabbalah*. Eleazar would eventually become one of the leading exponents of that esoteric discipline.

When Eleazar married, he and his wife, Dulcea, moved to a small, remote German village where they lived together as man and wife but only on the Sabbath. During the other six days of the week, Eleazar retreated to a small dacha located nearby in the forest where he studied and prayed at all hours of the day and night. His wife sold parchment scrolls to support the two of them.

Eleazar kept a spiritual diary where he described how he prayed during his retreats. He wrote that he would lie in bed, not moving. He liked to say that if people were to observe him during his prayers, they would think he was sleeping, but he wasn't sleeping; he had immersed himself into a deep trance state that he called "Constricted Consciousness" where he was "meditating on the Divine Presence" as it manifested in a "divine Light". This divine light kept changing as Eleazar watched it. He began to believe that these changes embodied the essential mystery associated with the practice of Kabbalah—that "the Light of your soul blazes forth, and you ascend to the Upper Universes". During the ascent, the meditating Kabbalist sees many visions of multi-colored lights that eventually transport the meditator into a space that Eleazar called the "lower *Shekhinah*". One of the visions of light that appear while the seer is in this space is "The Circle of the Special Cherub" that Eleazar described as looking like an "eye" with a dark inner pupil. This comment clearly shows that Eleazar knew how to use meditation to induce visions of light, including the visions of dark blue clouds that can become eye-like images. It's also clear from his diary entries that Eleazar pushed beyond the early-stage light visions to trigger the culminating vision of the fiery light, the vision of the *Shekhinah* itself. Here are two descriptions of what Eleazar said he saw when he penetrated into the *Shekhinah:*

> The Creator has no body, physical stature, image, or form at all… The glory is an appearance of the resplendent light… The appearance of His splendor, which is His glory, is like a consuming fire, and they call it the *Shekhinah* (*Sha'are ha-Sod*, pp. 147-148, quoted in Wolfson 1994, p. 214).

> The word of God is like white fire clothed in a black and dark cloud… The brightness blinds the eyes like one who looks at the sun when it is in its strength. Therefore, the glory, the will of His word, is fire; the form of a cloud and darkness surround it (MS Paris—BN 772, folios 157b-158a, as quoted in Wolfson, 1994, p. 244).

Eleazar's life of religious contemplation was suddenly upended by a tragedy that erupted at a time when many Christians in Germany were caught up in the fervor of the Crusades. Two men brimming with anti-Semitic animus attacked Eleazar and his family. They killed his wife and his two daughters and wounded Eleazar and his son. The father and son immediately left the forest home and traveled to the city of Worms that had a large Jewish community. Given Eleazar's visionary experiences, it's likely that he experienced the emergence of a temporal lobe behavioral syndrome that deepened his emotional life and that inspired him to become an influential religious leader. And, indeed, his reputation quickly spread far beyond the borders of the city of Worms as Jews who lived in many different countries found inspiration by reading his books about Jewish ethics and about the mystical practices of *Kabbalah*.

Jetsun Milarepa (1052-1135)

Milarepa was born into a prosperous Tibetan family, but his father died when he was only seven years old. The father's relatives stole all of the family's properties, forcing Milarepa and his mother to live in a state of abject poverty. In the traditional story of Milarepa's life, his mother urged her son to study sorcery so they could take revenge on the father's relatives. He followed her advice and became an expert sorcerer. Some of the traditional stories claim he used his magic skills to kill people, but eventually Milarepa became uncomfortable with his pursuit of the black arts. He decided to search for a guru who could teach him about how to live a better life. His quest led him to a Buddhist monk named Marpa the Translator, one of the missionaries who was among the first to import Buddhist ideas from India into Tibet. Marpa, who'd once been a disciple of the famous Buddhist teacher in Kashmir named Naropa, translated Naropa's anthology of advanced meditation techniques, *The Epitome of the Six Yogas*, into the Tibetan language. He then used the *Six Yogas* as a platform to help him organize monastic orders in Tibet that practiced a uniquely Tibetan version of Tantric Buddhism called *Vajrayana*, "The Vehicle of the Thunderbolt".

Milarepa's life was transformed when he became a disciple of Marpa the Translator. He often stayed awake all night practicing the advanced meditation techniques known in Tibet as "Highest Yoga Tantra". During those meditation vigils, Milarepa knew to look for visions of green light-rings described as "halos" by Marpa: "First one experiences the hallucination-like sign / That arises with the halo of five lights (Mullin, 1996, p. 167)." Also in Naropa's *Six Yogas* is the admonition to "Meditate on the four wheels, / Each shaped like an umbrella, / Or like the wheel of a chariot ('The Yoga of the Psychic Heat,' 1: 66)." Here the metaphor of the umbrella is used to draw an analogy between the ring-shaped rims of umbrellas that shrink in diameter while being closed and the wheel-shaped visions that shrink in diameter so it looks like they fly away.

One night Milarepa was disturbed by a nightmare in which he saw his mother and his sister appear. He became concerned and asked Marpa for permission to return home to see if something might be wrong. Marpa initially advised him against going, but Milarepa persisted. Marpa finally gave his permission, and Milarepa returned to his old home. There, to his horror, he discovered his mother's dead body. And his sister had vanished without a trace. The villagers would not tell him what had happened; they shunned him like they'd been shunning the house long before Milarepa arrived. Clearly something sinister had happened in that house, but Milarepa would never learn the real story.

After he buried his mother, Milarepa hiked to a remote mountain cave known today as Dragkar-Taso. Once there, he shed all his clothes and vowed to meditate continuously, following the example of the Buddha. He only took breaks from his meditation vigil when he needed to relieve himself or to replenish his energy with a meal of flour and nettle soup. Sometimes he was unable to prevent himself from falling asleep for short naps. This regimen of extreme austerities continued for years. Milarepa's body became almost skeletal and his skin took on a greenish tinge. Then, during one of his meditation vigils, Milarepa triggered a vision of fiery light. He said the vision transformed his physical body "into a blazing mass of fire, or into an expanse of flowing or calm water". He said that this was the vision that revealed to him the fundamental Truth of the Buddhist religion: "Thus was a hitherto unknown and transcendent knowledge born in me... What till now I regarded as an objective discrimination shone forth as the Dharma-Kaya (Evans-Wentz, *Tibet's Great Yogi, Milarepa*, 1969 [1928], pp. 208-9, 212)."

After seeing the vision of fiery light, Milarepa decided it was time for him to leave the cave and to begin sharing with others how his vision of the Dharma-Kaya inspired him with an intuition of transcendental Truth. First he made his way to a remote monastery of the Tibetan Buddhist Kagyu sect where he enrolled as a new initiate. He rose rapidly through the ranks to become an influential religious leader of the sect. His reputation as a monk who'd attained the ultimate spiritual experience spread throughout Tibet, attracting many visitors who came to the monastery to see Milarepa and seek his counsel.

Ibn al-Arabi (1165-1240)

Ibn al-Arabi was born in an active war zone where the inhabitants lived anxious lives amid an ongoing conflict. His father, a soldier fighting with the Almohad Islamic armies in southern Spain, was often absent from the home during al-Arabi's early childhood. The boy's first serious trauma occurred when he was twelve years old. He developed a serious illness and feel into a death-like coma. No one could wake him up. When his father returned from the front, he saw that his son was unconscious and couldn't be aroused. The father assumed that his boy was dying, so he began to recite the Muslim funeral chant at al-Arabi's bedside. It was then that the boy suddenly woke up. When al-Arabi mentioned his coma later in life, he said he'd seen many nightmares of "horrible-looking people who were trying to harm me" (Hirtenstein, *The Unlimited Mercifier: The Spiritual Life and Thought of Ibn 'Arabi*, 1999, p. 36).

When al-Arabi was sixteen years old, four years after his escape from the coma, a strong emotional turmoil began to well up inside of him. Feeling compelled to seek relief, he began wandering in a local cemetery. There al-Arabi discovered an empty tomb. That discovery sparked a plan to return with some supplies and spend time alone in that dark space, praying to Allah for guidance about what he should do with his life. Al-Arabi had never been able to find a Muslim teacher, so he didn't know to perform the prescribed Muslim ritual called *dhikr*, or "invocation", that was regarded as a foundation of proper mystical practice. But then al-Arabi prayed in the dark tomb, keeping his attention fixated on the empty visual field to receive whatever Allah might him, and he saw visions of green light begin to flow spontaneously. He was reminded of the stories he'd heard about *Khidr*, "The Green One", the spirit who's celebrated in Islamic mystical traditions as a hidden guide, as a "teacher to the prophets" who will "come to the aid of those seekers who don't have earthly teachers" (Hirtenstein, pp. 54-55). Later in life, Al-Arabi was reminiscing, he would tell people that *Khidr*, "The Green One", came to him and taught him what he needed to know to perform a proper invocation.

How did this concept of Khidr, the "teacher to the prophets", come about? There are verses in the *Holy Quran* that describe how a spirit messenger came to Moses to teach him how to think about things that Moses did not understand. The name *Khidr* does not appear in those verses, so how did that name come to be used by Islamic mystics to refer to a hidden guide called "The Green One"? The answer may be that the Arabic word for the color green is *Akhdar*, and if the initial letter, "A," is removed from that word, what's left is *Khdar*, which would be pronounced in a way that is a close approximation to the name, *Khidr*. That etymology suggests that, long before al-Arabi's time, there must have been Muslim mystics who taught themselves how to use meditation to induce the visions of light that appear early in a meditation-induced sequence, including the visions of green light rings that begin flowing spontaneously. In this view, the name *Khidr*, "The Green One", became a code that Muslim mystics could use to communicate with each other without drawing the attention of the religious authorities who would be suspicious of anyone claiming to see visions of green light-rings.

While al-Arabi was praying in the tomb, he imagined being visited by Moses, Jesus, and the Prophet Muhammed. He said each of them gave him important spiritual insights about how he should live his life. The Prophet Muhammed advised al-Arabi to study his life, his visions, and his career as the Prophet of Allah. That's what al-Arabi did after he left the tomb: he returned to his home and began studying the stories about the Prophet that had been published in the *Hadith*, the sayings of Muhammed collected from people who knew him personally or from people who'd passed along what they'd heard from other people who were contemporaries of the Prophet (Hirtenstein, pp. 55-56).

When young Al-Arabi ended his self-imposed burial in the vacant tomb, he decided that it was time for him to start searching again for a spiritual teacher who would agree to take him on as a pupil. He traveled first in southern Spain, then headed farther south into the Muslim territories of North Africa and resided there for many years. By the time he reached the age of thirty-two, al-Arabi had become known as a respected spiritual teacher in his own right. It was then that he began to see visions that were different from the green light of Khidr.

The first new vision arrived unbidden while Al-Arabi was leading a worship service. The description that follows is ambiguous, but it clearly refers to sensations of a bright light and includes hints that the light had a spherical shape:

> I was leading a group of people in prayer in the al-Azhar Mosque when I saw it as a light which was almost more visible than what was in front of me, except that I had lost all sense of behind. I no longer had a back or the nape of a neck. While the vision lasted, I had no sense of direction, as if I had become completely spherical (*Al-Futuhat al-Makkiyya*, II: 486, in Hirtenstein, p. 114).

A year later, al-Arabi saw a series of visions that he described in ways that made them seem similar to visions seen by the Prophet Muhammed. He claimed to have seen visions similar to what Muhammed saw during the *Mi'raj*, the famous "Night Journey" described in the *Quran*. The Prophet said that he physically ascended into Heaven during this vision and that, once there, he received commands from Allah about how Muslims should perform their prayers. When al-Arabi said he saw similar visions, he took care to avoid accusations of blasphemy by emphasizing that his visions were during a spiritual journey that didn't involve a physical ascent

Al-Arabi also claimed to have seen another vision similar to one attributed to Muhammed: "I came to the Lote-Tree of the Extreme Limit," he said, "and I stopped amidst its lowest and highest branches". This vision is described in al-Arabi's *Futuhat al-Makkiyya, "Book of the Night Journey"* (Chapter 367, quoted in Hirstenstein, pp. 113, 121-122). Here al-Arabi is clearly referring to the vision of the Lote Tree positioned at the boundary of

Allah's Abode that's described in Surah 53. In our discussion of Muhammed's visionary experiences in Chapter 11, we concluded that his vision of a lote tree most likely was a reference to his seeing visions of green light-rings as they became green disks and then disappeared. When al-Arabi said he saw a vision he described as the lote tree at the boundary of Allah's Abode, he reported that this vision instilled in him a "knowledge of entering and circularity", and he made a point of specifying that "This circularity is not a matter of not doing, it is actually what is happening" (*Book of the Night Journey*, III: 352, in Hirtenstein, p. 122). That description is consistent with what we concluded about Muhammed's vision of a Lote tree, "shrouded in what it was shrouded", that seemed most likely to be a reference to seeing the visions of green light-rings that appear first in a med-itation-induced sequence. The green light-rings have a circular shape, which could lead to a "knowledge of circularity," and the green rings recede away from the viewer, becoming green disks just before they disappear. It's easy to understand how someone might decide that those green disks shaped like the bowers of lote trees were passing through an invisible barrier and entered into a divine space where no human eye could follow. Watching that happen would give al-Arabi a rationale for saying that watching the vision of the lote tree gave him a "knowledge of entering".

Al-Arabi also claimed to have seen a third vision that was also seen by the Prophet Muhammed. He saw the vision of green "cushions" used by those who dwelled in Paradise: "Then I saw the cushions of the Litters of the Knowers," Muhammed some-times reported, "and I was enveloped in light until I became wholly light (*Quran* III: 350)." Al-Arabi said he'd seen those same visions of green cushions.

It would appear, then, that Al-Arabi saw visions of green lights on many occasions, beginning with the vision that came to him when he was sixteen years old and meditating in the empty tomb—the vision of *Khidr,* "The Green One"—and this continued when throughout his life. But al-Arabi made a point of waiting until he was an old man with a reputation as an inspired spiritual teacher before he felt sufficiently emboldened to compare the visions he saw to the visions seen by the Prophet Muhammed. It was only after he reached the advanced age of sixty-four that he felt compelled to share his experience of seeing a vision of a bright white light that manifested the "Divine Oneness" of Allah:

> I saw in a vision the exterior of the Divine Ipseity and its interior in a witnessing of verification, which I had not seen before in any of my witnessing. Through witnessing this there came to me knowledge, sweetness and joy, which cannot be known except by someone who has tasted it. The most beautiful of visions, and that is no lie or exaggeration... The figure is a white light on a red carpet; it was a white light in four layers... I have never seen, known or imagined, nor has a thought crossed my heart, anything like the image which I saw of this Ipseity (*Al-Futuhat al-Makkiyya,* II: 449, in Hirtenstein, pp. 214-5).

The life trajectory of al-Arabi diverges in many ways from the common pattern we've been investigating, but there are also similarities that warrant including him here. Clearly his experience of a deep and long-lasting coma with the accompanying nightmares that overtook him when he was only twelve years old would qualify as a serious trauma, one that was still haunting him four years later when he began living in an abandoned tomb in a cemetery and praying for spiritual guidance. This kind of psychological crisis, where the trauma and the upwelling of emotion occurs during the teenage years rather than at midlife, is a variation we'll see repeated in some of our other case studies. After the interlude in the cemetery, al-Arabi dedicated his life to religious activities—studying with many different spiritual leaders and eventually becoming a spiritual leader in his own right. These life choices suggest that al-Arabi experienced the emergence of a temporal lobe behavior syndrome while he was still very young. Perhaps some kind of epileptiform activity occurred in the limbic regions of his brain while he was unconscious during the coma. That might explain the obsession with religious concerns that governed his behavioral choices for the rest of his life. Especially noteworthy is the temporal lobe behavioral symptom of "hypergraphia". That symptom emerged when al-Arabi was an old man who wrote an account of his mystical experiences, the *Meccan Illuminations*, that filled thirty-six volumes. When al-Arabi was sixty-four years old and was finished writing his masterwork, he finally saw that vision of a bright fiery light filling the visual field that he called "The Divine Ipseit". After he saw that paroxysmal vision, he experienced the emergence of another strong temporal lobe behavior syndrome. Caught up in a resurgent symptom of hypergraphia, al-Arabi decided he needed to revise the *Meccan Illuminations*. He succeeded in accomplishing that momentous task shortly before he died at the age of seventy-one. It's reasonable to infer that the intensification of his temporal lobe behavior syndrome enhanced his sense of personal destiny to the point that he felt emboldened in writing the *Meccan Illuminations* to compare his visionary experiences to those of the Prophet Muhammed.

Ignatius of Loyola (1419-1590)

When Ignatius was born in Loyola, a Basque community in northern Spain. His mother died in childbirth. His father was a knight who was usually away from home on military campaigns, so Ignatius was raised by surrogate caregivers from early infancy on. In *Ignatius of Loyola: The Psychology of a Saint* (1992), a biography written by Dr. William W. Meissner, a psychoanalyst and a member of the Jesuit Order who is also a physician, Ignatius is portrayed as a young man known for his dandyish tastes—he relished stylish clothing, good food and drink, and amiable companions. He also chose to follow his father's example and joined the Spanish armies as a knight.

It was during one of the battles between the Christian armies from northern Spain and the armies of the Moors from the south that Ignatius received a serious wound. He was guarding the parapet of a castle when an incoming cannonball struck the stone wall near where he was standing. Fragments of metal and stone showered out in all directions, and some of those fragments struck Ignatius, shattering his leg. He had to submit to a long surgical operation performed without anesthetics. Tdo allow his leg to heal, he was forced to spend months in a hospital bed, immobilized. Then it became evident that wound wasn't healing, so he had to endure another excruciating surgery. His second convalescence lasted even longer than the first: he was confined to a bed for a full two years. For a man of action, this enforced inactivity was almost intolerable, but Ignatius had no choice. He also had to face the fact that his leg was not going to recover enough for him to return to his former career as a knight. He would have to find something else to do with his life.

During his convalescence, Ignatius was given some books about the lives of Christian saints. He was intrigued by the stories he found there, especially those in which the saints were portrayed as "soldiers for Christ". He realized that this might be the kind of career that would be open to him. When he was finally able to walk again, albeit with a pronounced limp, he decided to make a pilgrimage to the shrine of Our Blessed Lady at Monserrat to pray for guidance about how he might become a "soldier for Christ".

As he set off on his pilgrimage, Ignatius continued to suffer some misgivings about whether this decision to give up his old ways was in his best interest. He realized that if he were to follow the example of the saints whose lives he'd studied, he would have to purify his soul. That meant he would have to struggle mightily against his old inclinations—he would have to suppress his desire to wear stylish clothing, to stay in luxurious lodgings, to order good food and drink, to consort with young women, and to pursue all the other comforts that he'd cultivated in his former life. One night when he'd stopped at an inn on the way to Monserrat, he decided to test his professed dedication to live a religious life: he got down on his knees and continued praying all night long except for those occasions when he took a break to lash his bare back with a whip. His prayers convinced him that he was prepared to continue his quest to become "soldier for Christ". When he finally arrived in Monserrat, he bought a sackcloth tunic with a rope girdle and rope sandals—clothing suitable for a penitent pilgrim—and gave all the fine attire he'd been wearing during his journey to a poor man who was begging near the door of the church.

The Basilica of Santa Maria of Monserrat is a massive Gothic building that has attracted many pilgrims over the centuries. They come to be blessed by touching the hand of the famous statue of the Black Madonna. Ignatius went to one of the small chapels located inside the Basilica to complete the final stage of his pilgrimage by performing an all-night prayer vigil. In the morning when he stood up to depart, he removed his sword and dagger, the two possessions he'd cherished most during his earlier former life, and dropped them onto the floor of the chapel. He no longer needed those emblems of knighthood.

The regimen of self-denial that Ignatius adopted during his pilgrimage to Monserrat became part of his identity and his philosophy of life. He vowed that whenever he felt a positive attachment to something, he would judge whether he wanted to maintain that attachment by subjecting it to a test: he would ask himself if it helped him to discipline the unruly urges of his body and mind and thus to maintain the spiritual purity of his soul. If the feelings of attachment did not meet that test, he vowed to peremptorily reject his involvement with that person, place, or thing. This new philosophy of rejecting whatever seemed to bring him pleasure and while embracing what struck him as unpleasant became one of the core principles in the Ignatius's philosophy. Meissner, in his biography of Ignatius, points out that, late in life, when Ignatius wrote his autobiography, *Spiritual Exercises*, he advised others to adopt those the same strategies of self-reflection and self-deprivation that he felt had served him well: "If the soul chance to be inordinately attached or inclined to anything," he wrote, "it is proper that it rouse itself by the exertion of all its powers to desire the opposite of that to which it is wrongly attached (Exercise 16)."

After an all-night vigil in the chapel at Monserrat, Ignatius planned to return to his family home in Loyola, but on the way he passed through a small mountain town called Manresa that he struck him as a good site to begin exploring new ways to live his life. He volunteered to work in a hospital on the outskirts of town in exchange for being allowed to use of their beds. Later, when he decided to stay longer, he moved into one of the cells in a small priory managed by Dominican monks that was located near the hospital. He ended up spending a whole year in Manresa, even though that hadn't been part of his original plan.

Throughout his sojourn in Manresa, Ignatius continued to inflict his body and mind with a strict ascetic regimen. He would fast every day except Sunday and would only allow himself to eat the food he could get by begging. He let his hair grow wild and bushy. He rose every night at midnight to kneel on the stone floor of his small cell to pray. Sometimes those nightly prayer vigils extended for seven hours. He discovered a mountain cave that overlooked the valley and began using it to perform special prayers and penances. These self-inflicted privations affected his health. On several occasions, he became ill and had to be nursed back to health by some local women who had come to believe that he was a holy figure. One reason why Ignatius felt he had to punish himself was that once again he'd begun to be troubled by misgivings about having chosen this new path. In his autobiography, *Spiritual Exercises*, Ignatius felt a "darkness of soul, turmoil of spirit" as he found he was still struggling with "an inclination to what is low and earthly" and with "temptations which led to want of faith, want of hope, want of love (Exercise 317)."

During the year he spent in Manresa, Ignatius began seeing strange visions. When these visions first began to appear, Ignatius was pleased because he felt "great delight and consolation" while he was watching them. Sometimes those visions would appear even during the day when he felt tired and sleepy and found his attention drifting away from the task as hand. Here's how he described that vision:

> It often happened to him in broad daylight to see something in the air close to him, which gave him great consolation because it was very beautiful. He could not make out very clearly what the thing was, but somehow it appeared to have the form of a serpent. It was bright with objects that looked like eyes, although they were not eyes (Meissner, p. 71).

Early on Ignatius assumed that these otherworldly visions were probably a divine response to his nightly prayers. Then he began to wonder if that initial assessment was credible. He worried the visions did not arrive with any spiritual signs attached to them, and sometimes they interfered by intruding at night during the time when he wanted to sleep, which was always very limited.

Why might someone see visions like this—visions "having the form of a serpent" and filled with "objects that looked like eyes, although they were not eyes"? Meissner proposes a psychoanalytic explanation: that these visions represented a resurgence of images rising from the depths of Ignatius' unconscious. But what we've learned from our neurologically grounded investigation of meditation-induced light visions suggests a different interpretation. Ignatius was chronically exhausted, seriously sleep deprived, and undernourished. That combination of stressors would be likely to cause someone to inadvertently slip into a dissociated state on occasion, even in the middle of the day. And given that Ignatius spent most of his nights on his knees praying for guidance from God, he would have been intimately familiar with the altered state of consciousness that results when someone shuts out what's happening in his environment, keeps his mind free of distractions, focuses intently on the dark visual field with the hope and expectation that a moment will come when God filled that empty space with an important message. It's reasonable to assume that during his nightly prayer vigils Ignatius would have produced the same kind of neurophysiological reactions that occur when expert meditators induce empty-mind trance states. Those practices would activate the slow wave sleep rhythms that generate visions of green light-rings and then the dark blue clouds that condense into "Third Eyes". Given that Ignatius was chronically exhausted, sleep deprived, and malnourished, it's not unlikely that, even in the middle of the day, he might have rested on a bench and inadvertently slipped asleep for just a moment before jerking himself awake again. If there were brief sleep episodes that lasted long enough to activate the spindle bursts of Stage 2 NREM sleep before he jerked awake, it's not surprising that he saw visions of green light-rings even during the daylight hours. And those ring-shaped visions might well lead him to imagine that he was seeing something like a snake turning in on itself to bite its tail.

This was precisely what happened to a famous German scientist, Friedrich Kukulé, the man who discovered the atomic shape of benzene compounds. It was early in the evening and Kukulé was ensconced in an easy chair, his eyes closed, his mind resting in a state of reverie. He was on the cusp of falling asleep when saw the vision of a ring-shaped light. He was astonished to see something so unusual—a ring of light that he described as looking like a snake biting its tail. Kukulé sprang awake, filled with excitement, because he suddenly realized that a ring shape would explain how the benzene compounds he'd been studying performed certain functions.

The image of a snake biting its tail is also an ancient Egyptian symbol, the "*ouroboros*," which was adopted by the Gnostic and Hermetic religious cults that emerged in Europe during the early years of Christianity. So Ignatius was not the only seer to describe visions of light-rings as "having the form of a serpent". Ignatius also saw visions that he described as "objects that looked like eyes". This suggests that he also saw the visions of dark blue clouds stage 3 NREM sleep rhythms that have a bright "iris-like" ring surrounding a dark "pupil".

Seeing these visions made Ignatius feel good, but that concerned him. He'd vowed give up anything gave him pleasure, and he began to worry that the fact that these visions gave him pleasure might be a warning that they were not coming from God. What if they were being sent by the devil who was hoping that the pleasurable experience would distract Ignatius from the goal of achieving spiritual purity?

But often when he went to bed, great spiritual lights came to him, as did wonderful consolations, so that they took up most of the time he had set aside for sleep, which was not much. Now and then reflecting on this loss of sleep...

he came to doubt whether those lights came from the good spirit (Ignatius, *Obras Completas*, 3.26).

Ignatius couldn't decide what to do about those visions of light until one day when he was attending Mass in the cathedral he saw another, very different kind of vision, one that was so spiritually elevating that he was sure there could be no question about its source. It came to him while he was watching a priest elevate the sacred host to receive the divine blessing. He "saw with the inner eyes of the soul something like white rays that came from above," and, given the context in which the vision appeared, Ignatius assumed that this had to be a vision of Jesus, even if what he saw in his visual field was only the vision of a pure white light. After that first appearance, he began to see that same white light manifest on the many occasions when he was kneeling in prayer:

During prayer he often, and for an extended period of time, saw with inward eyes the humanity of Christ, whose form appeared to him as a white body, neither very large nor very small; nor did he see any differentiation of members. He often saw this at Manresa. He has also seen our Lady in similar form, without differentiation of members. / These things that he saw at that time fortified him and gave such great support to his faith that many times he thought to himself: if there were no Scriptures to teach us these matters of faith, he would still resolve to die for them on the basis of what he had seen (Ignatius, *Vita* 3: 29.4).

The visions of the white lights restored Ignatius' faith that he had chosen the right course of action when he determined to become a soldier for Christ. After seeing several visions of the bright white light, he realized that his concerns about those earlier visions of "snakes" and "eyes" were justified. And it wasn't long before he received confirmation that his new insight was correct. It happened on one occasion when Ignatius dropped to his knees in front of a crucifix to pray that he might see that miraculous vision of white light appear once again. What he saw instead were the visions that looked like "snakes" and "eyes", but now those visions were no longer giving him pleasure. He concluded that this must be because he was kneeling so close to a crucifix: "Before the cross, it did not have that beautiful color as before, and he understood very clearly, with a strong assent of his will, that it was the evil one (*Vita* 30-31)." Realizing that he was seeing visions sent by the Devil didn't make him afraid because now he'd seen the visions of white light that "fortified him and gave such great support to his faith".

Ignatius' determination to become a soldier for Christ was now even stronger than before, so he decided it was time to leave Manresa and to try to make his way to the Holy Land. He began walking south toward Barcelona where he hoped he would be able to catch a boat that would take him to Jerusalem. He was able to reach that destination, and, once there, he had many adventures that Meissner recounts in the biography. All the while, Ignatius continued to subject himself to the most extreme austerities. He eventually left Jerusalem and made his way back to Europe. He ended up studying religion at the Sorbonne University in Paris. While he was there, he formed a strong bond with his room-mates, all of whom shared a determination to do God's work. Ignatius convinced them to join him in a campaign to organize a brotherhood of mendicant monks who would commit their lives to being soldiers for Christ. To implement that plan, Ignatius and his new companions would have to get permission from the Pope in Rome. Ignatius was confident that they would be able to succeed in making their case to the Pope, and it turned out he was right: the petitioners were given permission to establish a new religious order called the Society of Jesus which came to be known as the Jesuits.

The trajectory of Ignatius's life follows the pattern that we've been investigating. We know his mother died when he was born and that he was raised by surrogate caregivers. As an adult, he faced a major life crisis when his leg was shattered in a battle, forcing him to endure two operations and several years immobilized in bed. When he recovered enough to be able to walk, he found he could suppress his feelings of disappointment and despair by subjecting himself to a regimen of extreme austerities designed discipline the unruly urges of his body and mind. His vow to be suspicious of anything that attracted him and gave him pleasure also helped him implement a dissociative coping strategy. His addiction to long prayer vigils that lasted most of the night would establish the preconditions for seeing the same kind of light visions that appear early in a meditation-induced sequence, the visions generated by slow wave sleep rhythms. Eventually his extreme ascetic regimens lowered the seizure threshold in his brain and set in motion the chain of events that triggered eruptions of the fiery light.

After Ignatius began seeing the visions of fiery light, he began to experience symptoms consistent with the emergence of a temporal lobe behavior syndrome. Seeing the visions of white light inspired him with an unshakeable faith and renewed his confidence that he'd chosen the right path in becoming a soldier for Christ. He experienced a deepening of his emotional life and acknowledged that he often found himself responding to feelings of sadness with the God-given "the gift of tears" that turned the sadness into joy. After seeing the fiery light, Ignatius was inspired by an enhanced sense of personal destiny that gradually coalesced into a plan to form a new organization in which young men would dedicate their lives, like him, to becoming soldiers for Christ. The sense of self-confidence that he'd acquired from seeing visions enabled him to overcome many obstacles and to eventually bring that plan to fruition. Ignatius also exhibits the symptom of hypergraphia: as the leader of the Jesuits, he became a prolific letter writer, and he also wrote several important books on religious subjects. He shared his ideas about how best to seek God's guidance in his book, *The Spiritual Exercises*, and in his autobiography, *The Pilgrim's Journey*, he revealed how he'd arrived at his spiritual insights by always seeking God's guidance and then proceeding by a process of trial and error.

John of the Cross (1542-1591)

Juan Yepes, also known as John of the Cross, was born in a small town near Avila, Spain. When he was three years old, his father died, leaving the family in a state of desperate poverty. The mother, Catalina, struggled to keep her three children fed, clothed, and sheltered. His older brother died two years after the father. When John was nine, his mother moved the family to Medina del Campo, a bigger town. She talked the local priests into admitting John to a school for poor children that provided students with food and shelter, a rudimentary education, and training for the jobs that would likely be available to them. John graduated from that school and found a job as a nurse in one of the local hospitals run by the Roman Catholic Church. While he was working at the hospital, he learned that there was an opening at a Jesuit school located nearby. It was a school that could provide the kind of basic educational background he'd missed out on as a young boy. He applied and was admitted. It was at that Jesuit school that John acquired the reading and writing skills that would serve him well in the future.

After graduating from the Jesuit school, John returned to his nursing job at the local hospital. His dedication to the job and his efficiency attracted the attention of the hospital administrator who offered to sponsor him for ordination into the priesthood. The administrator promised to appoint John to the position of hospital chaplain after he was ordained as a priest. But John decided he wanted to make a more dramatic change: he left the hospital and enrolled as a novitiate in a monastery in Medina run by the Carmelite order. The leaders of the Carmelite monastery soon became aware of John's talent and his potential to become an important resource for the monastery and for the local cathedral if he got a university education. They offered to send John to the University of Salamanca to study Scripture and theology in exchange for his promise to return. Four years later, when he graduated from the university, he did return to Medina and began to serve in various roles assigned by his superiors.

It was while he was working as a priest in Medina that he first encountered Teresa of Avila, an abbess known for having mystical experiences. She was looking for monks to help her implement a new program to reform how novice nuns were taught to live lives dedicated to contemplation and prayer. Teresa wanted to restore the spiritual purity of her Carmelite order by going back to basics—more periods of silence, more fasting, simpler clothing styles, and a restriction that forbade wearing shoes with covers. Teresa's nuns came to be known as the Order of Discalced Carmelites. When John apprenticed with Teresa to learn the reforms she was hoping to install, she was so impressed by his talents that she appointed him to become the spiritual director at one of her convents. She also asked John to be her personal spiritual director. He became Teresa's close confidant and adviser during the years when she was experiencing many of her most profound mystical raptures.

John's collaboration with Teresa of Avila also caused him to acquire some dangerous enemies. A faction of Carmelite monks in Toledo adamantly opposed Teresa's efforts to reform how the Carmelite Order worked with nuns realized that John was not only one of Teresa's most important advisers but also a threat in his own right. When Teresa sent John to organize a new monastery at Valladolid based on the teachings she'd prescribed to her nuns, the hostile faction in Toledo watched John's movements. When an opportunity arrived, they captured John and took him to their monastery in Toledo where they put him in solitary confinement. He was placed in a small, dark cell with only a single, tiny window high on the wall, just below the ceiling. That tiny window opened into the next cell, not out to the surrounding world. During the day, the window provided just enough light for John to read his breviary provided that he stood on his bench, tipped up on his toes, and held the breviary at an angle that allowed some faint light to fall on its pages. His captors left him alone in the dark except when they dropped off his daily ration that consisted of bread, water, and salted cod. Once a week his captures dragged him out of the cell to be flogged in the public square. John was imprisoned for almost eight months before he found a way to slip messages to supporters outside the walls of the monastery. They carefully plotted to find a way they could help John make a surreptitious escape, and it turned out to be successful.

During his solitary confinement, John began seeing visions. To remember what he'd seen and felt during these experiences, he composed poems that he later incorporated into a book, *The Spiritual Canticle*. He decided that the best way to describe the spiritual path that led him to feel a sense of union with God was to say that the seeker's soul had to learn how to ascend ever higher up through a dark, empty void John called the *nada*, "the nothingness." Even when a soul achieved the highest level of attainment, it would still be surrounded by that all-encompassing "nada" because "even on the Mountain, nothing".

The most graphic descriptions of the visions John saw are found in another of his books, *The Dark Night of the Soul*. There he describes how his soul, as it ascended through the dark nothingness, put on a series of disguises: "In the darkness of the night it changed its garments, and disguised itself in three colors, of which I shall speak hereafter. It sallied forth unknown to the whole of its household by a most secret ladder (Book II, Chapter 15.2)." To describe this spiritual ascent, John began by choosing words he knew would reassure the Roman Catholic authorities. He began by noting that a soul always begins its journey wrapped in the "white robe of faith" that protects all believers, but in his description of this vision he's so vague that it's clear, based on the comparison with what came later, that he's not describing one of the visions that he actually saw. He then moves on to describe the visions of light that will actually appear in the visual fields of expert meditators. The soul puts on a series of "disguises", John writes, and the first disguise worn by the soul is a green light that looks like an *almilla*. This is a word that would be familiar to his readers because an *almilla* was a ring-shaped pad that soldiers wore around the tops of their shoulders to cushion the weight of their armor. He also adds another metaphor to describe this vision and why it's part of the soul's disguise: it's because the vision of the ring of light functions like a soldier's helmet—like a helmet, the ring has only one opening to look through, an opening that directs the soul to look toward what lies ahead. Here in his own words is John's description of this first vision:

> The soul put on the white robe of faith on its going forth on this dark night... (21.6.) Over the white robe of faith, the soul puts on forthwith that of the second color, a green *almilla*, emblem of the virtue of hope, by which it is delivered and protected from its second enemy, the world (21.7)... The soul, then, thus disguised and clad in the vesture of hope, is secure from its second foe, the

world, for St. Paul calls hope the helmet of salvation. Now a helmet is armor which protects and covers the whole head, and has no openings except in one place, where the eyes may look through... It has one loophole only through which the eyes may look upwards only; this is the ordinary work of hope, to direct the eyes of the soul to God alone (*The Dark Night of the Soul*, Book II, 21.8, in Zimmerman B, *St. John of the Cross*, 1932, pp. 178-182).

Once the soul moves on, it gives up the green disguise and puts on the "robe of purple", the disguise it will use to ascend ever higher. This "going up of purple" elevates the seer's soul to the vision John calls the "seat of gold" where "the soul is on fire sweetly":

Over the white and green robes, as the crown and per- fection of its disguise, the soul puts on the third, the splendid robe of purple... This is the purple, spoken of in the Canticle [III. 10], by which the soul ascends to the seat where God reposes: "the seat of gold, the going up of purple". It is vested in this robe of purple that the soul journeys... when in the dark night it went out of itself, and from all created things, with anxious love inflamed, by the secret ladder of contemplation to the perfect union of the love of God its beloved Savior (Book II, Chapter 21, 2, 6-10).

When the soul reaches the "seat of gold", the ninth and final stage in its ascent, it feels itself consumed by fire: "On the ninth step, the soul is on fire sweetly. This step is that of the perfect who burn away sweetly in God... (Book II, 20.5)." A more detailed description of this final vision appears in another book that John wrote about his visionary experiences. Here's how he describes the vision of fire in *The Ascent of Mount Carmel:*

[W]hen God is pleased to grant this favor to the soul, He communicates to it that supernatural light whereof we speak... And it is at times as though a door were opened before it into a great brightness, through which the soul sees a light, after the manner of a lightning flash, which on a dark night, reveals things suddenly, and causes them to be clearly and distinctly seen, and then leaves them in darkness, although the forms and figures of them remain in the fancy (Book II, 24: 5).

In this review of the life trajectory of John of the Cross, we've encountered another example of the common pattern shared by many mystic seers. John's early childhood in a fatherless and impoverished family would have been difficult, but his mother was an important support. She was an effective advocate who got him started on an educational track that produced benefits far beyond what either of them expected. John clearly wanted to pursue a religious career, and as a young priest he most likely engaged in prolonged prayer vigils, but the event that catapulted him into a world of visionary experiences was being imprisoned for eight months in solitary confinement. In that situation, it would have been natural for him to resort to dissociative coping strategies to maintain his psychological equilibrium. After his escape from prison, John returned to his role as an important leader in the Order of Discalced Carmelites. He helped the Order found new convents and new monasteries. During those same years, he found time to write three books that have inspired many generations of readers: *The Spiritual Canticle, Dark Night of the Soul,* and *Ascent of Mount Carmel.* These accomplishments suggest that John of the Cross, after seeing the kinds of visions that are generated by the induction of limbic seizures, experienced the emergence of a temporal lobe behavior syndrome that deepened his emotional life, enabling him to express the most profound emotional and spiritual experiences in his writing. It also inspired an enhanced sense of personal destiny that helped him rise to the top leadership positions in the Carmelite Order.

Joseph Smith, Jr. (1805-1844)

The parents of Joseph Smith, Jr., often led their children in prayers and in singing their favorite hymns. They also shared stories about their own visions and their enigmatic dreams. The neighbors looked askance at the Smith family because they suspected them of engaging in the magic arts—and those suspicions were not unwarranted: the father, Joseph Smith, Sr., was an accomplished scryer who helped clients divine their futures or find lost items. His technique was to put his favorite seer-stones in his hat, place the hat over his face, and then let his mind wander wherever it might lead. Smith taught this esoteric skill to his son, Joseph Jr., who became a skilled scryer in his own right while he was still quite young.

When Joseph was seven years old, he suffered a serious physical trauma: a bone in his leg became seriously infected, and he had to endure a surgery in which the doctor cut open his leg and scraped the bones, all without anesthesia. Before the boy recovered from that first operation, the infection returned. A second operation had to be performed, and after that second surgery, young Joseph had to use crutches to move about for three years.

In addition to his physical challenges, Joseph had to struggle with inner doubts about the status of his soul. He described how "from the age of twelve years to fifteen, I pondered many things in my heart concerning the situation of the world of mankind, the contentions and divisions, the wickedness and abominations... my mind became exceedingly distressed for I became convicted of my Sins" (*Joseph Smith Letter Books*, pp. 1-2, in Hill D, *Joseph Smith: The First Mormon* (Doubleday, 1977, p. 47). When the young Joseph was fifteen years old, the family moved from Vermont to a farm outside of Palmyra, New York. That was a region of the country that often got caught up in "The Great Awakening" revivals that frequently swept through New England. Joseph often accompanied his mother when she attended the revivals that passed through their region. Joseph's father was opposed to all organized religions, and he refused to join them.

As Joseph was being bombarded by the hell-and-brimstone preaching of the revivalist preachers, his concerns about the status of his soul grew more acute. He spent a lot of time studying the Bible, searching for advice about how to alleviate his anxieties and his spiritual pain. During one of his readings, he came across a passage in the Epistle of James that caught his attention: "If any of you lack wisdom, let him ask of God, that giveth to all men liberally... and it shall be given him (James 1: 5)." After Joseph read that passage, he couldn't put those words out of mind. He became obsessed with figuring out what that advice might mean for him personally: "At length I came to the conclusion that I must either remain in darkness and confusion or else I must do as James directs, that is, ask of God" (Bushman, *Joseph Smith: Rough Stone Rolling*, 2005, pp. 38-39). Joseph decided that it was time for him to act on that Biblical advice. He headed into the forest that surrounded the family farm and searched for a spot where he could pray undisturbed for however long it might take to get the spiritual reassurance he so desperately needed. When he arrived at a meadow that was wide enough for him to look up and see the sky, he knew he'd found the right place. He knelt down on his knees to pray, and that's when he saw the vision that changed his life:

> I retired to the woods to make the attempt... Immediately
> I was seized upon by some power which entirely overcame

me and had such astonishing influence over me as to bind my tongue so that I could not speak. Thick darkness gathered around me, and it seemed to me for a time as if I were doomed to sudden destruction… Just at this moment of great alarm, I saw a pillar of light exactly over my head, above the brightness of the sun, which descended gradually until it fell upon me. It no sooner appeared than I found myself delivered from the enemy which held me bound. When the light rested upon me, I saw two personages, whose brightness and glory defy all description, standing above me in the air. One of them spake unto me calling me by name and said—pointing to the other—"This is my beloved Son; hear him."… When he came to, he found himself lying on his back in the woods, looking up at the sky (Smith, Jr., *History of the Church*, I, 1842, pp. 4-6, quoted in Hill D, *Joseph Smith: The First Mormon*, 1977, p. 52).

Joseph said he also saw another vision in which he received more explicit commands about what he should do. That vision came three years later. He was eighteen years old and kneeling beside his bed to pray before he retired for the night when a bright light suddenly filled the bedroom. A figure appeared in the light and told Joseph that he was being visited by the Angel Moroni. The angel told Joseph to go to a hill named Cumorah located nearby and to begin searching for plates of gold that had been buried there by an ancient culture that had vanished long ago. Joseph claimed that this vision of Moroni in the bright light reappeared three times that same night, then reappeared the next day. On that last occasion, seeing the vision caused Joseph to lose consciousness and collapse on the floor.

When young Joseph told his father about his vision, the two men agreed that the son should respect what had just happened to him and that he should treat the experience as an omen. Not long after that, Joseph reported that the Angel Moroni appeared again, led him to the hill named Cumorah, ad then pointed to the location where the ancient stone tablets were buried. But Moroni also told Joseph that he did not yet have permission to begin digging up those tablets. He ordered Joseph to come back to that same place at the same time every year. When the time was right, Moroni promised, would give Joseph permission to dig. It was only after Joseph returned for his fourth annual visit that Moroni gave him permission to begin. Joseph claimed that he dug up the tablets, took them home, and stored them in a large box. None of Joseph's contemporaries were allowed to look inside the box, so no one has ever been in a position to confirm Joseph's claim.

Joseph said that when he took the stones out the box and looked at them, he realized that he was facing a formidable challenge: the inscriptions on the tablets were written in an unintelligible language. He was only able to translate those inscriptions when God came to his aid and sent him a continuing stream of revelations. But those revelations did not appear spontaneously; Joseph had to use his scrying skills to put himself in a trance state before any revelations would begin. He put his green seer-stones in his hat, pulled the hat over his face, and concentrated his attention on the stones while he waited for revelations to begin. He would dictate the revelations in English as he "received" them, relying on one of the local men who knew how to write and who believed Joseph's claim that he had been assigned a divine mission. The translations that resulted from Joseph's scrying sessions were later published as *The Book of Mormon*. When that book was published, Joseph was only twenty-five years old, but he'd already attracted many followers who'd heard him recount his visionary experiences that had put him in contact with the divine realm. These followers helped him found a new religious sect called "The Church of Jesus Christ of Latter-Day Saints" which also came to be known as the Mormon Church.

The life trajectory of Joseph Smith, Jr., shows clear evidence of a traumatic childhood—the leg infection, the painful surgeries, the long convalescences, and the need to rely on crutches for three years after the second surgery. His frequent exposures to the fire-and-brimstone preaching at religious revivals inflicted another kind of trauma that left him morbidly concerned that his soul might end up in hell. We also know, based on Joseph's skill at scrying, that he knew how to empty his mind of distracting content and to concentrate his attention on the green seer stones in the dark interior of his hat. These are behaviors that would be effective in bringing on the kind of empty-mind meditative trance in which visions of green light-rings and dark blue clouds would begin to flow spontaneously. Joseph did not claim to have seen any of those light visions, but he did see a vision of fiery light "above the brightness of the sun" that was powerful enough to cause him to lose consciousness and collapse physically. That vision clearly qualifies as a paroxysmal vision of fiery light. That seizure-like vision clearly led to the emergence of a temporal lobe behavior syndrome. It was three years after that paroxysmal vision that he began to see visions of Angel Moroni bathed in a bright light. One of those visions also led to a loss of consciousness and a physical collapse. It was Joseph's visions of Moroni who inspired him to believe he'd been given a divinely inspired mission. Joseph describes how he would regularly put himself in a deep meditative trance state on many occasions, using his scrying skills to enter a trance that to contact Moroni or to channel God's instructions about how to translate the inscriptions on the golden tablets. He used the revelations he channeled by scrying with green stones placed in his hat to compose a substantial treatise, *The Book of Mormon*, that clearly points to his having experienced symptoms of hyper-religiosity and hypergraphia that often appear during the emergence of a temporal lobe behavior syndrome. That emergence of that syndrome also explains how Joseph acquired his enhanced sense of personal destiny that gave him an unshakeable self-confidence that he'd been chosen by God to become His prophet. That self-confidence helped generate the charisma that enabled him to attract many followers who were searching for some religious leaders who could point the way to salvation. That's why Joseph succeeded in founding a new sect within the Christian tradition known as The Church of Jesus Christ of Latter-Day Saints, a sect that has continued to prosper and to proselytize.

CHAPTER 13

The Trauma/Dissociation Complex

Psychoanalysis and the "Oceanic Feeling"

Sigmund Freud, the neurologist who invented psychoanalysis, published his theory about the origins of religions in a book, *The Future of an Illusion*. Soon after the book came out, Freud received a letter from a French writer named Romain Rolland who was living in India and writing a biography of the famous Hindu mystic, Sri Ramakrishna. Rolland congratulated Freud on the new publication but protested that Freud's analysis of the roots of religion did not take into account the kinds of mystical experiences that Rolland was hearing Ramakrishna describe: "I would have liked to see you do an analysis of spontaneous religious sentiment... without perceptible limits, like an oceanic experience." Rolland was thinking of the time that Ramakrishna told him about his first vision of "the presence of the Kali, the Divine Mother":

I saw an ocean... boundless, dazzling. In whatever direction I looked great luminous waves were rising. They bore down on me with a loud roar... They broke over me, they engulfed me... I lost all natural consciousness and I fell... Round me rolled an ocean of ineffable joy (Rolland, in Masson, 1980, p. 36).

Ramakrishna's account matches the vision described in the Hindu *Upanishads* as the "Abounding Brahma-Light". Meditators who attain this spiritual experience see "Brahman... the ocean of light. In it, indeed, the worshippers become dissolved like salt... It is oneness with Brahman for in it all desires are contained (*Maitri Upanishad*, 6: 35)."

Freud, who was not usually interested in mystical phenomena, responded to Rolland's letter. He suggested that for people to experience this kind of "oceanic feeling", they would have to abandon their normal reality orientation and experience a resurgence of memories that were implanted during the earliest stage of infant development—during the "oral stage" that begins at birth and continues for the first three years of life. During this oral stage, Freud explained, infants acquire memories of a blissful state when their needs are quickly met by their mothers or other caregivers, but the infants themselves do not realize what's really going on. They have not reached the stage of awareness where they would recognize that another person exists who's taking care of them. That realization, according to Freud, only arrives near the end of the oral stage. Until then, the young infants feel that they live in a magical world where they believe that their desires are omnipotent: if they feel distressed, the source of their pain will be removed, and if they wish to have something change, that will happen automatically.

Once infants reach the age where they recognize that another person is helping them to meet their needs, their interactions with the mother or some other nurturing caregiver inculcate a sense of well-being and emotional security and a confidence that other humans are worthy of trust and love. According to Freud, the memories of what it felt like to be an omnipotent infant whose needs were satisfied by magic wish-fulfillment get suppressed as the infant becomes a child and the child matures. Those early memories of omnipotence are no longer accessible. But there might be exceptions: Freud acknowledged that something might happen in the lives of adults to make them feel overwhelmed and unable to cope using their normal strategies of emotional defense. In that crisis situation, the old, repressed memories from early infancy might be allowed to resurface in the person's conscious awareness. Freud thought that was the best explanation for the kind of "oceanic feeling" that Rolland described. But Freud never mentioned what kinds of catastrophic events might trigger that effect. Psychoanalysts who came after Freud often agree in principle with the founder's theory that mystical consciousness is based on the nature of care that infants receive in their families of origins, but many of them have also contributed new insights.

Weston La Barre is an anthropologist who's also a psychoanalyst. He spent many years working in different cultures. At the end of his career he wrote his masterwork, *The Ghost Dance: The Origins of Religions* (1987), where he condensed what he'd learned from his field work and his collaborations with other influential anthropologists. In that book, La Barre revisits Freud's theory about mystical consciousness when he writes about the theories of Rudolf Otto, a Christian theologian who proposed that humans have an ability to sense a supernatural dimension of reality that is "Wholly Other" than themselves. Otto called this experience the perception of a *"Mysterium tremendum et fascinosum"*. La Barre responds that while humans might sense that they're somehow in contact with a supernatural dimension of reality, this experience is a legacy of the interpersonal dynamics that took place during infancy and early childhood in the nuclear family:

The Mysterium *is* in a sense objective, and, in fact, it *has* been experienced; but each individual has forgotten its erstwhile nature and original location... *The context is the universally nuclear family; the condition is individual human neotony.* In religion the projected parent still stands, as of yore, between us and physical reality... At the base of every religion is the familial experience, and all religions consequently contain some basic oedipal story in their myths (*The Ghost Dance*, p. 12).

La Barre also suggested that there are two different ways that infants and young children can acquire the sensitivities that enable them, as adults, to have such powerful experiences of the *Mysterium* described by Otto that they strive to be recognized as charismatic religious leaders. If the adults aspiring to become religious leaders do so because they experience a resurgence of repressed memories from the oral stage of development—memories of a time when feelings of omnipotence were still powerful and simply wishing for something was enough to make it so—La Barre predicts that they are likely to adopt a religious identity based on "psychic attitudes" that are "shaman-like". These religious leaders claim that they possess magical powers—that they can go on journeys to the spirit world, that they can heal the sick and conjure up miracles, or even that they can become a god themselves. La Barre, like Freud, traces the origins of this shaman-like psychic attitude to the oral stage of development when infants live in a world in which wishing often makes it so.

But La Barre also predicts that those who aspire to become religious leaders can take a different path: if their "psychic attitude" is "priest-like" rather than "shaman-like," the leaders will claim that they have developed a special relationship with God (or with some other supernatural entity) and were delegated the spiritual authority to serve as an intermediary when humans feel a need to communicate with their God. La Barre proposes that this "priest-like" predisposition is also acquired during early childhood, but it gets implanted during the "oedipal stage" of development said to take place between the ages of five and seven. During those years, young children begin to recognize that their fathers can be affectionate and fun-loving at times, but they can also demand obedience and take action to punish recalcitrant children. If children are able to preserve a loving relationship with their father throughout the oedipal period, despite his demands for obedience and his punishments, those children become adults who feel a deep need to reclaim that childhood experience of being nurtured in an intimate and safe family environment presided over by a powerful male who suc-cessfully combines authority and love. These adults can to attempt to replicate that childhood experience by dedicating their lives to being a servant of the God they regard as a Celestial Father. La Barre captures the essential difference between these two psychic attitudes of religious figures in this memorable passage:

> Insofar as he "masters" the spirits, and orders them about at will to do his bidding, the practitioner is a shaman... There is little ambiguity about who the "god" of the magician is: himself. In total submission to a personified God beyond his command, the practitioner is just as plainly a priest, presiding in group worship of an Omnipotent Father... The real difference between the shaman and priest is who and where the god is, inside or out (*The Ghost Dance*, p. 108).

An Alternative Theory

I was introduced to La Barre's *Ghost Dance* long before the time when I inadvertently induced the limbic seizure that generated my vision of fiery light. Back then I found his psychoanalytic theories about the origins of mystical consciousness to be provocative and wholly convincing. Then after having the visionary experience, I began to be more skeptical about theories that attempt to explain mystical consciousness as a resurgence of memories of oral stage omnipotence or memories of oedipal stage obedience to patriarchal authority. I'd discovered that a limbic seizure could be induced by someone who was not an epileptic and that when it erupted it could ignite an ecstatic rapture comparable to what many religious mystics described. My subsequent research revealed that people who suffer partial seizures often develop a cluster of post-seizure symptoms known as the temporal lobe behavior syndrome. The symptoms associated with that syndrome—the symptoms of hyper-emotionality, hyper-religiosity, hypergraphia, and hyposexuality—all overlap with what pious believers in many world religions expect to see exemplified in the lives of their favorite saints. Based on those insights, I began to believe that I'd discovered a new and neurologically grounded theory of ecstatic visionary experiences that would provide a credible alternative to the existing psychoanalytic theories. But then as the focus of my research expanded beyond brain mechanisms to include analysis of the life trajectories leading up to the visionary experiences of influential mystics, it became clear that the psychoanalytic emphasis on early child development was still relevant and still important.

Many founders of new religions who had legacies of child trauma resorted to dissociative coping strategies when they found themselves facing major life challenges. They chose to isolate themselves on solitary retreats to seek spiritual guidance from a supernatural entity they envisioned as being more trustworthy and more powerful than fellow humans. They chose to inflict their bodies and minds with extreme ascetic regimens designed to demonstrate their dedication, their spiritual purity, and their worthiness to receive some reward. They chose to immerse themselves in long prayer or meditation vigils, often continuing late into night or even all night which led them to gradually accumulate a substantial sleep deficit. This combination of behaviors, pushed to extremes, made it likely that their meditations would eventually destabilize sleep rhythm oscillators and initiate the onset of a hypersynchronous seizure. That would set in motion a chain of events with the potential to progress to the point of triggering a shift from hypersynchronous activity to the eruption of a paroxysmal seizure in the limbic and temporal lobe regions, the type of seizure that generates visions of fiery lights filling the visual field and the ecstatic emotional aura that accompanies that vision. That means childhood experiences do turn out to be very important. There is a demonstrable connection between what young children learn when they have to cope with trauma and the adult tendency to rely on dissociative coping strategies to respond to the pain imposed by some major life stress. But how does this correlation get established? What can happen in the lives of infants or young children to inculcate a predisposition to use dissociative defense strategies to cope with pain and distress?

Child Trauma, Adult Trance

In humans, the physiological level of arousal is mediated by the hypothalamic-pituitary-adrenal (HPA) axis. It can release stress hormones like cortisol that activate the sympathetic nervous system to mobilize a fight-or-flight response. The HPA axis can also produce the opposite effect: it can activate the parasympathetic nervous system to repress the level of arousal and restore the body to its normal state of homeostasis. When an infant is nurtured by a "good enough" mother, the HPA axis increases the level of oxytocin in the infant's bloodstream, activating a parasympathetic response that helps dampen the level of arousal. These experiences of being nurtured by a mother in a way that restores a state of calm teaches infants and young children that other people can be worthy of trust and that other people can provide effective support when it's needed. Those experiences of nurturing can also teach infants and young people the rudiments of how they can go about regulating their own emotional states, an important skill for everyone to acquire. The enduring effect of this kind of nurture-induced conditioning of the infant's HPA axis is underscored in an article written by Dr. Jean Decety of the Department of Psychiatry and Behavioral Neuroscience at the University of Chicago and her co-author, Dr. Margarita Svetlova:

> The social modulation of physiological stress responses not only lays the foundation for the development of emotional regulation competencies but continues to influence HPA activity in adolescents and adults by providing a buffer against stress and having a positive impact on measures of health and well-being (*Developmental Cognitive Neuroscience* 2012 Jan; 2[1]: 14).

By contrast, if the mother or other caregiver neglects the pressing needs of infants or young children, the pain and distress caused by that neglect will activate the sympathetic nervous system, mobilizing the fight-or-flight response. But the infants and young children are not able to fight or to flee; for them, the arousal mobilized by the fight-or-flight response is not only useless but also even more distressing because it exacerbates the pain and distress that's already present. If the infant's level of arousal rises enough to cross a threshold value, the HPA axis will intervene to restore the homeostatic equilibrium by triggering a neurophysiological reaction known as "conservation-withdrawal". In conservation-withdrawal, the parasympathetic nervous system takes over, allowing the infants and young children to slip into a deeply relaxed state. This state of parasympathetic collapse includes activation of the synchronous slow waves that would normally initiate a transition to Stage 2 NREM sleep. The activation of those slow-wave sleep rhythms directs the children's attention inward, away from the external environment and away from their feelings of pain and distress. The children's bodies also begin releasing endogenous opioids into the bloodstream, and that introduces a numbing effect that also helps dampen the pain and distress. Psychologist Allan Shore, a professor in the Department of Psychiatry at the UCLA School of Medicine and an important pioneer in the study of the effects of early trauma, gives a vivid description of the phenomenon of parasympathetic collapse:

> This intense psychophysiological distress state, phenomenologically experienced as a "spiraling downward," is proposed to reflect a sudden shift from energy-mobilizing sympathetic- to energy-conserving parasympathetic-dominant autonomic nervous system activity, a rapid transition from a hyper-aroused to a hypo-aroused state... This represents a shift into a low-keyed inhibitory state of parasympathetic conservation-withdrawal... that occurs in helpless and hopeless stressful situations in which the individual becomes inhibited and strives to avoid attention in order to become "unseen." This state is mediated by a different psychophysiological pattern than positive states... [and it activates] the opioid (endorphin) and corticotropin releasing factor in the brain (*Affect Dysregulation and Disorders of the Self*, 2003, p. 18).

The abrupt shift from sympathetic arousal to parasympathetic dominance is a phenomenon that was originally observed and described in the professional literature by the Russian physiologist, Ivan Pavlov. He performed many experiments in which he kept dogs in cages and administered electric shocks at unpredictable intervals. The pain produced by this intermittent stimulation elicited an autonomically driven alternation between sympathetic arousal and parasympathetic collapse. Eventually the dogs exhibited a conditioned response in which they simply gave up any attempt to escape the pain. Once they acquired this conditioned response, the dogs remained passive even when they were released from their cages and put in other situations where they were then exposed to other stressors. Pavlov called this reaction "learned helplessness". This same kind of conditioned response can be found in human infants and young children who have been mistreated (Seligman, 1972).

When children get traumatized at very young ages, their emotional reactions do not register in the brain as "declarative" memories, as memories that the adult could potentially recall and describe verbally. Instead, the traumatic experiences get imprinted as unconscious neurophysiological reactions—as chronic states of hyper-vigilance where the adult scans the environment to detect situations that feel threatening. If they do perceive a threat, there is an automatic and unconscious pulling away that can be both physical and psychological. These trauma-implanted memories that get embodied in neurophysiological reactions are called "implicit" or "procedural" memories. They're "implicit" memories because they usually can't be consciously recalled and communicated in words, and they're "procedural" memories because they continue to exert an important effect in determining how the person will proceed to act once an implicit memory causes the person to become alarmed. The implicit, procedural memories implanted in the neurophysiological circuits of traumatized children can continue to affect them in important ways throughout their lives without them ever becoming aware of the hidden forces that are driving some of their behavioral choices. This is especially true if the traumatic events occur when children have not yet reached the age of three. That's because most children are unable to recall any memories from before the age of three, even if they haven't been exposed to trauma. This is a generally recognized phenomenon called "childhood amnesia" in which the neurophysiological system preserves the memories as implicit, procedural reactions.

Robert Scaer is a neurologist who specializes in treating patients whose memories of trauma have been embedded as implicit memories that are difficult to retrieve by therapies that involve talking about early memories. In his book, *The Body Bears the Burden* (2001), Scaer explains that "Conservation-withdrawal is the earliest manifestation of dissociation, which if perpetuated becomes a lifelong tendency in the face of threat or stress... There is compelling evidence that the physical and chemical changes in the brain that result from inadequate maturation because of inadequate bonding and nurturing are relatively hardwired and permanent (pp. 121-122)." Scaer draws an analogy between the young child's predicament of having been exposed to pain and distress at a very young age without any hope of escape to the experiences of soldiers stationed in the trenches during World War I: those soldiers who had to passively endure the explosions of shells plummeting down from the enemy's artillery barrages "manifested relatively pure dissociative symptoms rather than the arousal, startle, and panic symptoms of PTSD. Shellshock was a relatively pure dissociative disorder (p. 184)."

If a child is regularly forced to use the conservation-withdrawal strategy to cope with pain and distress, that traumatic childhood can instill an unconscious, neurophysiological reflex that manifests in adult life as a predisposition to rely on some form of dissociation to cope with the threat posed by a major life crisis. This predisposition to dissociate remains unconscious because it is driven by the person's implicit memories of trauma. People who are suffering from this kind of "dissociative amnesia" tend to act in ways that are self-defeating and repetitive because they have no insight into their chosen behaviors or why those behaviors are not effective at producing the outcomes they want to achieve.

Child Trauma and Dissociative Amnesia

The diagnoses of childhood amnesia and dissociative amnesia have provoked many debates among academic psychologists and psychotherapists. The controversy is about whether those events experienced in early childhood, which did not get preserved as declarative memories, can actually resurface again much later in peoples' lives in ways that force them to struggle with feelings of anger, despair, shame, and a sense that their lives are careening out of control. One objection to the theory of dissociative amnesia is the claim that these so-called "recovered memories" often surface in psychotherapy sessions where the therapist's preconceptions about child trauma and the patient's suggestibility might interact in a way that conjures up a false set of "recovered memories" that match what the therapist was expecting to uncover. Fortunately, in our investigation this complicated issue does not arise, because we're focusing on mystic seers who lived long before psychotherapy was even invented.

Another objection put forward by opponents of recovered memories is that what happens in these cases is not an activation of implicit procedural memories, nor a case of "dissociative amnesia", but rather a case of the person making conscious use of the psychological defense of denial. In that view, what happens is that the patient never really forgets the events that took place in their early childhoods, but they remain determined, as adults, to never let themselves think about the memories of what happened.

The most important counterargument against those who challenge the concept of "recovered memories" and "dissociative amnesia" is that there are many well-designed and credible studies in the scientific literature, studies that cite evidence supporting the claim that implicit memories of child trauma can remain inaccessible to people's conscious awareness but still affect their behaviors in important ways. These studies document how the resurgence of emotional distress can reactivate the implicit, procedural memories implanted by child trauma, and a reactivation of those hidden memories can manifest in many different ways:

- As a welling up of an overt depression.
- As a depression that manifests as somatic complaints (e.g., anorexia).
- As alexithymia, where the sufferers can't recognize any emotions other than anger.
- As a propensity to always assign overly negative appraisals to life events.
- As problems maintaining relationships with other people.
- As moods that rapidly cycle up and down, a symptom called cyclothymia.
- As a predisposition to see visions or experience hallucinations.

These observations help explain a pattern that we saw surface again and again as we studied the life trajectories of the founders and other influential seers who had legacies of child trauma. As mature adults, these men and women usually assumed productive roles in their respective communities and appeared to be thriving in their adult lives, often with no visible signs that their lives were being affected by old wounds. But then, usually in midlife, when those men and women were confronted with some major life stress, they reacted to that challenge by resorting to the adult equivalent of conservation-withdrawal, the strategy that had served them so well as young children. They choose to rely on dissociative coping strategies—withdrawing from interaction with other people; going on solitary retreats to seek guidance from some supernatural being deemed to be more trustworthy than fellow humans; disciplining their bodies and minds with extreme ascetic practices to prove their worthiness to receive guidance; and immersing themselves in meditation or prayer vigils for hours on end. This constellation of events increases the odds that the seeker will set in motion the series of neurophysiological changes that can ultimately trigger a partial seizure that manifests as an ecstatic vision fiery light.

PART IV.

Seers and the Wellsprings of Creativity

CHAPTER 14

From Whence Cometh the Message?

The Empty Ecstasy of the Fiery Light

The visions of fiery light that transform the lives of many influential religious mystics are inherently "empty". There are no messages or dreamlike images contained in those visions because the seizure raging in the terminals of the visual pathways generates flashes of bright light that cut off that possibility. Other paroxysmal symptoms include sizzing sounds and muscle tremors. What the seer receives from the vision is the profound emotional experience generated by the seizure-driven stimulation of emotional association processing centers in the limbic brain.

What happens here is analogous to déjà vu experiences where people walk into a place they've never been before and suddenly feel that this scene before them is intimately familiar and deeply meaningful, even if they know that they've never actually been physically present in this place before. Those strong feelings motivate some people to confabulate stories about how they must have visited the site in their dreams or that they moved through it in a previous life. That's the same kind of confabulation that can occur when people have ecstatic mystical experiences that they are otherwise unable to explain. As we've discussed in earlier chapters, neurologists explain the déjà vu experience as the result of a sudden, transient discharge of neurons in the emotional association centers of the limbic brain. Those discharges create abnormal levels of neurotransmitters that then slosh around and imprint whatever the person is looking at with a strong sensation of familiarity and meaningfulness. Something similar happens when meditators trigger a vision of fiery light that sends a strong barrage of paroxysmal discharges into the limbic brain located downstream from the hippocampi. The stimulation of these limbic structures floods the seer's body and mind with ecstatic emotions and implants indelible memories of that ecstatic rapture with its erotic overlay. But there are no messages contained in those visions, no instructions about what to think or do; it's all about spectacle, trembling muscles, and surging emotions. So how is it that the seers come to believe that there's some critically important spiritual message embodied in their visions of pure light? Weston La Barre, the psychoanalytically oriented anthropologist whose Freudian ideas about the origins of mystical consciousness we discussed in the previous chapter, discussed this issue in his book, *The Ghost Dance: Origins of Religions.* He analyzed how and why traumatized children who come of age during an ongoing cultural crisis have the potential to become charismatic leaders who can succeed in founding a new religion.

Child Trauma and Crises of Acculturation

In the scenario described by La Barre, a cultural crisis occurs when a stronger, more technologically sophisticated culture challenges an older, more traditional culture. This intrusion raises alarms because it threatens to replace the values of the traditional culture. These kinds of cultural crises can disrupt the lives of families in many ways, but two kinds of dislocations are especially relevant for our investigation. The prevailing confusion and turmoil can undermine the ability of parents living in the traditional society to maintain the emotional balance needed to provide their children with a safe, nurturing environment—and that means it's likely that the incidence of child trauma will increase in that traditional society. But another kind of dislocation can also affect those traumatized children who live in the older, more traditional culture. As they mature, they're faced with the dilemma of whether to adopt their parents' traditional values or to model themselves instead on the values of the more powerful and more technologically sophisticated culture that is challenging traditional values. Adopting some of those new values might be an attractive option for those young people living in the traditional cultures who are hoping to succeed at achieving their goals in a world that's clearly dominated by the competing culture. According to La Barre, the question that these young people have to ask themselves as they come of age during these kinds of cultural crises is this: "Shall the models for my behavior be the old ambivalently loved persons of my tribe?—or the new ambivalently hated persons of a more powerful alien tribe? (*The Ghost Dance*, p. 338)."

George Devereux, a psychiatrist and anthropologist who was a close colleague of La Barre, provides some in-depth accounts of this acculturation crisis based on what he observed while working with members of various Native American tribes. He noticed that many of his clients felt severely disoriented by the conflicts they perceived between the values of their traditional Native American culture and the values championed by the dominant Anglo culture which had enveloped the tribe physically, mentally, and emotionally. The problems of acculturation became particularly acute for those youths who had legacies of child trauma. That trauma disrupted the internalization of the psychological structures that the young children needed to acquire during their development in order to become well-functioning adults. When those children matured, they found it to be increasingly difficult to repress thoughts and emotions that they would have been better able to repress if the values of their traditional culture were still firmly in place. The outcome, Devereux reports, was that some of these children with traumatic legacies acquired just enough of the traditional acculturation to be able to fit in as an accepted member of the tribe, but not enough of that acculturation to be seen by others as completely "normal". These children, when they grew up, were regarded by others in the tribe as being "deviant". That deviance could manifest in two different ways. Some of the young people regarded as deviant were nevertheless able to succeed at achieving recognition in their tribe because they found some way to embody what Devereux describes as the "unconscious segment of the ethnic personality". For example, there were some young people who had a mystical experience that marked them as being "different". Some of them were able to follow up on that experience by apprenticing themselves to tribal shamans and eventually being acknowledged as shamans in their own right. But there were other young people—those whose deviance was more severe and not consonant with the "unconscious segment of the ethnic personality"—who were stigmatized by the tribe as being mentally ill. Here is Devereux's explanation of the differences between "deviants" who became shamans and the outliers who were seen as being mentally ill:

> The crucial difference between the shaman and the "private" but unrecognized hysteric or psychotic lies in the fact that the shaman's conflicts are characteristically located in the unconscious segment of his ethnic personality rather

than in the idiosyncratic portion of his unconscious. He can express, control, and redirect his impulses and conflicts by using the many—usually ritualized—devices that each culture places at the disposal of those whose conflicts are of the "conventional" type... This explains why the normal members of the tribe echo the shaman's intrapsychic conflicts so readily and why they find his "symptoms" (ritual acts) so reassuring (Devereux, *Basic Problems of Ethnopsychiatry*, 1980, pp. 6-7, 16-17).

A similar phenomenon is occasionally observed in modern psychiatry where some patients who experience a mental breakdown or who are recovering from brain surgery are more successful than other patients at reintegrating themselves back into their previous lives and being accepted by their peers. For these patients, being able to demonstrate that they can conform to what Devereux called the "unconscious segment of the ethnic personality" can be an important ingredient of their recovery. Jose Fernando Muñoz Zúñiga, a psychiatrist who practices in Bogota, Columbia, specializes in treating patients with brain injuries. He gave a lecture at the International Neuropsychoanalytic Society in which he described how his seriously injured patients struggled to recover a normal identity after their surgery. Once the acute stages of medical treatment were over, Dr. Muñoz reported, there were patients who experienced behavioral problems that upset those with whom they had to interact. The crucial issue that determined if his patients recovered most of their normal functioning and reintegrated themselves to become fully accepted members of their society was if those patients found ways to link their new, abnormal symptoms to aspects of their formers lives that remained personally meaningful for them and that also could be understood and accepted by the people they encountered in their daily lives. The issue, then, was whether patients could create new narratives about who they'd become and about who they wanted to be. Those new narratives worked best if they incorporated the "unconscious segment of the ethnic personality" that they shared with other members of the same culture. If the patients could manage this—if they were able once again to feel comfortable with who they were when they were around other people—their feelings of self-acceptance made it easier for other people to feel comfortable around them.

Culture Crises, Wounded Healers, and the Resurrection of Hope

La Barre uses the insights that he and Devereux gleaned from their anthropological fieldwork to propose a more general theory about the type of person who will most likely surface at some future date to become the founder of a new religious vision that attracts many followers. When La Barre studied historical accounts describing the rise of charismatic prophets, he found that most of these innovators came from the ranks of traumatized children whose acculturation into the mores of their traditional culture got disrupted, not only by their individual experiences of trauma within their nuclear families, but also because they were exposed to the values of a more powerful culture that challenged the old ways of thinking and behaving. If there's someone living in the threatened culture who eventually succeeds at resolving their own inner struggles by finding a way to recombine fragments from the old and the new, forming a new, eclectic synthesis that appeals to other young men and women, then that person can become the kind of transformational leader that La Barre calls a "culture hero". But the culture hero walks a difficult path, as La Barre points out in this passage:

The predicament of the culture hero is precisely that of the neurotic: shall I operate with the defense mechanisms devised in my childhood (to which I am bound because they are compulsive, absolute, inviolable, and mostly unconscious in any case)? Shall I operate with the defense mechanisms of my society's past (to which, with complete loyalty, I have painfully, sometimes unwillingly, become enculturated, and which, all too often, actually conflict with the secular experiences of my personality)? Or shall I attempt new adaptations, heretic to both the native and alien tribal pasts I have learned? (*The Ghost Dance*, p. 338).

If the candidate for culture hero can reconcile the inherent contradictions between the old values and the new, and if that synthesis resonates with listeners who share the culture hero's traditional culture, inspiring them to adopt those new ideas themselves, then the candidate for culture hero has created a chrysalis that can give birth to a new crisis cult: "Each most catholicly established church was once a sect," La Barre writes, "each sect a cult, and in every revealed religion, the cult had its beginning in one person's revelation (p. 343)." In *The Ghost Dance*, La Barre provides many examples of how this phenomenon has surfaced again and again throughout the course of human history.

With the formation of a crisis cult, a new religious meme is born. But once that new religious meme is released out into the world, it has to prove its fitness to survive. Its fate is not unlike what happens in Nature where the Darwinian process of natural selection applies. In the natural world, a mutation in the genetic material of some creature that causes changes in the way that creature looks or behaves—changes that enhance or detract from its ability to reproduce and pass that mutated gene into the next generation—then that change will be an important determinant for whether that species will survive. Similarly, a new religious meme has to prove that it can survive and reproduce, and that success has to keep on happening even as the prevailing circumstances change, even as the new religious meme spreads into cultural environments that are very different from those in which it was first formulated. La Barre contends that this process in which culture heroes generate new religious memes by synthesizing the old and the new will inevitably surface again. That will happen, he predicts, when the circumstances that shape human life change in ways that require the threatened culture to make radical adjustments in its belief system to survive:

> Culture fantasies protect men from clear knowledge of their predicament at all times. But that is the function of sacred culture… When such fantasies are threatened, men are thrust back, shorn of defenses, to the same old anxieties and unmastered problems, and new dream work must be done by culture heroes. They must mend the fabric with new threads… And the mystic who is listened to, at best expresses only a current consensus. He dives deep, only to meet his own mind and the common problems of all… That is, the shaman is ill for conventional reasons, and in a conventional way characteristic of many others… For this reason, his symptoms (ritual acts), evolved as defenses for him, are found to be reassuring to his fellows (*The Ghost Dance,* p. 207).

Charisma and Conversion

Becoming a charismatic leader is a difficult task because it involves striking a delicate balance between the message that the new culture hero wants to convey and what the listeners want, what they need, what they can understand—and what they can tolerate. Charles Lindholm, a professor of anthropology and author of the book *Charisma* (1990), emphasizes that charisma is often misunderstood as a personal trait that the prospective leader either has or does not have. It's more accurate, Lindholm explains, to conceptualize charisma as a relationship between the person who aspires to become a culture hero and the people who desperately want to find answers and who come to hear what the person has to say that might make their lives better:

> Charisma appears only in interaction with others who lack it… Even though charisma is thought of as something intrinsic to the individual, a person cannot reveal this quality in isolation. It is only evident in interaction with those who are affected by it… Therefore, it follows that if the charismatic is able to compel, the follower has a matching capacity for being compelled, and we need to consider what makes up the personality configuration of the follower, as well as that of the leader, if we are to understand charisma (*Charisma*, p. 7).

Some of the considerations that will determine whether the culture hero's listeners will find the new ideas compelling can be found in the writings of behavioral economists who study the systematic biases that shape human thinking. Psychologist Daniel Kahneman describes some of those systematic human biases in his book, *Thinking, Fast and Slow* (2011):

- Confidence in the truth of a narrative is often unrelated to its empirical validity because people are more likely to accept and remember a story if it fits well with what they already think they know.

- People are predisposed to accept stories because of the "cognitive ease" involved, because it's easier to accept the story than to evaluate its truth quotient.
- People are often disposed to manipulate their beliefs in order to avoid the risk of undermining some important economic or interpersonal relationship.
- People want to ignore information that might set off some inner conflict.
- People want to feel confident that, at some future time, they will be able to become the kind of person they think they want to become, so they try to calculate what will likely be the "expected return" if they adopt a new idea.

Culture Heroes and Crisis Cults: Case Studies

In this chapter so far we've focused primarily on the theoretical aspects of La Barre's work, but in *The Ghost Dance* he also includes accounts of interesting crisis cults that emerged during the course of human history. With that theoretical background, we're now in a position to take a closer look at some of the examples of crisis cults La Barre includes in his book.

The Native American Ghost Dance

The ill-fated "Ghost Dances" of the Native American Sioux tribes took place on the Great Plains just before the turn of the twentieth century. La Barre recounts the story of a man named Wovoka, "The Cutter", who was born in a Paiute tribe around 1858. His father was a shaman who played a prominent role in a Native American messianic movement during the 1870s known as the Round Dance. When Wovoka was a teenager, he worked on a ranch owned by the David Wilson family of Nevada and became quite attached to the family. They also valued their relationship with him: they taught him English, instructed him in the beliefs of their Christian religion, and gave him the name, "Jack Wilson". He lived with other young Paiutes who also worked for the Wilsons and who'd set up camp near the ranch where they could maintain many of their traditional cultural practices. When "Jack Wilson" was in that camp, he used his original Paiute name, Wovoka.

When Wovoka became an adult, he left the Wilson ranch and joined his father's Round Dance movement. There he achieved recognition as a shaman and a spiritual leader in his own right. Then in 1889, when Wovoka was thirty-one years old, he fell sick with a high fever and slipped into a coma-like trance. When he recovered, Wovoka claimed that he'd been taken up to heaven to see God, and that while he was there, he saw that the deceased ancestors of the Native American tribes had been resurrected and that now they were enjoying themselves in heaven. He claimed that God put him in charge of the American West, that he'd been delegated by divine authority to organize to a new movement that would become powerful enough to free the tribes of the Great Plains from the dominance of the white settlers.

One of God's prescriptions, according to Wovoka, was that the members of all tribes should make special "Ghost Shirts" painted with images of the sun and moon and use them to per-form a new ritual Wovoka called the "Ghost Dance". Members of the tribes who wore Ghost Shirts and performed the Ghost Dance would be protected from all illnesses. Those who were warriors would be magically shielded from any bullets fired at them by hostile whites. Wovoka also claimed that, if the tribes complied with these commands, God would trigger a massive earthquake. During the upheaval, the second coming of Jesus would take place, and this new Jesus would take action to restore the world to the conditions that existed before the intrusions of the whites. Moreover, during this event, all of the tribes' deceased ancestors would come back to life. Wovoka predicted the earthquake would erupt sometime in the spring of 1891 or, if not then, shortly after when the Fourth of July arrived.

Wovoka's messianic predictions inspired many members of the Arapahoe, Cheyenne, Shoshone, Kiowa, Hualapai, and Sioux tribes, and he convinced them start performing the Ghost Dance. Most of the tribes assumed that, given Wovoka's prophecies of the earthquake and the second coming of Jesus, there would be no need for them to organize war parties to attack the whites themselves. They could just wait for God to take action.

But the Hunkapapa Sioux tribe that was living on the Pine Ridge Reservation in South Dakota chose a different option that turned out to have drastic consequences. During the years preceding 1890, the Hunkapapa tribe had been battered by a convergence of many catastrophic events. They didn't have enough food because white hunters had killed all the local buffalo herds; the whites kept breaking the treaties they'd just signed, most recently when white miners began flooding into the Black Hills in massive numbers to search for gold; and, not least, there had been recurring epidemics of measles, flu, and whooping cough that killed many members of the tribe. Then, to make matters worse, in 1891, when a devastating famine was spreading through the reservation, the U.S. Congress voted to cut in half the beef ration they'd promised to the Sioux. Reeling from all these disasters that had converged during the decade leading up to 1891, the desperate Sioux felt compelled to search for a way to revive their hopes for a livable future.

The charismatic chief of the Hunkpapa Sioux was a medicine man named Sitting Bull. He was impressed by Wovoka's vision, so he ordered his tribe to begin performing the Ghost Dance to help speed up the coming of the earthquake that Wovoka predicted. The Hunkpapa Ghost Dance was staged so often and with such enthusiasm that the white men who were serving as Indian agents at Pine Ridge became concerned. Worried that the situation might get out of control, they thought it would be prudent for them to have a troop of cavalry sent to the reservation to help keep the peace. But the agents didn't bother to inform the leaders of the tribes about this impending event, so when a troop of mounted cavalry rode unannounced into Pine Ridge, Chief Sitting Bull and his band of Hunkpapa Sioux became alarmed. They remembered the many deadly encounters they'd had with cavalry units in the not-so-distant past. The tribe quickly mobilized: they folded their teepees, packed their supplies, and fled the reservation, hoping to find a safe refuge in the remote canyons of the Badlands.

The cavalry troops pursued the escapees and initiated skirmishes. In one of these encounters, Sitting Bull, the chief of the Hunkpapa tribe, was killed. Not long after that, some of the cavalry men who'd been split off from the main band to form a search party discovered a small Hunkpapa camp filled with old men, women, and children. No warriors were present. The soldiers in the cavalry unit debated whether it was appropriate for them to attack an undefended camp. Some of men objected to the idea of attacking non-combatants and refused to participate, but most of the soldiers were willing to proceed. They attacked the Hunkpapa camp and killed everyone who was not able to hide or run away. This infamous incident, which came to be known as the Wounded Knee Massacre, shocked the Native American tribes and marked the end of the Ghost Dance movement.

La Barre proposes that the Native American Ghost Dance movement constitutes a paradigmatic example of how cultural crises spawn culture heroes who attract many followers from an older, more traditional culture that is being challenged by the intrusion of a more powerful, more technologically sophisticated culture. Wovoka was a culture hero who formed a crisis cult that synthesized the ancestral beliefs of the Sioux tribes and the beliefs of the Christian religion in a way that resonated with members of the threatened culture. The Ghost Dance flourished for a while, but only for as long as it could avoid making the kinds of choices that would end up provoking its own demise:

> The basic sameness of "Ghost Dance" movements everywhere in the Americas is quite remarkable. The repeated similarities in New World movements may be ascribed to four causes: to contact-borrowing of the same European elements of belief, to old culture traits common in both Americas, to a diffusion of traits of specific cults, and to the general psychic characteristics of a basic human nature (La Barre, *The Ghost Dance*, p. 232).

The Cargo Cults of Colonial New Guinea

Another example of a crisis cult described by La Barre is the "Vailala Madness" that erupted in the village of Vailala in the frontier region of New Guinea near the end of 1919. The native people worked hard to scratch a living out of the dense jungle. They were astonished to see that the white colonists, who'd only recently arrived in the region, were able by some mysterious process to summon huge vessels to dock in their newly constructed ports. They saw how the new docks enabled the whites to off-load containers filled with strange machines and myriad other supplies that the whites then used to consolidate their power and accumulate more wealth. To make matters worse, once those cargos had been off-loaded, the whites would order native workers to reload the ships with bails of copra and other natural resources that native farmers had been obliged to harvest in exchange for very meager pay. As the resentment of the native population festered, a man named Evara surfaced as the leader of a new cult.

Evara became famous as a mystic who would induce a trance he called *iki haveye,* or "belly-don't-know", and fall to the floor of his hut. He claimed that he received messages as the trance continued, messages sent to him by a spirit from the Otherworld. When people came to see for themselves how Evara behaved when he was inducing his trances, his example turned out to be contagious—many of the visitors begin fainting themselves and experiencing altered states of consciousness. Evara's main contribution to the new cult was his emphasis on incorporating the kinds of ceremonial practices he'd observed being used by the white people into the native rituals that had traditionally been performed to appease the ghosts of the tribal ancestors and keep the ghosts from harming the people who were still alive.

La Barre describes how the new cult attempted to combine old and new ideas to achieve magical effects. The ancestors were treated to the kinds of food and ceremonial practices that the natives had seen the whites perform during their feasts:

A major motif of the early movement was a tremendous interest in the dead. Indeed, the chief ritual was the making of mortuary feasts for them. Wooden benches and tables were set up for the feast and decorated, in imitation of white tables, with a clean loincloth table cover, neat beer-bottle vases and vivid croton leaf "flowers" in them. These feasts are obligatory to cultists, lest the ghosts visit sickness on them. Some say these meetings were not so much in imitation of the whites as a magic means and symbol of reversal in white-black roles (*The Ghost Dance,* p. 241).

The cargo cult movement also spawned another self-appointed leader, a man named Kori who insisted that the tribes would have to destroy all of their old sacred objects and abandon all of their traditional ceremonies. Kori claimed that these older traditions were now revealed to be hollow gestures that were pitifully ineffective compared to the practices of the white newcomers. In an important study of the Vailala Madness published in 1923, soon after the cults had begun to be formed, anthropologist Francis E. Williams described the basic elements of the conspiracy theory that was commonly preached by the leaders of the New Guinean "cargo cults":

> The cargo cultists preached that all these objects were actually forged by their own native ancestors in some far-off volcano, and were intended to be sent to them, only to be intercepted by the whites. If only the New Guineans would throw away their old native cult objects and ceremonies, and imitate the behavior of the whites, such as sitting solemnly and speechlessly around tables, then the cargoes would come to their rightful recipients (*The Ghost Dance*, p. 41).

In his report, Williams lamented that many of the traditional religious ceremonies and priceless art treasures of the native culture were destroyed by the natives themselves while they were caught up in the madness of the "Vailala Madness" crisis cult.

Pauline Christianity as a Crisis Cult

La Barre also examines the origins of the major religions that originated in the Mediterranean region, including Judaism and Christianity. When the Roman armies conquered Israel, they imposed a puppet king and only tolerated those religious authorities who were willing to collaborate with the occupiers. The Romans were only the latest in a long line of conquerors who provoked Hebrew resentments. A theme often revisited in the sacred scriptures of the Hebrew religion was that a Jewish Messiah would come to free the people of Israel from the dominance of the alien cultures. The Messiah would restore the traditional culture of righteousness and prepare the way for God to install His kingdom on earth. But that traditional aspiration had been overpowered, once again, by the dominance of yet another foreign culture more powerful and more technologically sophisticated than the traditional Hebrew culture.

It was during this ongoing clash between rival cultures that Jesus put himself forward as a charismatic religious figure in a manner that suggested he might well be the promised messiah. When Jesus and his disciples traveled to Jerusalem for the annual Passover, at a time when the Roman authorities were on special alert because they were wary of crowds, he chose to ride into the city on the back of a donkey instead of walking. This was a symbolic act that was immediately recognized as such by many Jews, all of whom would have been familiar with a prophecy in the sacred scriptures: "Shout in triumph, O daughter of Jerusalem! Behold, your king is coming to you; He is just and endowed with salvation, Humble, and mounted on a donkey (Zechariah 9: 8)." When Jesus arrived at the outskirts of the city, the enthusiastic crowds had already been alerted of his coming; they lined the street he traveled and cheered him on. That fact alone would have troubled the Romans and their puppet authorities in Jerusalem. Then when Jesus arrived at the Temple, according to one of the two accounts in the *New Testament* Gospels, he initiated a dramatic and provocative public protest: he strode around the perimeter of the Temple, turning over the tables of money changers and seats of merchants selling doves for sacrifice and berating them for their impiety: "It is written, 'My house shall be called a house of prayer, but you are making it a robbers' den (Mark 11: 15-18)." This evidence suggests that Jesus was deliberately choosing to challenge the Romans and the Temple leaders who served as the Roman enablers. And it's reasonable to infer that he acquired his self-confidence to take this dangerous stand and provoke a confrontation with the Romans because he'd been inspired by seeing the vision he interpreted as "Satan falling out of heaven in a hail of lightning." That vision of fiery light convinced him that a new dispensation was now at hand and that God was now prepared, at long last, to intervene in human affairs by helping Jesus succeed at doing what needed to be done to establish God's kingdom on earth.

The story of Jesus presents a classic example of La Barre's theory in action: a man with a legacy of child trauma, born into a traditional society, became an adult who worked as a humble carpenter in a small, rural village until one day he felt compelled to give up that life to become a disciple of John the Baptist. After his baptism by John, Jesus felt compelled to go on a solitary retreat into the wilderness and to immerse himself in prayer, seeking God's guidance about what he should do with his life. When Jesus saw the vision of lightning-like flashes, he took that as a sign of a momentous event—a sign that God had defeated Satan and that was why Jesus was seeing "Satan falling out of Heaven". This vision convinced Jesus that God was now ready, at long last, to install His kingdom on earth, and that, moreover, He'd just appointed Jesus to be the leader who would take charge of mobilizing the Jewish people to implement the divine plan. The message proclaimed by Jesus resonated with many Jews who'd adhered to the traditions of the Hebrew religion but who were demoralized to see their culture subjugated by the pagan Romans. Jesus recruited twelve men to become his disciples to form the nucleus of a crisis cult. When Jesus and his disciples staged their ceremonial approach to Jerusalem during the Passover, the Romans and their Jewish collaborators realized that this man named Jesus posed a serious danger to the status quo. That's why they ordered him to be captured, put on trial, and sentenced to a cruel death. They wanted to send a clear message to other Jews who might be thinking about rebellion. This sequence of events fits well with La Barre's description of Jesus as a "culture hero" who proclaimed a new message in which some of the ideas enshrined in the existing Hebrew traditions were intermixed with new ideas in a way that excited many Jews and that challenged the ideas of the ruling authorities:

> Indeed, to take a firmly secular view of it, Christianity itself was a crisis cult. Initially it was an ordinary politico-military revolt in the traditional Hebrew mold of secular messiahs, one of whom the Roman governor Pilate straightforwardly regarded a rebellious would-be King of the Jews in the Davidic line and executed in the usual fashion between two *lestai* or "brigands" as the Romans called the Zealot resistance fighters. The alleged crucifixion of their own messiah by the Jews themselves is historical nonsense, indeed quite non-textual, and obviously a tendentious later distortion by Christians (*The Ghost Dance*, p. 254).

The crisis cult formed by Jesus and his disciples continued to exist after Jesus' death by keeping a low profile, meeting in secret, and waiting for Jesus's prophecies to come true. But the nascent Jesus movement did not begin to attract huge numbers of followers until another man stepped forward, a new "culture hero" who transformed Jesus' original teachings by creating a new synthesis of ideas drawn from wildly different sources—from the pagan land of Tarsus where he'd been born and raised, from the traditional Hebrew religion taught by the Temple authorities who presided in Jerusalem, from the new Jesus Movement led by Peter and James, from teachings attributed to his predecessor, Jesus of Nazareth, and from his own visionary experiences. That new "culture hero" was Paul of Tarsus.

Paul first appears in the Biblical record as a member of a team of enforcers sent to the city of Damascus by the Temple authorities in Jerusalem. Their assignment was to attack the new Jesus Movement that was rumored to be attracting many new followers in the local synagogues. While Paul was walking on road to Damascus, he was suddenly struck to the ground by a vision of a bright flash of light that left him blind for three days. He had to be led into the city of Damascus by his fellow enforcers who hired a room for him to use until he recovered. As languished in solitude, wondering why he'd been struck down by that vision and why he was still blind, he was visited by an elder from a Damascus synagogue named Anaias, a member of the Jesus Movement. The visitor convinced Paul that the vision was a summons for him to switch allegiances and to become a convert to the Jesus Movement. When Anaias put his hands on Paul's head and offered a prayer, Paul's blindness suddenly disappeared. Given all of these extraordinary experiences, Paul decided that he did indeed need to convert.

After his conversion, Paul left Damascus. According to the Biblical record, he spent three years in "Arabia", but there's no information about what he was doing while he was there. Then when he finally returned to Jerusalem, he contacted Jesus' disciples, Peter and James, who'd become the leaders of the Jesus Movement, and asked to meet with them. In that meeting, Paul presented his new ideas about the meaning of Jesus' life and death, ideas that he claimed to have received in visions that had been sent to him by Jesus himself. Paul's new ideas initiated heated debates, but eventually he was able to convince Peter and James to let him become a missionary who'd carry the good news of

Jesus' teachings and his miraculous resurrection, not to Jewish synagogues like the missionaries sent out by the Jesus Movement in Jerusalem, but rather to Gentile communities along the shores of the Mediterranean Sea. When Paul set out on that mission, he ended up preaching a message was significantly different from what he'd told the leaders of the Jesus movement and even from the teachings of Jesus himself.

Paul had grown up in Tarsus, a city located in the country we now call Turkey, and that meant that even though he grew up in a Jewish family, he was exposed to an environment in which there were many religious ideas and practices that were significantly different from the traditional Hebrew religion. He would have known about the raucous Dionysian revels celebrated by pagan groups in the area. He would also have known about the values of the Hellenic Greek culture that had prevailed in the region long before coming of the Romans. And the writer of Luke's gospel wrote that Paul came from a family was granted Roman citizenship because it was wealthy and influential enough to merit special treatment. This background in pagan religions and Hellenic cultures influenced Paul in ways that shaped how he interpreted the meaning of Jesus' life and death.

Paul taught that Jesus was not just an influential rabbi who might someday return as the long-awaited Messiah of the Hebrew nation. Paul claimed that Jesus was a divine spirit, a "Son of God" who'd been incarnated in a human body to provide humans with a *Kristos*, a "Savior" figure, a being whose life and death would demonstrate that God understood human suffering and that He wanted humans to know that, like His divine son, Jesus, they could look forward to having their souls resurrected after their deaths, provided that they proclaimed allegiance to this new, Christ-based faith. Paul's interpretation of the meaning of Jesus's life and death was an anathema to traditional Jews who were prepared to acknowledge Jesus was an influential teacher but would vehemently reject the claim that he was a god in his own right. Paul's missions to Gentile communities distributed throughout the Mediterranean region attracted many followers who organized new Christian congregations.

Here is La Barre's description of Paul's role as a "culture hero" who created his own new crisis cult in which Jesus was idolizing as a Christ figure, a crisis cult that transformed the earlier crisis cult that had been organized by Jesus' original disciples:

> With a long history of secular messiahs, the Jews simply never accepted a supernatural Hellenistic one. But in subsequent centuries the failed secular messiah was transcendentalized in a new heresy of Judaism, Christianity, and the messiah blasphemously made God. This heresy drew also from a Neolithic vegetation spirit, the "dying god" of the Near East, the paschal scapegoat in a tradition going back to Abraham, and from the Essene sect as many Dead Sea Scrolls have shown. Christianity is still cognitively troubled and imperfectly melded Hellenistic "ghost dances" of the Hellenic and Semitic people crushed by Rome. As Fokke Sierksma has pointed out, Christianity was a standard messianic movement in an acculturative context, with a royal court adopting an alien culture under the Roman occupation... with a typical prophet predicting the destruction and renewal of the world (*The Ghost Dance*, p. 254).

The comprehensive scope of La Barre's analysis of crisis cults in *The Ghost Dance* can be appreciated by consulting his subject index where, under the heading "Cult movements and leaders," there are references to more than a hundred examples, some dating back to ancient human history but others that refer to relatively recent crisis cults.

How Myths Form Families

When mystic seers are caught up in a culture crisis, the competing sets of values they struggle to interpret will inevitably contain fragments of stories inherited from other cultures that preceded them. Dr. Michael Witzel, the Wales professor of Sanskrit and Indian Studies at Harvard University and author of *The Origins of the World's Mythologies* (2012), has pioneered a new methodology for the study of human myths that adopts some of the analytical techniques that helped scholars revolutionize their attempts to reconstruct the histories of human languages. Witzel's innovative approach reveals how all religious myths can be sorted into one of two over-arching family groups. He labels these two familial myth groups using geological terms that refer to the two sections of the ancient supercontinent of Pangea, sections that eventually split off from each other and then drifting farther apart.

The southern portion of the ancient supercontinent that kept moving south after the split is called "Gondwana", and that's the name that Witzel assigns to a "Gondwanan" family of myths. The myths in the Gondwanan family that survive today are found in tribal cultures that are still organized in small bands—like the cultures of the San Bushmen of South Africa, the Australian Aborigines, and the Tukano Indians of South America. The primary characteristic of myths in the Gondwanan family is an acceptance of the natural world as it is and an acceptance of the social group into which a human is born: "The ultimate questions on first origins are not asked in Gondwanan myths," Witzel writes, "one is interested, at best, in the origins of one's land or of humans and their condition (p. 290)." Gondwanan myths typically instruct a petitioner about how to contact spirits that would otherwise remain invisible and about how to persuade those spirits to help solve some practical, real-life problem.

The section of the ancient supercontinent of Pangea that moved north after the split is called "Laurasia". That's the name Witzel adopts for a "Laurasian" family of myths. The myths in the Laurasian family are very different from the "Gondwanan" family. Here's Witzel's description of those differences:

Once complete mythologies are compared across time and space, this soon leads to the discovery of an underlying structure—that of a *storyline*, extending from the creation of the world to its final destruction. This narrative system, however, is not found globally. It is certainly widespread but not universal: the mythologies of the Aborigines of Australia, the Melanesians of New Guinea and its neighboring islands, and most populations of sub-Sahara Africa lack it. / Due to its wide spread [across] Eurasia and the Americas, I will call this mythological system the "Laurasian" one, following established geological and biological usage… It is thrilling to observe that the Laurasian system can be traced back, step by step, to the later Paleolithic, some 40,000 years ago, when aspects of it appeared in the first cave paintings. Conversely, the Gondwana scheme must have been that of our African ancestors: a small group of them ventured out of Africa some 65,000 years ago… They became the ancestors of all non-African people. A subset of them developed the Laurasian mythological system that became increasingly dominant after the last two ice ages, some 50,000 to 20,000 years ago (Witzel, *The Origins of the World's Mythologies*, p. xi).

The Laurasian myths were adopted by cultures that developed more complex levels of social organization, beginning with the ancient civilizations that evolved in India, Persia, Egypt, Israel, China, and Mesoamerica. The primary characteristic of the

Laurasian family is that the myths reassure listeners that there is a fundamental order that underpins the universe. The basic ideology is that the universe evolves following the same linear trajectory as a human life:

> Laurasian mythology… represents our *oldest complex story*. It is a *novel* of creation, growth, and destruction of the world, of divine and human evolution and decay, from birth to death, from creation to destruction… According to this worldview, the universe is ultimately regarded as a living body, not surprisingly in analogy to the human one: it is born, grows, and finally dies (Witzel, Ibid., pp. 54-55).

Witzel points out that the Laurasian myths incorporated some fragments of stories that originally appeared in the Gondwana family, but those fragments got integrated into the "novelistic" storylines of the Laurasian myths. Once the core features of the Laurasian family of myths coalesced, those basic ideas got passed on from older cultures that were waning in power to newer cultures that were in the process of replacing the old. Witzel's analysis shows how that Laurasian storyline eventually percolated into the worldviews that now proliferate over much of the globe:

> Identical or very similar patterns of development can be seen in Old Egypt, Mesopotamia, Vedic India, China, Japan, and Polynesia as well as with the Aztecs, the Mayans, and Incas. The resulting similarity of ideas about the divine origin of just the ruling classes cannot be attributed to diffusion… / … path dependencies were at work. Their long trail was established by the early shamans of c. 65,000 BCE, who emigrated out of Africa into Eurasia, carrying along their idea of human descent from a High God in heaven (p. 407).

Witzel goes on to describe how the concept of the Laurasian storyline eventually evolved the concept of a monotheistic god. He points out that it was in Zoroastrian Iran that this momentous idea first appeared with Zoroaster's concept of the god, *Ahura Mazda:*

The foundational development of monotheism in Zoroastrian Iran (with Ahuramazda as creator god) [occurred] about 3,000 years ago. The Zoroastrian concept was adopted around the mid-first millennium BCE by Hebrew and subsequently by Christian religion, with major repercussions for the Roman Empire, the rest of Europe, and beyond. Finally, after the emergence of its Islamic form nearly 1,400 years ago, it affected much of Africa, the Near East, and South and Southeast Asia. The Christian and Islamic versions are the currently dominant forms of Laurasian myth worldwide… The Christian offshoot presents a curious mixture of the Hebrew version of Laurasian myth as found in the first chapters of Genesis, of Zoroastrian-inspired monotheism, and of New Eastern mystery cults with a heavy dose of ancient, Neolithic theories of sacrifice… Regular, repeated animal sacrifice in Judaism was substituted in Christian religion by the onetime momentous killing of a divine "lamb" in human form, a feature that is reenacted in daily or weekly ritual (Witzel, p. 408).

Witzel concludes his magisterial analysis of the two myth families developed by humans with a postscript in which he anticipates that "for those who are tired of the old mythologies and are looking for 'something new', I am sure someone will come up with a new myth, supported entirely by new ideas for humanity in the global society of the 21st century—for a very simple reason: we have to look back at our small blue planet from outer space (p. 439)."

CHAPTER 15

Visions of Light and Human Religions

Visions of Light: A Universal Phenomenon

During the course of this investigation, I've shown that meditation-induced light visions have a virtually universal distribution in human religious cultures. We've discussed how light visions inspired the original founders of all the world's major religions, including Hinduism, Zoroastrianism, Judaism, Buddhism, Daoism, Christianity, Manicheism, and Islam. We've also examined how visions of colored light induced by meditation or by rituals of extreme stimulus overload have been used by many other religions to create important mythical symbols, a phenomenon that helped shape the religions of ancient Egypt, Aboriginal Australia, classical Mesoamerica, and the religious practices of tribal groups in North and South America.

My neurologically-grounded, reverse-engineering analysis of the clear light visions that can appear to skilled practitioners of empty-mind meditation—the analysis of the shapes, colors, timing intervals, and sequences of those light visions—makes it possible, for the first time ever, to provide a detailed, comprehensive, and vertically integrated explanation of how the human brain generates that sequence of light visions. The theory I've proposed fits seamlessly with the findings of neuroscientists who've published experimental studies in the subject domains that turn out to be relevant for explaining this complex phenomenon—subject domains that include the visual system, the sleep/wake complex, epileptic seizures, psychogenic seizures, ecstatic auras, and the post-seizure emergence of temporal lobe behavior syndromes. The causal theories I've presented are detailed, comprehensive, elegantly simple, and consistent with what's known about specific brain mechanisms.

But it's also important to acknowledge that the causal explanations I've presented here are clearly *post hoc*, which is to say, these theories were developed after the event they purport to explain and they have not yet been subjected to the kind of hypothesis testing that is a fundamental requirement of the scientific process. As it happens, I have neither the skills nor the resources that would enable me to take the next step in the scientific process—to use these theories to extrapolate specific predictions that could be tested by well-designed experiments. But it is often the case that when scientists are just beginning to study a subject about which there is little known at the outset that they begin with a pilot study designed to identify the kinds of variables that would need to be subjected to more rigorous scientific tests. The use of pilot studies is particularly relevant in the social sciences—in psychology, sociology, anthropology, and medicine—where many practitioners agree that there is often a need to begin with a "grounded theorizing" approach. An investigator using a grounded theorizing approach begins by proposing a tentative theory that's based on what they've experienced themselves in their clinical work. They use their provisional theory to extrapolate some predictions and then subject those predictions to an initial empirical test, all the while keeping in mind that their goal at this initial stage in the inquiry is to identify variables that need to be examined by future studies that employ a more rigorous scientific protocol. I think it's appropriate for me to describe the methodology I've used in this investigation as an example of the "ground theorizing" approach.

The new insights that have surfaced in this investigation have already proved to be useful: I've shown how these insights can be used to reconsider the conclusions of researchers who used EEGs to study the brains of expert meditators while they induced their "peak experiences". Most of the EEG studies we reviewed reported that there was a recurring correlation between the meditators' peak experiences and the surges of high-amplitude excitation with tabletop or earmuff patterns that appeared in the EEGs. Those findings are consistent with an eruption of a partial seizure of temporal lobe or limbic origin. But in the studies we reviewed, the researchers either ignored that possibility or rejected it and instead attributed the abnormal, high-amplitude EEG patterns to hidden muscle movements that they didn't actually observe. The researchers' reluctance to consider evidence in favor of an alternative diagnosis of self-induced partial seizures underscores the importance of disseminating the new insights we've uncovered.

Our investigation reveals that those brain mechanisms that generate the visions of light that appear early in a meditation-induced sequence—the green light-rings and the dark blue clouds—are the same brain mechanisms that govern the normal nightly transition from waking to the three first stages of NREM sleep. It also reveals that sleep rhythm oscillators in the brainstem are vulnerable to becoming destabilized if their target cortical neurons happen, for some reason, to be in a hyperexcitable condition when the synchronous sleep rhythms begin to arrive. If the hyperexcitable cortical neurons respond to the arrival of the synchronous spindle waves by joining in firing bursts that mirror the same rhythms of the spindle waves, that sends synchronous waves flowing back and forth between sleep rhythm oscillators in the brain stem and neuron networks in the cortical regions, creating a positive feedback loop. Those synchronous oscillations can build to the point that they destabilize the sleep rhythm oscillators. Research shows that this kind of destabilization can happen "with surprising ease" to trigger the onset of a hypersynchronous seizure. That seizure can then keep building strength until it pushes neurons in the most vulnerable hippocampus to fire paroxysmal discharges that spread through intra-hippocampal circuits and out into the temporolimbic regions of the brain. This sequence of events has long been established as the cause of sleep-onset seizures in epileptic patients, but my investigation shows that meditators who do not have any epileptic disorders can nevertheless trigger these sleep-onset seizures if they attempt to meditate at a time when their cortical neurons are already hyperexcitable. Two risk factors known to stimulate cortical neurons to become hyperexcitable are the accumulation of a sleep deficit and a depressed mood.

This theory provides a credible explanation for the question we set out to solve when we began this investigation. We asked how it would be possible for the founders of all the world's major religions to be inspired by seeing visions of light that they all described in remarkably similar ways. The answers I've uncovered, based on my analysis of what the founders were doing when they saw their visions and on what they said they saw, turns out to be surprisingly simple. The evidence suggests that many founders were driven by feelings of depression to engage in behaviors that increased the odds of them triggering a destabilization of sleep rhythm oscillators: they withdrew from other people to isolate themselves on solitary spiritual quests; they subjected themselves to extreme ascetic regimens; and they performed long meditation vigils that extended late into the night, thereby accumulating substantial sleep deficits. But there were also other mystics, including some founders of world religions, who induced visions of fiery light by performing tribal rituals designed to overstimulate the participants' levels of arousal to the cusp of triggering a parasympathetic collapse. We've seen how both behavioral strategies can end up producing a similar effect because, in the end, they stimulate the same brain mechanisms.

Is There a "God Module" in the Brain?

In 1997, neuroscientist V. S. Ramachandran gave a presentation at the annual meeting of the Society for Neuroscience in which he proposed that someday it might be possible to demonstrate that there is a "specialized neural circuitry for the sole purpose of mediating religious experience." Many scientists have since engaged in that debate. Some argue that there is indeed a "god module" while others reject that hypothesis. But our investigation reveals that Ramachandran's question is misleading: his question implies that scientists will eventually be able to identify a specific brain structure that is "specialized" for the "sole purpose" of "mediating religious experience". What we've discovered in our investigation is that there is indeed a specific set of neural mechanisms that can generate the kinds of ecstatic experiences that many people would associate with a "god module", but it turns out that those neural mechanisms are not "specialized" for the "sole purpose" of "mediating religious experience". The neural mechanisms that generate the visions of fiery light and other kinds of ecstatic seizures are the very same neural mechanisms that put all of us to sleep at night. I'm deeply moved by that insight—by the recognition that the mundane processes of our brain that can be transformed, albeit temporarily, into a "god module".

Mechanisms Don't Have Meanings

The theory I've presented in this book identifying the brain mechanisms that generate meditation-induced light visions provides a *necessary* explanation for this religious phenomenon, but that does not mean I've also provided a *sufficient* explanation. We humans typically ascribe a wide range of meanings to what we see, hear, and feel, and we often adjust our attributions of meaning according to whether other people in our community agree with the way we've interpreted the significance of a situation. That's why it's always important to assess how a neuroscientific theory about the operation of brain mechanisms relates to the psychological states generated by those mechanisms and to the meanings that humans want to assign to our states of consciousness.

The contrasts between these two aspects of human thought stand out in an example a friend pointed out—the birth of a new baby. Physicians know a lot about the physiological processes that take place when a baby is born, but that physiological explanation, while it's critically important for many reasons—especially because it enables the physicians and nurses to safeguard the health of the mother and the newborn—does not and cannot account for the profound emotional significance that the new birth has, not only for the baby, but also for other humans who happen to be involved—for the mother and father, for siblings and grandparents, and perhaps also for the local community. Moreover, the significance of a child's birth might eventually have an important effect on an entire society or even for all humans if that child happens to grow up to become the kind of "culture hero" described by anthropologist Weston La Barre, if that child becomes someone who brings a new religious meme into the world.

For those of us who are interested in the neuroscientific analysis of the visionary experiences that give rise to human religions, this analogy is instructive. It helps us remember that we humans create a sense of self by telling ourselves stories—stories about where and when we came into being, stories about our early lives, stories about who we've now become, and stories about where we're going. Some of the most profound and inspiring stories in human history have been created by mystic seers whose lives were transformed when they saw visions of the fiery light. Being able to recognize that Truth about the power of human storytelling is as important as knowing the neuroscientific explanation of what happened in the brain to trigger the visions of fiery light.

By Their Fruits Ye Shall Know Them

Mystic seers, especially those whose visions inspired them to launch new careers as religious leaders, hope that the stories they tell about their visions will not be interpreted by their listeners as simply the idiosyncratic musings of an eccentric man or woman. They hope that the stories they tell will convince their listeners that Reality has a supernatural dimension that we humans can contact to seek help and learn how to live better lives. But how can the listeners judge whether the stories being told by a particular mystic seer are worth heeding?

William James, the famous psychologist and author of *The Varieties of Religious Experience*, pointed out that the merits of a new idea should not be based solely on the reputation of the person who proposed it. To denigrate a religious idea because of the personal shortcomings of the originator is to commit what he calls the "genetic fallacy". James gives a specific example of a genetic fallacy that I feel speaks directly to me and to the subject of this investigation: he insists that it would be intellectually dishonest to dismiss someone's religious idea because it was inspired by what the person experienced during or after an epileptic seizure. I know James is talking to me because I'm inclined to be skeptical of ideas that coalesce when a person who experiences a limbic seizure then experiences the emergence of a temporal lobe behavior syndrome. Why does this make me skeptical? Because the ideas generated by that process often turn out to be similar in a predictable way. But my stance clearly violates the genetic fallacy, so I'm willing to reconsider. What would William James recommend as an alternative?

What James proposes as an appropriate test for assessing the worth of a new religious idea is the "empiricist criterion". By that he means a pragmatic test that assesses "the way in which it works on the whole". This kind of pragmatic criterion is one that rational people will find easy to accept and easy to apply, but James insists that this same criterion is also used by even by the most pious believers, even by those who insist that God has given humans a complete and detailed set of commands about what is proper to do in every situation. It's inevitable, James insists, that even the most adamant fundamentalists will be obliged to make personal judgments when they choose which divine command is relevant for addressing the problem and when they decide what that command requires them to do in that situation. Making those interpretations is inevitably a subjective process in which the believers have to decide for themselves what they *think* God wants them to do or what they *think* a passage in the sacred scriptures prescribes. Here is James' explanation for why using the pragmatic criterion to make ethical judgments is ultimately unavoidable:

> This is our own empiricist criterion; and this criterion the stoutest insisters on supernatural origin have also been forced to use in the end. Among visions and messages,

some have always been too patently silly, among the trances and convulsive seizures, some have been too fruitless for conduct and character to pass themselves off as significant, still less as divine. In the history of Christian mysticism, the problem of how to discriminate between such messages and experiences as were really divine miracles, and such others as the demon in his malice was able to counterfeit… has always been a difficult one to solve, needing all the sagacity and experience of the best directors of conscience. In the end it had come to our empiricist criterion: By their fruits ye shall know them, not by their roots (William James, *The Varieties of Religious Experience*, p. 34).

Fruitful Visions: Why Psychedelic Hallucinations Don't Make the Cut

In Michael Pollan's fascinating book, *How to Change Your Mind: What the New Science of Psychedelics Teaches Us About Consciousness, Dying, Addiction, Depression and Transcendence* (2018), he includes interviews with people who describe their personal experiences with taking psychedelic drugs of various kinds in various settings. As I read what Pollan wrote, I realized that meditating to induce visions of pure light produces very different outcomes from what happens to people who ingest psychedelic drugs. One important difference is that the meditation-induced light visions are predictable while the drug-induced experiences are inherently unpredictable. Pollan interviewed a researcher who told him that "she has been struck by the similarities between the phenomenon of the LSD experience and her understanding of the consciousness of children: hotter searches, diffused attention, more mental noise (or entropy), magical thinking, and little sense of a self that is continuous over time (p. 328)." Another researcher offered a similar observation: "The brain appears to become less specialized and more globally interconnected, with considerably more intercourse, or 'cross talk,' among its various neighborhoods (p. 317)."

While these idiosyncratic, dreamlike scenarios generated by psychedelic drugs can be immensely stimulating and emotionally evocative for the individual involved, the story of what happened during the "high" has little relevance for anyone other than the user. It's difficult to see how the highly individualized, chaotic, and kaleidoscopic experiences produced by hallucinogens could ever result in the creation of new religious ideas that could be shared with other people in a way that inspires those listeners to live more rewarding lives. The drug-induced experiences just don't have the kind of story-telling potential that aspiring "culture heroes" use to articulate new religious ideas that resonate with their fellow humans. The usual advice that experienced drug users give to friends who are thinking about experimenting with taking drugs is, "Try it; you'll like it! You'll be amazed at what you see and what you feel!" And, indeed, it's often the case that the person who acts on that advice will end up being amazed and delighted by what happened, but that "high" will almost certainly remain an inherently private experience.

When a reporter asked Pollan to say something about his own experiences taking the hallucinogenic drugs he discusses in his book, he replied that it was very difficult to describe his own drug-related experiences without boring his readers. One of the major obstacles he faced in writing the book, Pollan said, was describing his personal experiences in a way that would interest other people. He found it was hard to avoid becoming one of those insensitive monologuists who keeps blabbing on and on with a description of what happened in a recent dream.

When hallucinogenic drugs stimulate the emotional association centers in the user's limbic brain, the outcome is quite different from what happens to someone experiencing a mediation-induced partial seizure. In the case of the drug user, the sensation of excess meaningfulness gets associated with whatever is in front of that person's eyes or with the chaotic images flashing in the mind's eye. By contrast, in the case of a meditator who's induced a partial seizure, that sensation of excess meaningfulness gets projected onto the same set of light visions that have been seen by many other mystic seers living in many different cultures and in many different historical eras. Some of those earlier mystics were inspired by their visions to search within themselves for new insights about how we humans can live better lives. Some of them succeeded, and by so doing, they established themselves as models for contemporary mystics whose meditations trigger ecstatic visions of fiery light. The new seers, inspired by the examples set by the seers who proceeded them, might decide to search within themselves in the hope of discovering new stories about the meaning of human lives, stories that would not only help them ovecome their own problems but also resonate with others who hear what they have to say. Some of those seers will succeed in using their visions to invent new religious symbols or perhaps even create a new religious meme that ends up changing the course of human history.

What I found to be surprising about Pollan's investigation was that while he interviewed many people who'd participated in psychedelic sessions and who felt deeply moved by having caught a glimpse of what they interpreted as another dimension of reality, the scientists that Pollan interviewed did not express much interest in finding out *why* it was that those hallucinogenic drugs caused the users to feel so deeply moved. They showed little interest in finding out how the drugs produced their effects by stimulating neurons in the emotional association centers of the users' brains. And Pollan did not seem all that interested in pushing them to say more about what caused the emotional high.

We've discussed the same mechanism as being responsible for the phenomenon of déjà vu. Neurologists explain that experience as what happens when a transient discharge in the emotional association centers of the limbic brain coats whatever happens to be in front of a person's eyes with a patina of familiarity and meaning. That's also the same mechanism that generates ecstatic auras during the kinds of partial seizures we've been studying. It would be reasonable, then, to expect that something similar must happen when people ingest hallucinogenic drugs and experience a strong emotional reaction to whatever images surface in their visual fields during that experience. When there's a strong emotional reaction, it might be positive or negative, but, in either case, it's likely to create an indelible memory and it might well end up becoming a powerful influence that changes the person's life. That's why it seems strange to me that the researchers featured in Pollan's book appear to be so uninterested in how the hallucinogenic drugs interact with a drug user's limbic system. That's a stark contrast with our investigation where we've shown how meditation-induced seizures stimulate neurons in the emotional association centers of the limbic brain in a way that adds emotional content to the visual signals that are surfacing in the person's conscious awareness.

How Much Meditation Is Too Much? (What I Think I've Learned)

If my theory about the neural correlates of light visions is correct, then a meditator who succeeds at inducing the lightning-like flashes, tremors, and ecstatic raptures so highly prized by mystics the world over will almost certainly damage some of the inhibitory neurons in the hippocampi, neurons that the seer can ill afford to lose. The loss of hippocampal neurons can, with the passing of time, lower the person's seizure threshold. It can also compromise the person's short-term memory in ways that increase the person's vulnerability to dementia. These risks suggest that inducing paroxysmal visions of fiery light on a recurring basis is, in effect, a form of self-injury that can potentially lead to serious consequences.

Does the prospect of damaging neurons in the brain constitute a good reason for abandoning the pursuit of meditation-induced light visions? I would think so, especially for someone who is obliged to continue making his or her own way in the world. That's why I made the decision to stop inducing light visions after I discovered what happened inside my brain on that one occasion when I saw a paroxysmal vision of fiery light. But will other people have that same reaction? What about those religious traditions that encourage meditators to keep inducing visions of fiery light and its accompanying ecstasy with the goal of achieving a state in which that vision and that ecstasy become continuous? Are those religious traditions prepared to make changes in the kinds of meditational practices they prescribe so as to make them safer for their adherents? Perhaps. But, then again, perhaps not. I suspect that there will always be individuals who are obsessed with transcending mundane reality by triggering the visions and ecstatic raptures that we've discussed in this book. And for some people, learning that there are risks involved might constitute a lure, not a deterrent. That appears to be a dynamic that's relevant in many other high-risk activities—rope-free rock-climbing, sport parachuting, and the like.

For those mystics who experience ecstatic seizures triggered by temporal lobe epilepsy, self-inducing the ecstatic rapture may be so incredibly rewarding that this overrides all concerns that these raptures might cause the underlying condition to become worse. The great Russian novelist Fyodor Dostoevsky captured the dilemma facing those mystics who realize that the elation they're experiencing is also the symptom of a disease. Dostoevsky experienced seizures himself, and he was diagnosed with epilepsy, so it's tempting to conclude, as many eminent epileptologists have concluded, that he experienced himself an ecstatic seizure of the sort he attributes to Prince Myshkin, one of the principal characters in Dostoevsky's novel, *The Idiot:*

> Reflecting on that moment afterwards when he had recovered, he often used to tell himself that all these gleams and lightning-flashes of heightened self-awareness, and hence also of "higher existence," were nothing more than the illness itself, violating the normal state of things as it did, and thus it was not a higher mode of existence at all—on the contrary, it should be regarded as the lowest. And yet he arrived at length at a paradoxical conclusion: "What if it is the illness then?" he decided finally. "What does it matter if it is some abnormal tension, if the end-result, the instant of apprehension, recalled and analyzed during recovery, turns out to be the highest pitch of harmony and beauty, conferring a sense of some hitherto-unknown and unguessed completeness, proportion, reconciliation, an ecstatic, prayerful fusion with the supreme synthesis of life?"… If in that second, in the final conscious moment before the attack, he could have managed to tell himself clearly and deliberately: "Yes, for this moment one could give one's whole life!" then of course, that moment on its own would be worth one's whole life (Dostoevsky, *The Idiot*, 1992 [1868], p. 237).

For some people, the chance of experiencing a moment of true ecstasy and having one's life seemingly showered with an intuition of transcendent meaning will remain an irresistible challenge, a goal made even more alluring because of the dangers involved. There will, however, be many meditators who, like me, want to practice meditation in a way that does not entail the kinds of risks that we've mentioned in this investigation. For those meditators, there is already an alternative method of meditation available that's taught by the Theravadan Buddhist tradition of Southeast Asia and by the New Age meditation centers in the West that teach Insight meditation. The goal of Insight practice is to achieve the recognition that everything we humans see, hear, touch, think, and feel—everything that appears to us to have a substantive existence—will ultimately be revealed to have only an illusory reality that masks the impermanence and emptiness of the phenomena we think we perceive. But that goal of Insight as interpreted by the Theravadans turns out to be the same goal envisioned by the Tibetan Vajrayana Buddhists. The Tibetan Buddhists rely on a very different strategy to pursue the goal of Enlightenment—they believe that the sequence of light visions induced by Highest Yoga Tantra provides humans with the most effective and expeditious vehicle for attaining Enlightenment in a single lifetime—but when meditators attain that goal, they experience an Enlightenment that is described as having the same qualities as those professed by the Theravadan Buddhists. Both traditions claim that the attainment of Enlightenment reveal the Insight that all of the phenomena we humans perceive as having some kind of substantive existence are only apparitions that mask the ultimate formlessness and ever-changing nature of the universe: "When illusory forms contact the Formless... one gains understanding of the Pervading and the Real, / And mastery of the Very Bright and of the Enduring, and of the Siddhi of Transformation (Naropa, *The Six Yogas*, 'The Yoga of Clear Light' 4: 35-36)."

As for myself, I seldom feel inclined to meditate, but if I were to begin again, I'd shift to using the Theravadan approach that emphasizes empty-mind meditation but not cultivating visions of light. I might not follow all the rules—I'd probably dally a bit to watch the beautiful visions of clear light that appear early in a meditation-induced sequence when everything remains calm—but I'd be very careful to not push beyond those early visions and the calm state of mind they accompany. I wouldn't want to incur the risk of doing something that might inadvertently trigger another eruption of the paroxysmal fiery light. If by chance I were to see hints of a faint, white smudge in the upper right quadrant of the visual field—that same white smudge that kept appearing for a few days after my paroxysmal vision—I would immediately back off, divert my attention, get out of bed, go downstairs, have a snack, and spend some time engrossed in reading a good book. That's how I intend to preserve the benefits of an occasional resort to a relaxed and inspiring meditation experience without incurring any more neuron damage than what has already occurred.

So how much meditation is too much?

It depends. It depends on the type of meditation you practice. It depends on the strength of your attraction to the lure of a mystical ecstasy. And it depends on your tolerance for high-risk behaviors. People make that decision for themselves. I hope this book helps you make the decision that's right for you.

About the Author

Philip Taylor Nicholson, a professional medical writer, studied philosophy at Princeton, law and psychiatry at Stanford Law School, and health education at the Harvard School of Public Health. After being drafted during the Vietnam War, he served first as a judge advocate stationed at England AFB, Louisiana, but then, based on his professional training, he was reassigned to Air Force Headquarters in the Pentagon to be the legal representative on a new Social Actions Mobile Assistance Team. The team was tasked with traveling worldwide to consult with local base commanders about changes in policies relating to race relations and drug abuse. After discharge, Nicholson and his wife moved to Boston and began raising a family. He worked as a professional medical writer producing scripts for videos about new scientific breakthroughs that were used for the continuing education of physicians and other medical professionals.

Nicholson is the author of *Meditation & Light Visions: A Neurological Analysis* (2009), and a co-author of *Your Self: An Introduction to Psychology* (1976). He's also published many articles in academic journals. Some examples include "The Soma Code: Luminous Visions in the Rig Veda" in *The Electronic Journal of Vedic Studies* (2002), and "Psychosis and Paroxysmal Visions in the Lives of the Founders of World Religions" in *The Journal of Neuropsychiatry and Clinical Neurosciences* (2014). The author's website, www.religiousvisionsoflight.com, features video animations of each vision of light in a meditation-induced sequence along with descriptions of each vision by famous mystics.

Acknowledgments

I'm profoundly how grateful for all the help I received from Joel Pitney, Laura Pitney, Sayde Walker, and the rest of the staff at LaunchMyBook as they transformed my manuscript into real book. I also want to thank editors Rachel Weaver, Lynnette Horner, and Brad Wetzler who gave me perceptive advice about what I could do to make this book more interesting while I was still in the process of writing and revising.

A key moment that inspired me to begin writing about my experiences with visions was when Dr. Michael Witzel, the Wales Professor of Sanskrit at Harvard University, agreed to meet me, someone whom he'd never met and who wasn't an academic, to follow up on why I'd left a message for him asking about the Sanskrit word, *nimnam*. In the ancient Hindu scripture, the *Rig Veda*, there is a vision described as *nimnam*, but no one knew what that vision actually looked like. I'd just seen a sequence of meditation-induced light visions that paralleled descriptions in the *Rig Veda*, so when Dr. Witzel translated *nimnam* as "a bulbous protrusion", I was able to draw an image of what I'd seen that matched that description. Our initial exchange inaugurated a long, collegial relationship that has provided many opportunities for me to make presentations to academic audiences. Dr. Witzel's work continues to inspire me, including, most recently, his masterwork, *The Origins of the World's Mythologies* (Oxford University Press, 2012).

In closing, I'd like to acknowledge that the most important and most rewarding moments in my life have come from loving—and being loved by—the people with whom I share the intimacies of daily life. No one is more aware of that truth than a person who engages in the solitary pursuits of research and writing. That's why I want to express my deepest thanks to my wife, my three daughters, and my brother and sister, for the affection, support, and frequent forbearance that they've directed my way. Some of the ideas and writing strategies that I incorporated in this book originated in conversations with my daughters, and there were many occasions when they helped me with suggestions for editing changes and graphic design issues. They never lost patience with my queries and their advice always turned out to be perceptive, appropriate, and much appreciated. I feel very fortunate to live in a family where that kind of sharing can happen.

Sources

Allen JP. 2005. Translation of The Ancient Egyptian Pyramid Texts. No. 23. In: *Writings from the Ancient World Series* (Society of Biblical Literature & Brill NV: Leiden, The Netherlands)

Andersen RA 1989. Visual and eye movement functions of the posterior parietal cortex. *Annual Reviews of Neuroscience* 12: 377-403.

Andersen RA and Mountcastle VB. 1983. The influence of the angle of gaze upon the excitability of the light-sensitive neurons of the posterior parietal cortex. *Journal of Neuroscience* 3(3): 532-548.

Andersen RA, Essick GK and Siegel RM 1987. Neurons of area 7 activated by both visual stimuli and oculomotor behavior. *Experimental Brain Research* 67: 316-322.

Assmann J. 2001. *The Search for God in Ancient Egypt* (Cornell University Press: Ithaca, New York).

Assmann J. 2005. *Death and Salvation in Ancient Egypt* (Cornell University Press: Ithaca, New York).

Austin JH. 1999. *Zen and the Brain: Toward an Understanding of Meditation and Consciousness* (MIT Press: Cambridge, MA).

Baduel N. 2008. Tegumentary Paint and Cosmetic Palettes in predynastic Egypt: Impact of those Artefacts on the Birth of the Monarchy. In: Midant-Reyens B, Tristant Y, eds., Egypt at Its Origins 2: Proceedings of the International Conference "Origin of the State, Predynastic and Early Dynastic Egypt," Toulouse, France, September 2005 (*Orientalia Lovaniensia Analecta* 172, Uitgeverij Peeters en Departement Oosterse Studies: Leuven, Belgium).

Bamberger JE. 1970. *Evagrius Ponticus: The Praktikos* (Cisterian Publications).

Bausch SB, Chavkin C. 1997. Changes in hippocampal circuitry after pilocarbine-induced seizures as revealed by opioid receptor distribution and activation. *Journal of Neuroscience* 17(1): 477-492.

Bazil C, Walczak T. 1997. Effects of Sleep and Sleep Stage on Epileptic and Nonepileptic Seizures. *Epilepsia* 38(1): 56-62.

Bear D and Fideo P. 1977. Quantitative Analysis of Interictal Behavior in Temporal Lobe Epilepsy. *Archives of Neurology* 34: 454-467.

Bear D. 1979. Temporal lobe epilepsy: A syndrome of sensory-limbic hyperconnection. *Cortex* 15(3): 357-384.

Bear D. 1986. Hemispheric Asymmetries in Emotional Function: A Reflection of Lateral Specialization in Cortical-Limbic Connections. In Doane BK and Livingston KE, eds., *The Limbic System: Functional Organization and Clinical Disorders* (Raven Press: New York, pp. 29-41.

Bell R. 1934. Muhammad's Visions. *The Muslim World* 1934; 24(2): 145-54.

Benson A, Sehgal L. 1987. The Light at the End of the Tunnel. In: Hedges K, ed., *Rock Art Papers* 5(23): 1-6 (Museum of Man: San Diego).

Bhawe SS. 1957, 1960, 1962. *The Soma Hymns of the Rig Veda, Parts I-III*, as quoted in Wasson RG. *Soma: Divine Mushroom of Immortality* (Harcourt Brace Jovanovich: New York, 1971).

Bishop MP, Elder ST, and Heath RG. Intracranial self-stimulation in man. *Science* 140: 394-396.

Black Elk W, Lyon WS. 1991. *Black Elk: The Sacred Ways of a Lakota* (HarperCollins: San Francisco).

Blackmore S, Troscianko T. The Physiology of the Tunnel (*Journal of Near-Death Studies* 1989 Fall; 8(1): 15-28.

Boehme J. No date. *Dialogues on the Suprasensual Life*, William Law, transl. (Frederick Ungar Publishing Co: New York).

Bokenkamp SR. 1996. Declarations of the Perfected. In: Lopez DS, Jr. *Religions of China in Practice* (Princeton University Press: Princeton, NJ), pp. 166-179.

Bokenkamp SR. 1997. *Early Daoist Scriptures* (University of California Press: Berkeley and Los Angeles).

Boston Globe. "A Study on the 'God Module': Finding Faith in the Brain," October 29, 1997, p. A14.

Bower B. "Into the Mystics: Scientists Confront the Hazy Realm of Spiritual Enlightenment," *Science News* 2001; 159(97): 104-106.

Bowie F, Davies O. 1990. *Hildegard of Bingen: Mystical Writings* (Crossroad Classic, Reprint). Boyce M. 1984. *Textual Sources for the Study of Zoroastrianism* (Oxford University Press: London).

Bukhari's Hadith [e.g., *Sahih al-Bukhari* (Mohee Uddin Book Depository)].

Bushman RL. 2005. *Joseph Smith: Rough Stone Rolling* (Vintage Books: New York, NY).

Butler N, Salamone F. 2004. !Kung Healing, Ritual and Possession. In: Walter MN, Fridmans EJN, eds., *Shamanism: An Encyclopedia of World Beliefs, Practices and Culture* (ABC/CLIO: Santa Barbara), pp. 891-894.

Buzsáki G, Penttonen M Bragin A, Nádasdy Z, Chrobak JJ. 1995. Possible physiological role of the perforant path-CA1 projection. *Hippocampus* 5: 141-146.

Cavalli-Sorza LL. 2000. *Genes, People and Languages* (North Point Press: New York).

Chagmé K. 2000. *Naked Awareness: Practical Instructions on the Union of Mahamudra and Dzogchen.* Wallace BA, transl. (Snow Lion: Ithaca, New York).

Chilton B. 2000. *Rabbi Jesus: An Intimate Biography* (Doubleday/Random House: New York).

Cirignotta F, Todesco CV, Lugaresi L. 1980. Temporal lobe epilepsy with ecstatic seizures (co-called Dostoevsky epilepsy). *Epilepsia* 21: 705-710.

Benson EP, de la Fuente B. 1996. *Olmec Art of Ancient Mexico* (National Gallery of Art/ Harry N. Abrams: New York, NY).

Coe MD. 2005 [1996]. *The Maya, 7ᵗʰ Edition* (Thames & Hudson: New York).

Cohen A. 1992. *Autobiography of an Awakening* (Enlightenment Media).

Connolly M, Van Essen D. 1984. Representation of the visual field in parvicellular and magnocellular layers of the lateral geniculate nucleus in the macaque monkey. *Journal of Comparative Neurology* 226: 544-564.

d'Aquili E, Newberg A. 1993. Religious and Mystical States: A Neuro-psychological Model, *Zygon* 28: 177-199.

d'Aquili E, Newberg A. 1999. *The Mystical Mind: Probing the Biology of Religious Experience* (Fortress Press: Minneapolis, MN).

Da Love Ananda. 1988. The Knee of Listening (DawnHorse Press).

Davidson R, Goleman D. "How Meditation Changes Your Brain—and Your Life," *Lion's Roar,* May 7, 2018.

Decety J, Svetlova M. Putting together phylogenetic and ontogenetic perspectives on empathy. *Developmental Cognitive Neuroscience* 2012 Jan; 2(1): 1-24.

DeLuca JW, Daly R. 2003. The inner alchemy of Buddhist Tantric meditation: a QEEG case study using low resolution electromagnetic tomography (LORETA). *Subtle Energies and Energy Medicine* 13(2): 155-208.

DeLuca JW. 2005. Generating Wisdom and Compassion: QEEG and LORETTA Findings. Presentation delivered at a September conference sponsored by the International Society for Neuronal Regulation. Abstract available in PDF format at www.fearlessheart.com.

Devereux G. 1980. *Basic Problems of Ethnopsychiatry* (University of Chicago Press: Chicago).

Dick PK. 2011 [1991]. *Valis* (Mariner Books, Reissue edition).

Diehl RA. 2004. *The Olmecs: America's First Civilization* (Thames & Hudson: London).

Dolgoff-Kaspar R, Ettinger AB, Golub SA, Perrine K, Harden C, Croll SD. 2011. Numinous-like auras and spirituality in persons with partial seizures. *Epilepsia* 52(2): 640-644.

Doniger W [O'Flaherty W]. 1971. *The Rig Veda: An Anthology* (Penguin Books: London).

Dostoevsky F. 1992 [1868]. *The Idiot.* Myers A, transl. (Oxford University Press: Oxford).

Duvernoy H. 1988. *The Human Hippocampus: An Atlas of Applied Anatomy* (J. F. Bergmann Verlag: Munich).

Eliade M. 1964. *Shamanism: Archaic Techniques of Ecstasy* (Princeton University Press: Princeton).

Elkin AP. 1994 [1970]. *Aboriginal Men of High Degree: Initiation and Sorcery in the World's Oldest Tradition* (Reprint by Inner Traditions International: Rochester, Vermont, USA).

Engels and Rocha. Interictal behavioral disturbances: a search for molecular substrates. *Epilepsy Research Supplement* 1992; 9: 341-9.

Epstein P. 1978. *Kabbalah: The Way of the Jewish Mystic* (Shambhala Press, Boston).

Evans-Wentz WY, ed. 1958. *Tibetan Yoga and Secret Doctrines.* Lama Kazi Dawa-Samdup, Transl. (Oxford University Press: New York).

Evans-Wentz WY, ed. 1969 [1928]. *Tibet's Great Yogi Milarepa: A Biography from the Tibetan* (Oxford University Press: London).

Fanning S. 2001. *Mystics of the Christian Tradition* (Routledge: New York).

Farmer S, Henderson JB and Witzel M. 2002 (2000). Neurobiology, Layered Texts, and Correlative Cosmologies. *Bulletin of the Museum of Far Eastern Antiquities* 72: 48-90.

Faught E, Falgout J, Nidiffer FD, Dreifuss FE. 1986. Self-induced photosensitive absence seizures with ictal pleasure. *Archives of Neurology* 43: 408-410.

Federn W. 1960. The 'Transformations' in the Coffin Texts: A New Approach. In: *Journal of Near Eastern Studies* (University of Chicago Press), Vol. 19, No. 4, pp. 241-257.

Feuerstein G. 1989. *The Yoga-Sutra of Patañjali: A New Translation and Commentary* (Inner Traditions International: Rochester, VT).

Firmage JP, *The Boston Globe*, 1/24/1999.

Flattery DS, Schwartz M. 1989. *Haoma and Harmaline: The Botanical Identity of the Indo-Iranian Sacred Hallucinogen Somo and Its Legacy in Religion, Language and Middle East Folklore* (University of California Press: Los Angeles).

Fox M. 1985. *The Illuminations of Hildegard of Bingen* (Bear & Company: Rochester, VT).

Freidel D, Schele L, Parker J. 1993. *Maya Cosmos: Three Thousand Years on the Shaman's Path* (Perennial Publishers: New York).

Gardner I, Lieu SNC. 2004. *Manichaean Texts from the Roman Empire* (Cambridge U Press).

Geschwind N. 1983. Interictal behavioral changes in epilepsy. *Epilepsia* 24 [Suppl. 1]: S23-S30, p. 258.

Geschwind N. 1984 [1961]. Dostoevsky's Epilepsy. In: Blumer D. *Psychiatric Aspects of Epilepsy* (American Psychiatric Press: Washington, D.C.), pp. 325-333.

Gloor P. 1997. *The Temporal Lobe and Limbic System* (Oxford University Press: London).

Goetz D and Morley SG. 1950. *Popol Vuh: The Sacred Book of the Ancient Quiché Maya* (University of Oklahoma: Norman).

Gonda J. 1963. *The Vision of the Vedic Poets* (Mouton & Co.: The Hague, Netherlands).

Griffith RTH. 1971[1889]. *The Hymns of the Rig Veda, Vols. I-II* (Chowkhamba Series: Varanasi, India).

Guenther M. 1999. *Tricksters and Trancers: Bushman Religion and Society* (Indiana University Press: Bloomington, Indiana).

Hampton OW. 1999. *Culture of Stone: Sacred and Profane Uses of Stone Among the Dani* (Texas A&M University Press: College Station).

Hansen BA, Brodtkorb E. Partial epilepsy with "ecstatic" seizures. *Journal of Epilepsy and Behavior* 2003 Dec; 4(6): 667-673.

Heath RG, ed. 1964. *The Role of Pleasure in Behavior: A Symposium by 24 Authors* (Hoeber Medical Division, Harper & Row: New York, NY).

Heath RG. Pleasure and brain activity in man: Deep and surface electroencephalograms during orgasm. *Journal of Mental Diseases* 1972; 154(1): 3-18.

Heider K. 1997. *Grand Valley Dani: Peaceful Warriors, Case Studies in Anthropology, 3rd Edition* (Holt, Rinehart and Winston: New York).

Hill D. 1999 [1977]. *Joseph Smith: The First Mormon* (Signature Books: Salt Lake City, UT).

Hirtenstein S. 1999. *The Unlimited Mercifier: The Spiritual Life and Thought of ibn Arabi* (Anqa Publishing, an independent publisher based in the United Kingdom).

Holtved, E. 1967. Eskimo Shamanism. In: *Studies in Shamanism*, Edsman CM., ed. (Almqvist and Wiksell: Stockholm).

Horgan J. 2003. *Rational Mysticism: Dispatches from the Border Between Science and Spirituality* (Houghton Mifflin Co.: Boston).

Hughes JR. 2005. The idiosyncratic aspects of the epilepsy of Fyodor Dostoevsky. *Epilepsy and Behavior* 7: 531-538.

Hume L. 1992. *Ancestral Power: The Dreaming, Consciousness and Aboriginal Australians* (Melbourne University Press: Victoria, Australia).

James W. 1961(1902). *The Varieties of Religious Experience: A Study in Human Nature* (Collier MacMillan: New York).

Jaseja H. 2005. Meditation may predispose to epilepsy: an insight into the alteration of brain environment induced by meditation. *Medical Hypotheses* 2005;64(3): 464-467.

John of the Cross. 1958 Edition. *Ascent of Mount Carmel* (Doubleday Image Books, NY)

John of the Cross. 1973 [Reprint of 3rd Edition (1903)]. *The Dark Night of the Soul* (Attic Press: Greenwood, SC)

Joralemon PD. 1976. The Olmec Dragon: A Study in Pre-Columbian Iconography. In: Nicholson HB. *Origins of Religious Art & Iconography in Preclassical Mesoamerica* (UCLA Latin American Center Publications: Los Angeles, CA).

Joralemon PD. 1996. In Search of the Olmec Cosmos: Reconstructing the World View of Mexico's First Civilization. In: Benson EP and de la Fuente B. *Olmec Art of Ancient Mexico* (National Gallery of Art: Washington, D.C.).

Kahle W, Leonhardt H and Platzer W. 1993. *Color Atlas/Text of Human Anatomy, Vol. 3: Nervous System and Sensory Organs* (Georg Thieme Verlag: Stuttgart).

Kahneman D. 2011. *Thinking, Fast and Slow* (Farrer, Straus and Giroux: New York).

Katz R. The Kung Approach to Healing. In: Znamenski AA, ed., *Shamanism: Critical Concepts in Sociology, Vol. 2* (RoutledgeCurzon: London), pp. 425-442.

Kavanaugh K, ed. 1987. *John of the Cross: Selected Writings* (Paulist Press, NY)

Keeley B, ed. 1999. *Kalahari Bushmen Healers* (Ringing Rock: Philadelphia, USA).

Keeley B, ed. 2003. *Ropes to God: Experiencing the Bushman Spiritual Universe* (Ringing Rock: Philadelphia, USA).

Kellogg R, Knoll M and Kugler J. 1965. Form-Similarity Between Phosphenes of Adults and Pre-School Children's Scribblings. *Nature* 208: 1129-130.

Ketter TA, Andreason PJ, George MS, Lee C, Gill DS, Parekh PI, Willis MW, Herscovitch P and Post RM. 1996. Anterior paralimbic mediation of procaine-induced emotional and psychosensory experiences. *Archives of General Psychiatry* 53: 59-69.

Kieffer G. 1988. *Kundalini for the New Age: Selected Writings by Gopi Krishna* (Bantam Books: NY).

Kirsch J. 1998. *Moses: A Life* (Ballantine Books: New York).

Klüver, H. 1966 [1942]. *Mescal and Mechanisms of Hallucinations* (University of Chicago Press: Chicago).

Knoll M and Kugler J. 1959. Subjective Light Pattern Spectroscopy in the Encephalographic Frequency Range. *Nature* 184: 1823-1824.

Knoll M, Kugler J, Eichmeier J and Höfer O. 1962. Note on the Spectroscopy of Subjective Light Patterns. *The Journal of Analytical Psychology* 7: 55-69.

Knoll M, Kugler J, Eichmeier J., and Höfer O. 1962. Note on the Spectroscopy of Subjective Light Patterns. *The Journal of Analytical Psychology* 7: 55-69.

Knoll M, Kugler J, Höfer O and Lawder SD. 1963. Effects of Chemical Stimulation of Electrically-Induced Phosphenes on their Bandwidth, Shape, Number and Intensity. *Confinia Neurologica* 23: 201-226.

Kohn L. 1993. *The Taoist Experience: An Anthology* (State University of New York Press: Albany).

Krishna, G. 1971 [1967]. *Kundalini: The Evolutionary Energy in Man, 2nd edition* (Shambhala Publications: Boulder, CO).

Kroll PW. 1996. Body Gods and Inner Vision: The Scripture of the Yellow Court. In: Lopez DS, Jr. *Religions of China in Practice* (Princeton University Press: Princeton), pp. 149-155.

La Barre W. 1970. *The Ghost Dance: The Origins of Religion* (Doubleday & Co., Garden City, New Jersey).

La Plante, Eve. 1993. *Seized: Temporal Lobe Epilepsy as a Medical, Historical and Artistic Phenomenon* (HarperCollins).

Landsborough D. St. Paul and temporal lobe epilepsy. *Journal of Neurology, Neurosurgery and Psychiatry* 1987 Jun; 50(6): 659-664.

Lawlor R. 1991. *Voices of the First Day: Awakening in the Aboriginal Dreamtime* (Inner Traditions International: Rochester, VT).

Lazar S, Kerr CE, Wasserman RH, Gray JR, Greve DN and Treadway MT, McGarvey M, Quinn BT, Dusek JA, Benson H, Rauch SL, Moore CI and Fischl B. 2005. Meditation experience is associated with increased cortical thickness. *Neuroreport* 16(17): 1893-1897.

Le Gros Clark WE. 1940-41. The laminar organization and cell content of the lateral geniculate body in the monkey. *Journal of Anatomy* 75: 419-433.

Lehmann D, Faber P, Achermann P, Jeanmonod D, Gianotti I, Pizzagalli D. 2001. Brain sources of EEG gamma frequency during volitionally meditation-induced altered states of consciousness, and experience of self. *Psychiatry Research: Neuroimaging Section* 108: 111-121.

Lewis IW. 1971. *Ecstatic Religion* (Routledge: London and New York).

Lewis-Williams JD and Dowson T. 1988. The Signs of All Times: Entoptic Phenomena in Upper Paleolithic Art. *Current Anthropology* 29(2): 201-245.

Lewis-Williams JD and Dowson T. 1993. On Vision and Power in the Neolithic: Evidence from the Decorated Monuments. *Current Anthropology* 34: 55-65.

Lewis-Williams JD. 1995a. Modeling the Production and Consumption of Rock Art. *South African Archaeological Bulletin* 50: 143-154.

Lewis-Williams JD. 1995b. Seeing and Construing: The Making and 'Meaning' of a Southern African Rock Art Motif. *Cambridge Archaeological Journal.* 5(1): 3-23.

Lindholm C. 1990. *Charisma* (Basil Blackwell Publishing: Oxford, England).

Little S, Eichman S. 2000. *Taoism and the Arts of China* (The Art Institute of Chicago and the University of Chicago Press: Berkeley).

Lutz A, Greischar LL, Rawlings NB, Matthieu R and Davidson RJ. 2004. Long-term meditators self-induce high-amplitude gamma synchrony during mental practice. *Proceedings of the National Academy of Science* 2004; 101(46): 16369-16373.

Maddocks F. 2001. *Hildegard of Bingen: The Woman of Her Age* (Doubleday: New York).

Maeda E, Robinson HPC and Kwana A. 1995. The mechanisms of generation and propagation of synchronous bursting in developing networks of cortical neurons. *Journal of Neuroscience* 15(10): 6834-6845.

Mails T. 1978. *Sundancing at Rosebud & Pine Ridge* (University of Nebraska Press: Lincoln).

Margalit R. "Built on Sand: King David's story has been told for millennia: Archeologists are still fighting over whether it's true," *The New Yorker,* June 29, 2020, pp. 42-51.

Markham RH and Markham PT. 1994 (1992). *The Flayed God: The Mythology of Mesoamerica* (HarperCollins: San Francisco).

Masson JM. 1980. *The Oceanic Feeling: The Origins of Religious Sentiment in Ancient India* (D. Reidel Publishing Company: Dordrecht, Holland).

Mavromatis A. 1987. *Hypnagogia: The unique state of consciousness between wakefulness and sleep* (Routledge & Kegan Paul: London).

McClenon J. 2002. *Wondrous Healing: Shamanism, Human Evolution and the Origin of Religion* (Northern Illinois University Press: Dekalb, Illinois).

McDaniel J. 1989. *The Madness of the Saints: Ecstatic Religion in Bengal* (University of Chicago Press: Chicago).

McKnight D. 1999 [1992]. *People, Countries, and the Rainbow Serpent: Systems of Classification among the Lardil of Mornington Island* (Oxford University Press, Oxford).

Meissner WW. 1992. *Ignatius of Loyola: The Psychology of a Saint* (Vail-Ballou Press: Binghamton: New York).

Meggit MJ. 1960. *Desert People* (University of Chicago Press: Chicago IL).

Miller A and Taube K. 1993. *An Illustrated Dictionary of the Gods and Symbols of Ancient Mexico and the Maya* (Thames & Hudson: London).

Mirabai. 1993. *For Love of the Dark One: Songs of Mirabai* Shambhala Press, Boston).

Mishra R S. 1987. *The Textbook of Yoga Psychology: The Definitive Translation and Interpretation of Patanjali's Yogasutras* (Crown Publishers, New York, NY).

Morgan H. 1990. Dostoevsky's epilepsy: A case report and comparison. *Surgical Neurology* 33: 413-146).

Morphy H. 1999. Encoding the Dreaming—A Theoretical Framework for the Analysis of Representational Processes in Australian Aboriginal Art. *Australian Archaeology* 49: 13-22).

Motter BC, Steinmetz MA, Duffy CJ and Mountcastle VB. 1987. Functional properties of properties of parietal visual neurons: mechanisms of directionality along a single axis. *Journal of Neuroscience* 7(1): 154-176.

Mountcastle VB, Andersen RA and Motter BC. 1981. The influence of attentive fixation upon the excitability of the light-sensitive neurons of the posterior parietal cortex. *Journal of Neuroscience* 1(11): 1218-1235.

Mountford CP. 1976. *Nomads of the Australian Desert* (Rigby Ltd.: Adelaide, Australia).

Muktananda S. 1978. *The Play of Consciousness, 4th Edition* (SYDA Foundation: South Fallsburg, NY).

Mullin GH. 1996. *Tsongkhapa's Six Yogas of Naropa* (Snow Lion: Ithaca, New York).

Naito H and Matsui N. Temporal lobe epilepsy with ictal ecstatic state and interictal behavior of hypergraphia. *Journal of Nervous and Mental Disease* 176(2): 123-124.

Nanamoli B. 1991[1975]. *The Path of Purification (Visuddhimagga) by Bhudan-tacariya Buddhaghosa, 5th edition* (Buddhist Publishing Co.: Kandy, Sri Lanka).

Nelson, EW. 1899. The Eskimos About Bering Strait. In: *The 14th Annual Report of American Ethnology*, pp. 653

Newberg A and d'Aquili E. 2001. *Why God Won't Go Away: Brain Science and the Biology of Belief* (Ballantine Books: NY).

Newberg A, Alavi A, Baime M and Pourdehnad M. 2000. Cerebral Blood Flow During Meditation: Comparison of Different Cognitive Tasks. *European Journal of Nuclear Medicine* 27, 8, p. 1104 (PS. 375).

Newberg A, Alavi A, Baime M, Santanna J and d'Aquili E. 2001. The Measurement of Regional Cerebral Blood Flow During the Complex Cognitive Task of Meditation: A Preliminary SPECT Study. *Psychiatry Research: Neuroimaging* 106: 113-122.

Newberg A, Pourdehnad M, Alavi A and d'Aquili E. 2003. Cerebral blood flow during meditative prayer: preliminary findings and methodological issues. *Perceptual and Motor Skills* 97: 625-630.

Newberg AB and Iversen J. 2003. The neural basis of the complex mental task of meditation: neurotransmitters and neurochemical considerations. *Medical Hypotheses.* 61(2): 282-291.

Newberg AB and Lee BY. 2005. The neuroscientific study of religious and spiritual phenomena: Or why God doesn't use biostatistics. *Zygon* 40(2): 469-489.

Nicholson P. 1992. Dissociation, Dream-Sleep, and Self-Induction of Thalamo-Occipital Seizures with Ecstatic Auras and Interictal Behavior. *Proceedings of the 4th International Montreux Congress on Stress* (American Institute of Stress), February 16-20, pp. 82-83.

Nicholson PT. 1996a. Phosphene images of thalamic sleep rhythms induced by self-hypnosis. *Journal of Subtle Energies and Energy Medicine* 7(2): 111-148.

Nicholson PT. 1996b. Dialogue: Phosphene images of thalamic sleep rhythms induced by self-hypnosis. *Journal of Subtle Energies and Energy Medicine* 7(3): 273-283.

Nicholson PT. 1999. Phosphene Epiphenomena of Hypersynchronous Activity Emerging in Thalamocortical Circuits and Triggering a Hippocampal Seizure. *Epilepsia* 40 [Suppl 2]: 27 & 203.

Nicholson PT. 2002a. The Soma Code, Part I: Luminous Visions in the Rig Veda. Electronic Journal of Vedic Studies. *The Electronic Journal of Vedic Studies* 8(3): 31-52.

Nicholson PT. 2002b. The Soma Code, Part II: Soma's Birth, Purification, and Transformation into Indra. *The Electronic Journal of Vedic Studies* 8(3): 53-69.

Nicholson PT. 2002c. The Soma Code, Part III: Visions, Myths, and Drugs. *The Electronic Journal of Vedic Studies* 8(3): 70-92.

Nicholson PT. 2002d. Meditation, Slow Wave Sleep, and Ecstatic Seizures: The Etiology of Kundalini Visions. *Journal of Subtle Energies and Energy Medicine* 12(3): 186-227.

Nicholson PT. 2002e. Empirical Studies of Meditation: Does a Sleep Rhythm Hypothesis Explain the Data? *Journal of Subtle Energies and Energy Medicine* 13(2): 109-129.

Nicholson PT. 2004. Restoring the One: Meditation and Light Visions in Early Daoist Texts. In: Bai Gengsheng, ed., *Papers from the 7ʰ International Conference of the International Society for Shamanistic Research* (Changchun, China, August 2004).

Nicholson PT. 2006. Does Meditation Predispose to Epilepsy? EEG Studies of Expert Meditators Self-Inducing Simple Partial Seizures. *Medical Hypotheses* 66(3): 674-676.

Nicholson PT. 2006. Light Visions, Shaman Control Fantasies and the Creation of Myths. In: Witzel, M., Editor, *Papers from the Harvard-Peking University International Conference on Comparative Mythology* (Beijing, China, May 2006).

Nicholson PT. 2010. *Meditation & Light Visions: A Neurological Analysis* (CreateSpace Books: Online

Nicholson PT. 2011. Drama of the Gifted Seer: Trauma, Trance, and Seizure. Poster Presentation, Annual Meeting of the American Psychoanalytic Association, New York.

Nicholson PT. 2011. Website: www.religiousvisionsoflight.com

Nicholson PT. 2014. Psychosis and Paroxysmal Visions in the Lives of the Founders of World Religions, *The Journal of Neuropsychiatry and Clinical Neuroscience* Jan. 1; 26(1): E113-4.

Nicholson PT and Firnhaber RP. 2003 [2001]. Autohypnotic Induction of Sleep Rhythms Generates Visions of Light with Form-Constant Patterns. In: Leete A & Firnhaber RP, eds., *Shamanism in the Interdisciplinary Context* (BrownWalker Press: Boca Raton, Florida).

O'Flaherty WD (nee Doniger). 1971. *The Rig Veda: An Anthology* (Penguin Books: London).

Oppenheimer S. 2003. *The Real Eve: Modern Man's Journey Out of Africa* (Carroll & Graf: New York).

Pacia S, Ebersole J. 1997. Intracranial Substrates of Scalp Ictal Patterns from Temporal Lobe Foci. *Epilepsia* 38, 6, pp. 642-654.

Parker S. Training attention for conscious non-REM sleep: The yogic practice of yoga-nidra and its implications for neuroscience research. *Progress in Brain Research* 2019; 244: 255-272.

Penfield W and Jasper H. 1954. *Epilepsy and the Functional Anatomy of the Human Brain* (Little, Brown and Company: Boston).

Persinger MA. 1984. Striking EEG Profiles from Single Episodes of Glossolalia and Transcendental Meditation. *Perceptual and Motor Skills* 58(1): 127-133.

Persinger MA. 1987. *Neuropsychological Basis of God Beliefs* (Praeger Press: New York).

Persinger MA. 1993a. Transcendental meditation (TM) and general meditation are associated with enhanced complex partial epileptic-like signs: evidence for "cognitive kindling"? *Perceptual and Motor Skills* 76: 80-2.

Persinger, M. 1993b. Paranormal and Religious Beliefs May Be Mediated Differentially By Subcortical and Cortical Phenomenological Processes of the Temporal (Limbic) Lobes, *Perceptual and Motor Skills* 76(11): 247-251.

Persinger MA. 2001. The neuropsychiatry of paranormal experiences. *Journal of Neuropsychiatry and Clinical Neuroscience* 13(4): 515-523.

Persinger MA, Fisher S. 1990. Elevated Specific Temporal Lobe Signs in a Population Engaged in Psychic Studies. *Perceptual and Motor Skills* 71(3 Pt 1): 817-818.

Persinger MA, Makarec K. 1993. Complex Partial Epileptic Signs as a Continuum from Normals to Epileptics: Normative Data and Clinical Populations. *Journal of Clinical Psychology* 49(1): 33-45.

Peters FE. 1994. *Muhammed and the Origins of Islam* (State University of New York Press: Albany).

Polland M. 2018. *How to Change Your Mind: What the New Science of Psychedelics Teaches Us About Consciousness, Dying, Addiction, Depression, and Transcendence* (Penguin/Random House: New York, NY).

Powers, WK. 1975. *Oglala Religion* (University of Nebraska Press: Lincoln).

Preuss MH. 1988. *Gods of the Popol Vuh* (Labyrinthos: Culver City, California).

Puett MJ. 2002. *To Become a God: Cosmology, Sacrifice and Self-Divinization in Early China* (Harvard-Yenching Institute: Cambridge, MA).

Radhakrishnan S. 1992. *The Principal Upanishads* (Humanities Press International: Atlantic Highlands, NJ).

Rajna P, Veres J. 1993. Correlations between night sleep duration and seizure frequency in temporal lobe epilepsy. *Epilepsia* 34(3): 574-579.

Ramachandran V, Blakeslee S. 1997. *Phantoms in the Brain: Probing the Mysteries of the Human Mind* (William Morrow & Co.: New York).

Rasmussen K. 1930. *The Intellectual Culture of the Iglulik Eskimos* (Copenhagen).

Raphael, transl. 2003. *Shankara Atmanbodhi: Self-Knowledge* (Aurea Vidya).

Rauch SL, van der Kolk BA, Fisler RE, Alpert NM, Orr SP, Savage CR, Fischman AJ, Jenike MA, Pitman RK. 1993. A symptom provocation study of posttraumatic stress disorder using positron emission tomography and script-driven imagery. *Archives of General Psychiatry* 53: 387-390.

Ray DJ. 1967 [1975]. *Eskimo Masks: Art and Ceremony* (University of Washington Press: Seattle).

Ray RA. 1994. *Buddhist Saints in India: A Study of Buddhist Values and Orientations* (Oxford University Press: New York).

Reichel-Dolmatoff G. 1972. The Cultural Context of an Aboriginal Hallucination: Banisteriopsis caapi. In: *Flesh of the Gods: The Ritual Use of Hallucinogens*, Furst, PT, ed., pp. 84-113 (Allen and Unwin: London).

Reichel-Dolmatoff G. 1975. *The Shaman and the Jaguar: A Study of Narcotic Drugs Among the Indians of Columbia* (Temple University Press: Philadelphia).

Reichel-Dolmatoff G. 1978. *Beyond the Milky Way: Hallucinatory Imagery of the Tukano Indians* (UCLA Latin American Center: Los Angeles).

Reichel-Dolmatoff G. 1987. *Shamanism and the Art of the Eastern Tukanoan Indians* (E. J. Brill: New York).

Reichel-Dolmatoff G. 1996. *The Forest Within: The World-View of the Tukano Amazonian Indians* (Themis Books: Devon, UK).

Reza. 1996. Pilgrimage to China's Buddhist Caves. *National Geographic* 189(4): 53-63.

Robinet I. 1993. *Taoist Meditation: The Mao-Shan Tradition of Great Purity* (State University of New York Press: Albany, New York).

Robinet I. 1997 [1992]. *Taoism: The Growth of a Religion* (Stanford University Press: Stanford, California).

Rodin E and Schmaltz S. 1984. The Bear-Fideo personality inventory and temporal lobe epilepsy. *Neurology* 34: 591-6.

Rodinson M. 1961. *Muhammed* (American University in Cairo).

Sabom M. 1998. *Light & Death: One Doctor's Fascinating Account of Near-Death Experiences* (Zondervan Publishing: Grand Rapids, Michigan).

Sabom M. 1981. *Recollection of Death: A Medical Investigation* (HarperCollins, New York).

Sankara. 2003. Raphael, transl., *Atmabodha: Self-Knowledge* (Aurea Vidya: New York, NY).

Sargant W. 1974. *The Mind Possessed: A Physiology of Possession, Mysticism, and Faith Healing* (J. B. Lippincott: New York).

Saint Romain P. 1991. *Kundalini Energy and Christian Spirituality* (Crossroads Publications).

Saver JL and Rabin JR. 1997. The Neural Substrates of Religious Experience. In: Salloway S, Malloy P and Cummings JL, eds., *The Neuropsychiatry of Limbic and Subcortical Disorders* (American Psychiatric Press: Washington, D.C.), pp. 195-207.

Scaer R. 2001. *The Body Bears the Burden: Trauma, Dissociation, and Disease* (The Haworth Press: Philadelphia, PA).

Schipper K. 1993. *The Taoist Body* (University of California Press: Berkeley).

Scollo-Lavizzari G and Scollo-Lavizzari GR. 1974. Sleep, sleep deprivation, photosensitivity and epilepsy. *European Journal of Neurology* 11: 1-21.

Seigel RK and Jarvik ME. 1975. Drug-Induced Hallucinations in Animals and Man. In: *Hallucinations: Behavior, Experience, and Theory*, Siegel RK and West LJ., eds., pp. 81-161 (John Wiley & Sons: New York).

Seligman MEP. 1972. Learned Helplessness. Annual Review of Medicine 23: 407-412.

Shore A. 2003. *Affect Dysregulation of Disorders of the Self* (W. W. Norton & Co.: New York).

Shukla GD, Srivastava ON, Katiyar BC. Sexual disturbances in temporal lobe epilepsy: a controlled study. *British Journal of Psychiatry* 1979 March; 134: 288-292.

Silburn L. 1988. *Kundalini: The Energy of the Depths*. Gontier J, Transl. (State University of New York Press: Albany).

Silvas A. 1999. *Jutta and Hildegard: Biographical Sources* (Brepols Publishers: Belgium).

Stewart C. 1998 [1656]. *Cassian the Monk* (Oxford University Press).

Steriade M, McCarley RW. 1990. *Brainstem Control of Wakefulness and Sleep* (Plenum Press: New York).

Steriade M, Contreras D. 1995. Relations between cortical and thalamic cellular events during transition from sleep patterns to paroxysmal activity. *Journal of Neuroscience* 15(1): 623-642.

Steriade M, Contreras D, Amzica F, Timofeev I. 1996. Synchronization of fast (30-40 Hz) spontaneous oscillations in intrathalamic and thalamocortical networks. *Journal of Neuroscience* 16(8): 2788-2808; see also Contreras D and Steriade M. (1997) State-dependent fluctuations of low-frequency rhythms in corticothalamic networks. *Neuroscience* 76(1): 25-38.

Steriade M, Contreras D, Curro Dossi R, Nunez A. 1993a. The slow (< 1 Hz) oscillation in reticular thalamic and thalamocortical neurons: scenario of sleep rhythm generation in interacting thalamic and neocortical networks. *Journal of Neuroscience* 13(8): 3284-3299.

Steriade M, McCormick DA and Sejnowski T. 1993b. Thalamocortical oscillations in the sleeping and aroused brain, *Science* 262: 679-685

Steriade M, Nuñez A, Amzica F. 1993c. Intracellular analysis of relations between the slow (< 1 Hz) neocortical oscillation and other sleep rhythms of the electroencephalogram. *Journal of Neuroscience* 13(8): 3266-3283.

Steriade M, Timofeev I and Grenier F. 2001. Natural waking and sleep states: a view from inside neocortical neurons. *Journal of Neurophysiology* 85: 1969-1985.

Steriade M. 1991. Alertness, quiet sleep, and dreaming. In: Peters A and Jones EG, Editors. *Cerebral Cortex, Vol. 9* (Plenum Press: New York), pp. 279-357.

Steriade M. 1993. Cellular substrates of brain rhythms. In: Niedermeyer E and Lopez da Silva F, Editors. *Electroencephalography: Basic Principles,*

Clinical Applications, and Related Fields, 3rd Edition (Williams and Wilkins: Baltimore), pp. 27-92.

Steriade M, Contreras D. 1998. Spike-wave complexes and fast components of cortically generated seizures. I. Role of the neocortex. *Journal of Neurophysiology* 80(3): 1439-1455.

Steriade M, Amzica F, Neckelmann D, Timofeev I. 1998. I. Spike-wave complexes and fast components of cortically generated seizures. II. Extracellular patterns. *Journal of Neurophysiology* 80(3): 1456-1479.

Steriade M, Timofeev I. 2003. Neuronal Plasticity in Thalamocortical Networks during Sleep and Waking Oscillations. *Neuron* 37: 563-576.

Stevens JR, Mark VH, Erwin R, Pacheco, Suematsu K. Deep temporal stimulation in man: long latency, long lasting psychological changes. *Archives of Neurology* 1969 Aug; 21(2): 157-169.

Stoffels C, Munari C, Bonis A, Bancaud J, Talairach J. 1980. Genital and sexual manifestations occurring in the course of partial seizures in man. *Revue d'electroencephalographie et de neurophysiologie clinique* 10(4): 386-392.

Stringer JL, Lothman EW. 1992. Reverberatory seizure discharges in hippocampal-parahippocampal circuits. *Experimental Neurology* 116: 198-203.

Surbeck W, Bouthillier A, Nguyen DK. 2013. Bilateral cortical representation of orgasmic epilepsy localized by depth electrodes. *Epilepsy Behavior Case Reports* 2013; 13; 1: 62-65.

Swedenborg E. 1995 [1890]. Heaven and Its Wonders and Hell from Things Heard and Seen (Swedenborg Foundation: West Chester, Pennsylvania).

Taylor JH. 2001. *Death and the Afterlife in Ancient Egypt* (University of Chicago Press: Chicago).

Taylor P, ed. 1988. *After 200 years: Photographic Essays of Aboriginal and Islander Australia Today* (Cambridge University Press: Cambridge).

Thibaut G., transl. 2011. *The Vedanta Sutras of Badarayana, Part 1-2* (Literary Licensing Book Publishers: Whitefish, MT).

Theissen G, Merz A. 1998 [1996]. Bowden J., transl., *The Historical Jesus: A Comprehensive Guide* (Fortress Press: Minneapolis, Minnesota).

Trevisol-Bittencourt P, Troliano A. Interictal personality syndrome in non-dominant temporal lobe epilepsy: case report. *Arquivos de neuro-psiquiatria* 2000 Jun; 58(2B): 548-555.

Uchida S, Atsumi Y and Kojima T. 1994. Dynamic relationships between sleep spindles and delta waves during a NREM period. *Brain Research Bulletin* 33: 351-355.

Underhill PA. Y chromosome sequence variation and the history of human populations. *Nature Genetics* 2000 Nov; 26(93): 358-361.

Vasktokas JM. 1977. The Shamanic Tree of Life. In: *Stones, Bones, and Skin: Ritual and Shamanic Art*, pp. 93-117, Brodzley AT, Daresewich R and Johnson N, eds (Society for Art Publications: Toronto).

Vermes G. 1981 [1973]. *Jesus the Jew: A Historian's Reading of the Gospels* (Fortress Press: Philadelphia).

Voskuil PHA. 1983. The epilepsy of Fyodor Mikhailovitch Dostoevsky (1821-1881). *Epilepsia* 24: 658-667.

W. Bill. 1957. *Alcoholics Anonymous Comes of Age* (Alcoholics Anonymous World Services).

Wallace BA, ed. 2003. *Buddhism and Science: Breaking New Ground* (Cambridge University Press: New York).

Wasson RG. 1971. *Soma: Divine Mushroom of Immortality* (Harcourt Brace Jovanovich: New York).

Waxman S, Geschwind N. 1975. The Interictal Behavioral Syndrome of Temporal Lobe Epilepsy. *Archives of General Psychiatry* 32: 1580-1586.

Wenke RJ. 2009. T*he Ancient Egyptian State: The Origins of Egyptian Culture (c. 8000-2000 BC* (Cambridge University Press: New York.)

Wente EF. 1982. Mysticism in Pharaonic Egypt? In: *Journal of Near Eastern Studies* (University of Chicago Press, Vol. 41, No. 3, pp. 161-179.

Williamson PD and Engel J Jr. 1997. Complex partial seizures. In: Engel J Jr, Pedley TA, eds. *Epilepsy: A Comprehensive Textbook, Vol. I* (Lippincott-Raven: Philadelphia), pp. 557-566.

Wilson E. 1994. The Transits of Consciousness. *Journal of Subtle Energies and Energy Medicine* 4(2): 171-185.

Wilson HH. 1888. *Rig-Veda Samhita: A Collection of Ancient Hindu Hymns, Vols. I-VI* (Trubner & Co.: London).

Winkelman MJ. 1992. *Shamans, Priests and Witches: A Cross-Cultural Study of Magico-Religious Practitioners.* (Arizona State University, Anthropological Research Papers, No. 44: Tempe).

Winkelman MJ. 2000. *Shamanism: The Neural Ecology of Consciousness and Healing* (Bergin & Garvey [Acquired by Greenwood Publishing Group: Santa Barbara, California]).

Witzel M. 2001. Comparison and Reconstruction: Language and Mythology. *Mother Tongue: Journal of the Association for the Study of Language in History* Issue 6: 45-62.

Witzel M. 2005. Vala and Iwato: The Myth of the Hidden Sun in India, Japan and Beyond. The *Electronic Journal of Vedic Studies*, 12(1): 1-65.

Witzel M. 2006. Creation Myths. In: *Proceedings of the Pre-Symposium of RIHN and 7th ESCA Harvard-Kyoto Roundtable*, Osaka T and Hase N, eds., pp. 284-318 (Research Institute for Humanity and Nature: Kyoto, Japan).

Witzel M. 2012. *The Origins of the World's Mythologies* (Oxford University Press: London).

Wolf P. 1997. Isolated seizures. In: Engel J, Jr., Pedley, TA, eds. *Epilepsy: A Comprehensive Textbook, Vol. I* (Lippincott-Raven: Philadelphia), pp. 2475-2481.

Wolfson ER. 1994. *Through a Speculum that Shines: Vision and Imagination in Medieval Jewish Mysticism* (Princeton University Press: Princeton, NJ).

Zalesky C. 1987. *Otherworldly Journeys: Accounts of Near-Death Experiences in Medieval and Modern Times* (Oxford University Press: New York).

Zeki S. 1993. *A Vision of the Brain* (Blackwell Scientific Publications: London).

Zimmerman B, ed. 1932. *St. John of the Cross* (Sheed & Ward: London).

Index

Author's Drawings of Light Visions

**Video animations of light visions
are featured on the author's website:**

www.religiousvisionsoflight.com

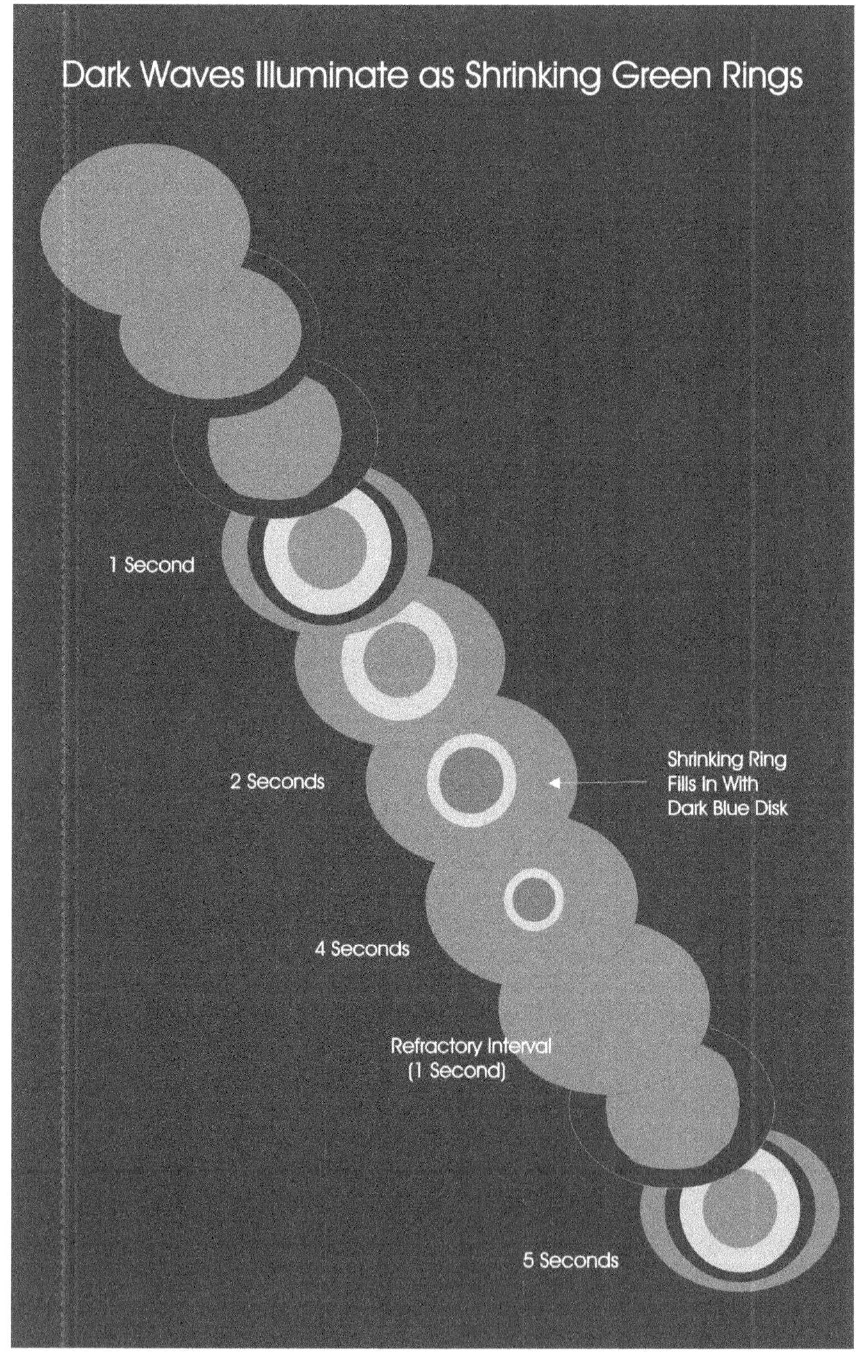

Dark Waves Illuminate as Shrinking Green Rings
1 Second
2 Seconds
Shrinking Ring
Fills In With
Dark Blue Disk
4 Seconds
Refractory Interval
(1 Second)
5 Seconds

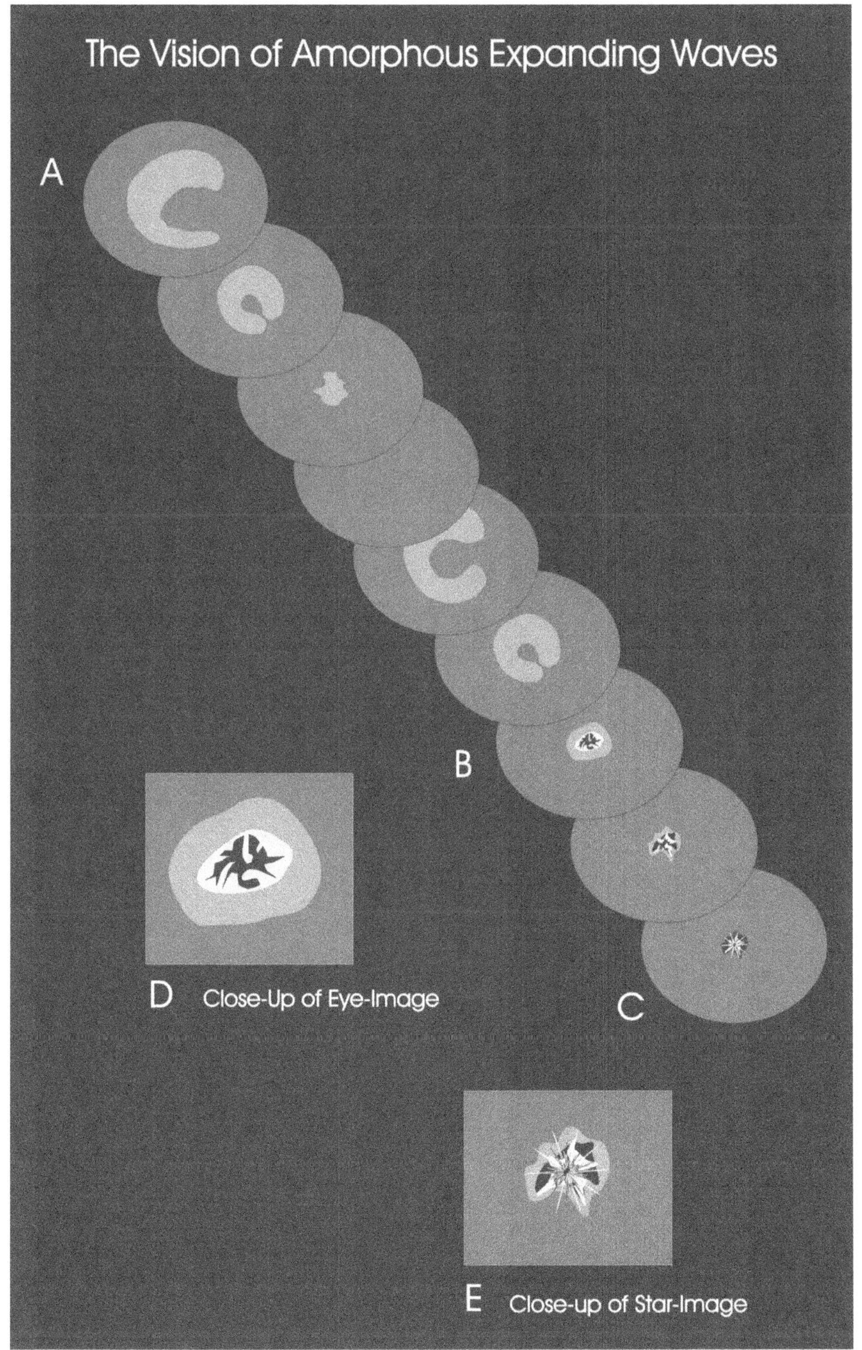

The Vision of Amorphous Expanding Waves
A
B
C
D   Close-Up of Eye-Image
E   Close-up of Star-Image

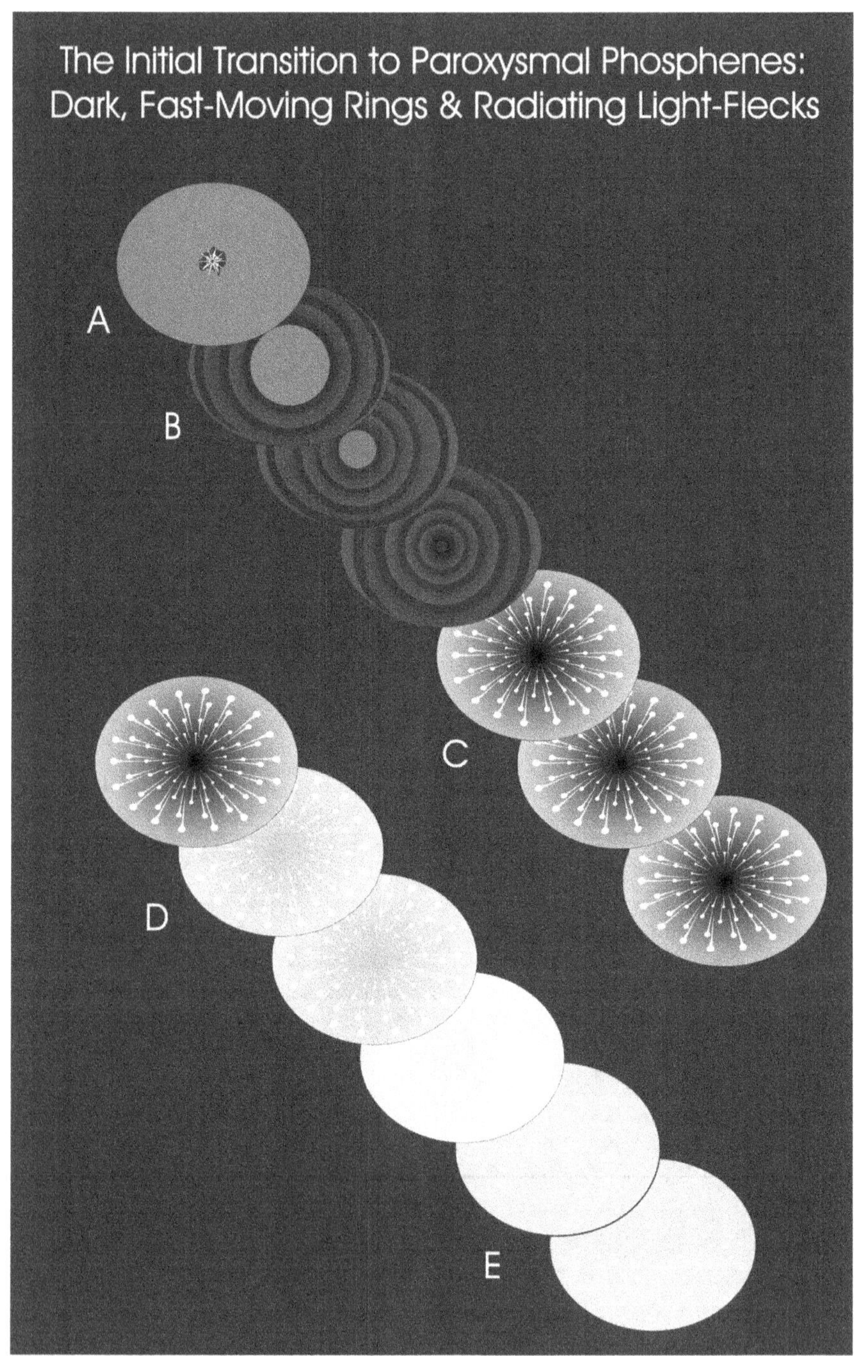
The Initial Transition to Paroxysmal Phosphenes:
Dark, Fast-Moving Rings & Radiating Light-Flecks
A
B
C
D
E

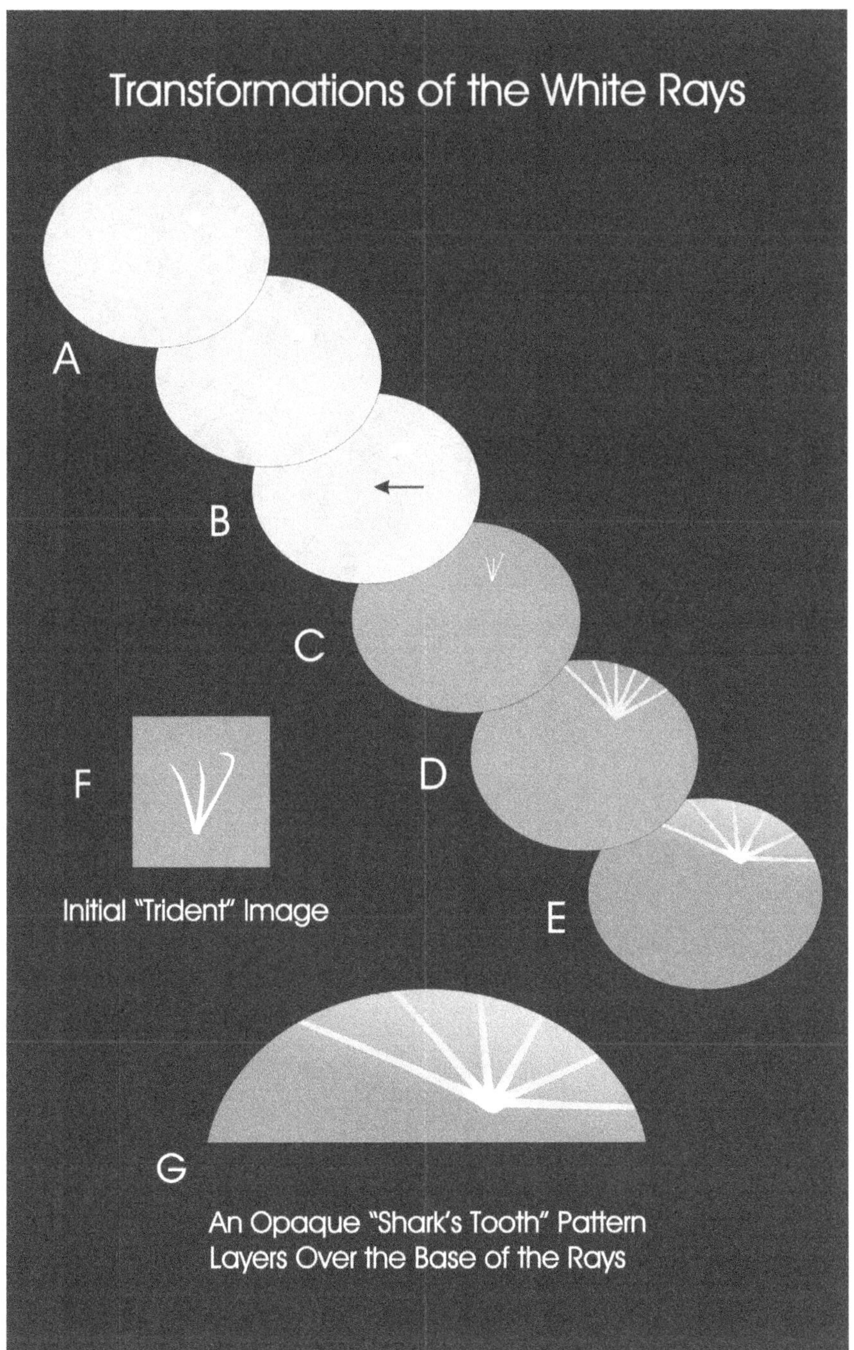

Transformations of the White Rays
A
B
C
D
E
F
Initial "Trident" Image
G
An Opaque "Shark's Tooth" Pattern
Layers Over the Base of the Rays

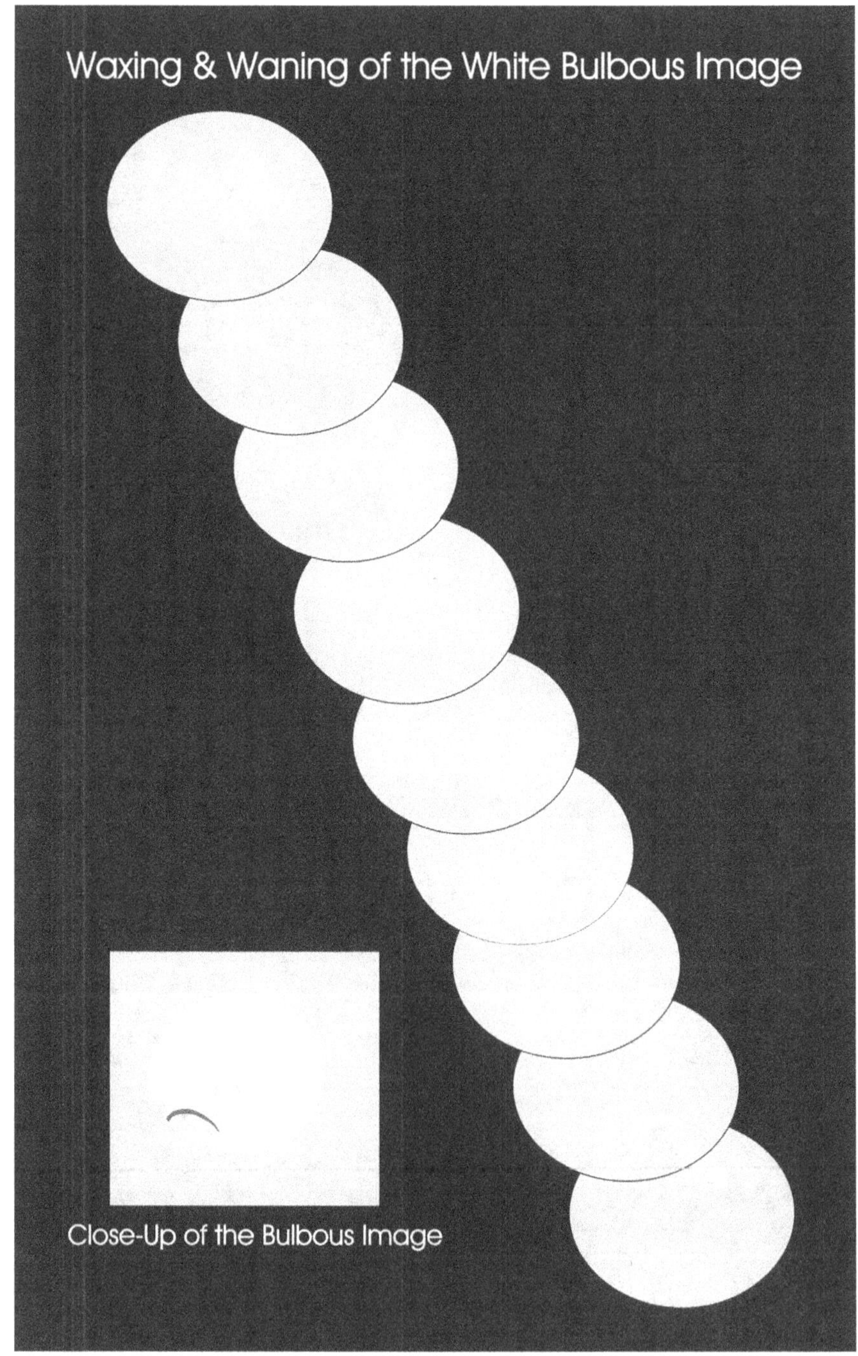
Waxing & Waning of the White Bulbous Image
Close-Up of the Bulbous Image

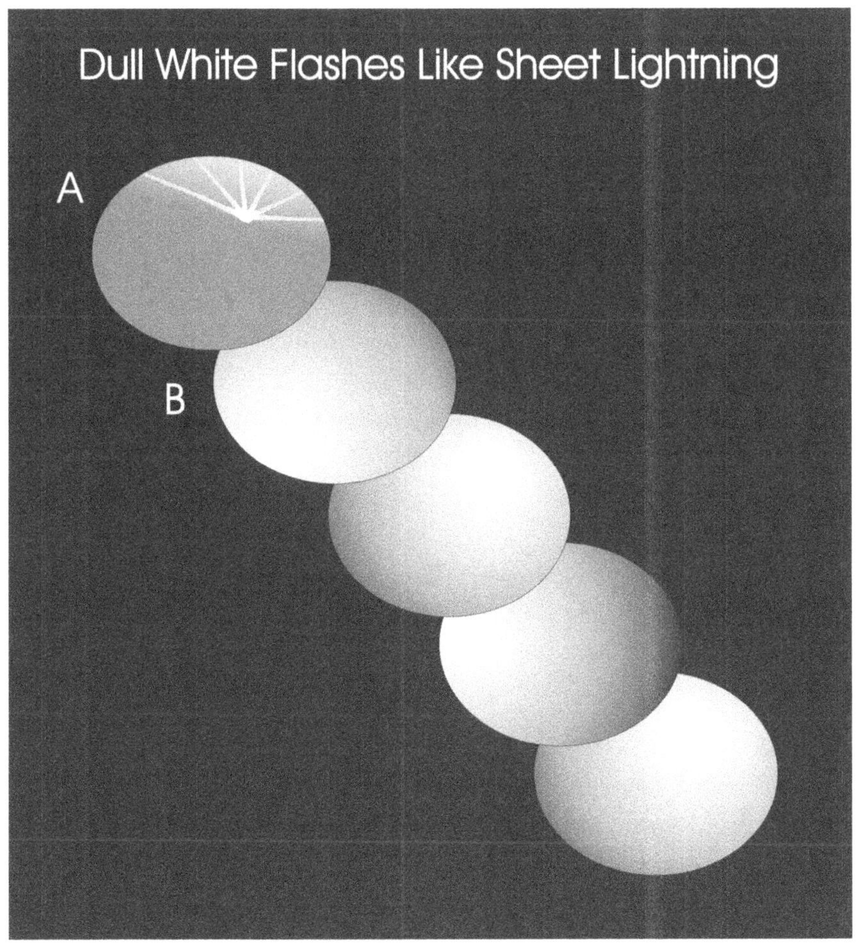

Dull White Flashes Like Sheet Lightning
A
B